Forever

A True Story of Love and War

Daniel J. Quinley

Feather Merchant Publishing

Printed in the United States of America on acid-free paper.

Feather Merchant Publishing

First Edition

For information about bulk purchases, please contact:

FeatherMerchantPublishing@yahoo.com

or visit

www.BookLocker.com

Acknowledgement

During World War II, in the European Theater of Operations, the 8th Air Force alone suffered more than 47,000 casualties. Of that, more than 26,000 were killed in action. Thank you for your sacrifices.

This book is dedicated to my mother and father. Their unwavering dedication and love for each other since 1936 serves as an inspiration to all who know them. Thank you for your dedication to each other, your service to us, your country, and for picking me to be your son.

I would like to also dedicate this book to all the veterans of all our wars. Those who came home, and those who did not. To their spouses and family members left behind. To the spouses and family members who suffered the long unknown. Not knowing if or when their loved ones would come home.

To the veterans who kept the peace between wars.

Thank you all for your service

Contents

High Flight

Oh! I have slipped the surly bonds of earth

And danced the skies on laughter-silvered wings;

Sunward I've climbed, and joined the tumbling mirth

Of sun-split clouds, and done a hundred things

You have not dreamed of.

Wheeled and soared and swung. High in the sunlit Silence.

Hov'ring there, I've chased the shouting wind along,

And flung my eager craft through footless halls of air

Up, up the long delirious burning blue

I've topped the wind-swept heights with easy grace

Where never lark, or ever eagle flew.

And, while with silent, lifting mind I've trod

The high untrespassed sanctity of space,

Put out my hand, and touched the face of God.

— John Gillespie Magee, Jr

Can You Take It?

Found on the wall at Dulag Luft
German interrogation center

It's easy to be nice boys,
When everything's okay.
It's easy to be cheerful,
When you're having things your way.
But can you hold your head up,
And take it on the chin,
When your heart is breaking,
And you feel like giving in.

It was easy back in England,
Among the friends and folks.
But now you miss the friendly hand,
The joys, and songs, and jokes.
The road ahead is stormy,
And unless you're strong in mind,
You'll find it isn't long before,
You're dragging far behind.

You've got to climb the hills boys,
It's no use turning back.
There's only one way home boys,
And it's off the beaten track.
Remember you're American,
And when you reach the crest,
You'll see a valley cool and green,
Our country at its best.

You know there is a saying,
That sunshine follows rain.
And sure enough you'll realize,
That joy will follow pain.
Let courage be your password,
Make fortitude your guide,
And then instead of grousing,
Just remember those who died.

ix

Prologue

If we are to heed the past to prepare for the future, we should listen to these quiet voices of a generation that speaks to us of duty and honor, sacrifice and accomplishment. I hope more of their stories will be preserved and cherished as reminders of all that we owe them and all that we can learn from them.[1]

In 1943 2nd Lt. Cecil W. Quinley is the co-pilot of the "Feather Merchant," a B-17F bomber (42-30009) (VE-G) assigned to the 381st bomb group (H), 532nd Squadron at Ridgewell station 167 in Essex, England. Before the war he moved from his family home in Ceres, California, to Sacramento on his 21st birthday in 1936. There, he is set up on a blind date with Margaret Farley to attend the California State Fair. Margaret is a 20 year old college student studying to be a teacher. It's love at first sight and the couple begin seeing each other on a regular basis. Cecil and Margaret marry in 1939. 70 years later, in 2009, family and friends celebrated their 70th wedding anniversary as they renewed their vows. What transpired through the years between that blind date and today is nothing short of a true and everlasting love that legends are made of. The couple thrived through good times, and bad, keeping faith through their church and each other.

Cecil is a veteran of 14 combat missions in the European Theater of operations during WWII. He was shot down and injured on his 14th mission and imprisoned in the infamous Stalag Luft III and Stalag VII-A. He survived a winter "death march" when the Germans evacuated the former camp as the Russian Army neared. Margaret survived the blues in Sacramento as depression over her imprisoned husband set in. She feared for Cecil's life in a far-away land and became active with the American Red Cross to contribute to the war effort and stay busy. She lit ten candles each week in her church for the missing ten airmen of the "Feather Merchant." Eventually, the war ends and the two are reunited to continue their long love affair.

After the war Cecil and Margaret move to Chico, California, and begin their family by adopting three sons. Cecil remained in the Air Force reserve obtaining the rank of captain. After fifty years of avoiding the subject of his

---

1 Tom Brokaw. "The Greatest Generation." Random House, 1998.

war years, Cecil is convinced by Margaret to become active in putting together Veterans and Memorial Day exhibits and becoming involved in local history projects and interviews. One such interview is on file in the United States Library of Congress. Throughout their early relationship and war years the couple wrote to each other every day when possible. Those letters are featured here and are used in the telling of their story in every chapter. The letters provide a window, witnessed firsthand, of many historical events. This epistolary format is blended with their memoir in a creative non-fiction style. The events are historically accurate as remembered by Cecil and Margaret. Every effort was made to verify their memories through other resources to compile the most accurate account possible in the telling of their story.

The people are real. The places are real. The events are real. The letters are real.[2]

---

[2] All family letters and photographs are used by permission of Cecil and Margaret Quinley. Historical photographs were taken by Army and Air Corps personnel and are not part of personal collections.

Chapter 1
8 October 1943

The air was crisp and clean as the formation climbed through the clouds over the North Sea. Contrails formed behind the mass of B-17 bombers that were struggling ever higher with their heavy loads. A deadly giveaway to the enemy that would see them because of it. Higher and higher they climbed as they made their way toward Germany, and their destiny:

The day started like any other when we had a mission to fly; it began the night before. We knew that a mission was called for October 8th, but we didn't know where we'd be going, or any further details. Our destination was always a closely guarded secret. Although our enemy always seemed to know more than we did. It was about 0400 hours when I woke up with a light shining on my face. I say woke up, but there was no real sleep the night before a raid, not for the veterans who already knew what to expect, not for the sober. October 8th would be my 14th mission. Some of the crew had more mission credits than I did, so we all knew what we'd be doing in a few hours and that made sleep hard to come by. The man holding the flashlight was Lieutenant Robinson, the 532nd Squadron Operations Officer. His flashlight scanned each bed in our Nissen hut as he called out each name when the light hit our face,

"Lieutenant Pry, Lieutenant Quinley, Lieutenant Burwell, Lieutenant Snyder, wake up, you're flying today! Briefing at 0600!"

He did the same to Captain Baltrusaitis' crew, who we shared the hut with. We'd been flying a pretty light schedule for the last part of September because of the Schweinfurt and Stuttgart losses, so we knew our luck would be running out soon. I stayed behind on the October 4th mission to Frankfurt because our ship was flying deputy group lead. Lt. Colonel Hall flew in my seat. During the flight Jack lost the number two engine to a mechanical failure and barely made it back to Ridgewell by diving and cloud hopping to dodge German fighters that were trying to get at him. He and Lt. Col. Hall fought about it because Jack said that they'd gone too far to turn back. It would have been safer to stay with the formation, even with only three engines, but the colonel ordered him under threat of court-martial to turn around. So instead of having the safety of the formation, they had to run from fighters by themselves, all the way back to the channel.

Jack was considered one of the best pilots in the 381st. He was a perfectionist and knew just about everything there was to know about a B-17. Jack Pry entered the service as an enlisted man and worked his way up. He was a sergeant and aircraft mechanic before he went to cadet flight school, and he had even become a B-17 instructor at one point. When I was assigned as his co-pilot at Walla Walla, Washington, I actually outranked him. He was a flight officer at the time, but was promoted to 2nd lieutenant just prior to our leaving the states. My main goal, as was everyone's, was to survive the mandated 25 missions so I could go home. I graduated single engine school and, although I wanted to transition into the twin engine P-38 fighter, my instructor told me I was probably too old to get the appointment. I would have been 28 by the time I graduated, an old man in fighter pilot years, which is what earned me the sometime nickname Pappy. Instead of risking it, and getting something I really didn't care for, I put down B-17 or instructor on my wish list shortly before graduation from pilot training. What I hadn't counted on was being dropped into Jack's lap as an inexperienced co-pilot who had never flown a multi-engine plane. Jack wasn't happy to see me at first and I can't say that I blamed him. I think at this stage of the game the co-pilot should be able to fly the airplane, but I guess there was a shortage of co-pilots right then due to the push to get more crews ready for deployment to England in a big hurry. Nearly my whole class was in the same boat as I was. The scuttlebutt was that I'd be getting my own plane and crew on my next mission, but for the time being I was happy flying with Jack and the boys. Captain Baltrusaitis had me fly with him on a recent mission to see if I was ready. He had me fly left seat and he didn't do anything I didn't ask him to do. "Baldy," as we called him, was a rough and tough man of Lithuanian descent and was one of the original pilots of the 381st Group. He flew hard and drank hard, as did many of us who watched our friends die nearly every time we went up.

The engine problem Jack encountered on the way to Frankfurt had been fixed and the ship was ready to go, so we figured we'd be flying today. The first order of business was to get cleaned up, shaved, and dressed. We shaved before a mission because it made our oxygen masks seal better on our faces. Long johns and two pairs of socks were typical. Coveralls and a jacket would go over our regular clothes, but not until shortly before take-off. If we bundled up too soon we'd begin to sweat, then the sweat would freeze when we got up to altitude where the temperature could reach thirty to fifty below zero. We rode our bicycles to the combat mess. The base was large, and soon after our arrival in July we learned that obtaining a bicycle was the best way to get around. At combat mess they served us bacon and real eggs which, although was much appreciated, was never a good sign. Real eggs meant we were going to be assigned a rough mission, probably somewhere deep in Germany, surrounded by hundreds of fighters and thousands of anti-aircraft gun emplacements. I had two or three cups of coffee to try to wake up. For some reason none of us were our normal selves. There was an uneasiness about the morning. An unspoken anxiousness that wasn't usually there. Normally, we were all a pretty sad bunch trying to wake up. Today, everyone was quite chipper, chatting non-stop, making nervous gestures and talk. It doesn't sound alarming to the casual observer, but it just wasn't normal, not for us, not before a raid. If you weren't superstitious when you arrived in England, you soon were. It could be a distraction, or it could be something to hold on to when you needed it. A false sense of security, I suppose, but it was what we had. After breakfast, with my Chesterfield smokes in hand, we made our way to briefing, chain smoking the entire way.

Jack, Ted, Roger, and I took our seats in the mission briefing room. Colonel Nazzaro, the 381st Group Commander, walked through the door and the room was called to attention. He advised us to be seated and he stood there on the stage for several moments looking around the room. That was unusual too. He normally pulled the curtain right away and got right to the briefing. After his dramatic pause in front of all the officers he exposed the huge map on the wall at the head of the room. When he did so there were the usual collective moans and groans from all in attendance. The moans were a normal reaction, but today they were louder and longer than usual, reflecting the distance and increased dangers of today's raid that was now in full view of us on the map. There were long pieces of string indicating our route into and out of Germany. Our minds were still fresh with the memories of the disastrous Schweinfurt raid where we lost so many ships and friends. Colonel Nazzaro spoke,

"Gentlemen, our target today is Bremen, Germany."

The radio and intelligence officer gave us the usual information about weather, launch times, form-up procedures, our route to and from the target, expected enemy fighter numbers and so on. It was going to be a rough one alright. We were going all the way to Bremen, where the city is surrounded by some of the heaviest concentrations of anti-aircraft batteries in Germany. It had all the makings of another Schweinfurt.

Since arriving in England I tried hard to write to my wife every day. It was a tradition we'd started even before we were married. It was tough to do sometimes, because I was so limited on the information I could share from the war zone. I wouldn't have time to write before leaving today, but I'd finished one yesterday and got it mailed off just in time. It was a short letter that I'd planned on adding to, but something told me to just seal it up and drop it in the outgoing mail. It was on my mind as we left the briefing.

> Hello again, darling! Here it is another night, so I'll tell you once again that you are my sweetheart and that I'm still in love with you an awful lot. Even if I didn't get any mail from you again today, because I know that it isn't any fault of yours. Although, I wish it was your fault, because then I know it would be remedied right quick, but probably tomorrow I'll get some. Sure haven't any news again tonight, so this will naturally be another short note. Just got in and had chow and it's already time to get myself into bed just in case I have to get up before breakfast. I sure did have a dream last night. I dreamt that it was Christmas day and I came flying into Sacramento and you were down in Ceres, so I went out and hitchhiked down there. Then I came walking in and you greeted me with open arms. That's when I woke up, but it was swell while it lasted. No fooling, wish it would all come true. I'll say goodnight now darling, much as I hate to, but I don't have any news, anyway, except that I love you, and I said that once, but it's still very much true. Also, naturally, I sure do miss you too. God bless you darling. Love and kisses, Cecil.

After getting the rest of our gear we hopped a truck out to the hardstand where we found the enlisted members of the crew readying their guns. Jack briefed them as I performed a walk around inspection of our ship, the "Feather Merchant." She was one of the original ships of the 381st Group that came over from the states, a B-17F (42-30009). I could hear Jack telling the men, over their own moans and groans, what we'd be facing today. With all the groups combined our force numbered just under 400 B-17 and B-24 bombers and about 250 P-47 fighters. There'd also be the usual Spitfires from the RAF to escort us across the English Channel until the P-47's could join up. On today's mission the fighters would stay with us to the border of Holland and Germany, probably farther than they'd ever escorted us before.

But after our "little friends" leave us, we'd have to fight the rest of the way to the target and back without fighter cover until they could meet up with us again on our way home. Our launch time was scheduled for 1115-1130 hours. Our squadron, the 532nd, would be flying the low formation at about 26,000 feet, and we'd be carrying twelve 500 pound bombs. Low formation made us easier targets for the flak gunners. I was assigned left seat on this flight because we'd be flying second flight lead. Jack had to fly right seat so we could keep proper position from the squadron lead plane. In this case that was our roommate Captain "Baldy" Baltrusaitis in "The Joker." Jack just hated giving up his seat for any reason, but I have to admit, I liked seeing him get antsy in the right seat, It made me chuckle. Make no mistake about it though, it was still Jack's ship, he's just that way. The "Feather Merchant" became our assigned ship about two weeks after the Schweinfurt mission. Our first assigned ship was "Ole Flak Sack," another 381st original, but she'd received some pretty extensive damage during a belly landing by our friend Lt. Leo Jarvis, who was getting some training time while his ship was having battle damage repaired. We flew "Ole Flack Sack" in training and on our first three missions. Our other ships were "The Hellion," on the Schweinfurt raid and, much to the dismay of our wives, "Old Coffins" a couple of times after that.

Shortly after being assigned the "Feather Merchant" we experienced severe oxygen problems that forced us to abort two missions which we never received credit for. Jack managed to get those ironed out. Not without difficulty, however. The maintenance major kept insisting that there was nothing wrong with the system, but we kept running out of oxygen way too soon. The major never actually said it, but he acted like he was questioning our aborts and whether or not we were telling the truth about the leak. Jack was called into Colonel Nazzaro's office and read the riot act and practically accused of being a coward because of some aborted flights. It was a mistake for the major to question Jack's bravery regarding the aborts, and his perceived notion that there was nothing wrong with the oxygen system. I think the major resented Jack because of his expertise and prior experience as an aircraft mechanic. Certainly, some career officers didn't much care for the guys who worked their way up through the ranks like Jack did. On this occasion we tricked the major into coming on a check ride with us that turned into, well, a kidnapping. We took him up to 25,000 feet out over the North Sea to prove our point. Sure enough, at altitude, we began rapidly losing pressure in the oxygen system, just like we'd been telling him. The major kept yelling at us to land the aircraft and was getting awfully upset with Jack and I, but Jack would have none of it. He told that major we were going to keep flying until he admitted there was something wrong with it and promise to fix it, instead of claiming we were cowards behind our backs, and to never question his or our bravery or resolve again. At first that he did an awful lot of yelling for us to land the plane, and Jack did an awful lot of yelling back at him. I could see my career flashing before my eyes. Eventually, however, the major finally calmed down, admitted he was wrong, and promised he'd get the system fixed. Thank God for that, I thought we were going to get court martialed for sure. The "Feather Merchant" was repaired that same day and we never heard another word about the kidnapping. I think Jack and the major made a deal that Jack and I wouldn't get court martialed and no one would hear about his crew not being able to fix the plane, or his excitable nature up at altitude when he thought he was going to die without oxygen. From then on, the maintenance crew took Jack seriously when he said something was wrong with the aircraft, but they still didn't like him much.

Chapter 2
Bremen

I was thinking what a beautiful day it was as we climbed out over the English Channel. We were flying at an indicated 160 knots, or about 185 miles per hour. The colors were amazing and were the bluest I'd ever seen. Once we reached land the sky was contrasted with the lush landscape below us. The white contrails were amazingly beautiful and there were even circular contrails coming off the props of the ships around us. It was magical, even mesmerizing, and hard to imagine that soon there would be a sky full of enemy fighters intent on killing us all. During long flights you have to remain observant but your mind can't help wandering to things you'd rather be doing; places you'd rather be. There were usually always delays of some sort after all the pre-flight checks, and then what followed was the infernal waiting. Sometimes Jack and I would talk; sometimes we'd be off in our own worlds. We'd write letters, or read letters. Ted would most likely be taking a nap and Roger reading his navigation charts. The rest of the boys would be gabbing in the back, maybe playing cards. Today, while waiting for the green flare that signaled engine start, I was reading the last letter I received from Margaret. My mind drifted back to it as I stared out the window at the rest of our squadron.

> Hiya Honey. Greetings on our 53 month anniversary. I still love you, darling, very-very much, and miss you as much, or more (if possible) than ever. But there is some consolation in the realization that these past few months apart are that much closer to the day when you'll be home again. Sure hope it will be real soon too, because that would really make me a happy gal.

> I didn't get a letter from sweet you again today. Darling. I know this isn't much of a letter, but I'm awful lonesome for you tonight. So much so that I can't think of anything but you to write about. I sure hope and pray that this old war will end in a hurry (now) so that you and a lot of other boys can come home. Things look good in the news tonight. At least we're holding our own against the Germans, and Japs too. You boys did another nice job over France last night. Congratulations and stuff.

It's only 9 O'clock dearest darling, but I'm tired, so I'm going to dash to bed after a nice bath. I'll do better on a letter tomorrow, honey. I'm not much of a morale builder tonight. I love you with all my heart and visit the cathedral twice every day to say a couple of extra prayers for my sweetheart. Hope they help a little to keep you safe. Until tomorrow, and always darling, May God bless you and protect you and bring you home to me very soon. Good night for this time honey-bun. All my love and kisses. Margaret.

My day dreaming was interrupted as a few enemy fighters showed up over Holland and tried to get to us, but our P-47 little friends kept them away. As we approached the German border, however, our little friends reached the limit of their fuel supply. If they were to safely make it back to base they'd have to leave us, and just like that, they were gone. Now, every eye in our ship scanned the sky intently looking for little black specks that would turn into enemy fighters hoping to chalk up another B-17 kill for their Fatherland.

We were late taking off, something to do with our decoy force, so we figured the Luftwaffe would have plenty of warning that we were coming. They'd be ready for us. As I said, Jack didn't seem himself today. No one did. There was a lot of talking on the intercom and the noise was getting on our nerves. Finally, he yelled at everyone,

"Can the chatter. Watch for Jerry fighters. Call out when you see them."

We were headed toward our turning point at Rastede, Germany. From there we'd head to our Initial Point (IP) at Vegesack and turn south toward Bremen for the bomb run. At that point I'd turn the ship over to Ted, our Bombardier, and the ship is controlled by autopilot through his Norden Bomb Sight. Just as we were afraid of, though, as soon as the P-47's left the Jerries were all over us. There were twin engine ME-210's and JU-88's firing rockets at us from our six O'clock, just out of gun range. Tex, our tail gunner, was swearing up a storm because the Jerries were too far away to hit with his twin .50 caliber machine guns. It was frustrating for the gunners. They could see the Jerries back there, but they couldn't do anything about it. I hated the rockets, they were like flying death goblins. They didn't fly a whole lot faster than us, at least it seemed that way to me. If coming from behind, they'd appear out my side window and pass on by, like a faster car passing us on the highway. Your natural instinct was to veer away from them, but there was only so much evasive action we could take in a tight formation, and staying in a tight formation with an overlapping field of fire from our gunner's was the only real defense we had against fighter attack. It was the Schweinfurt mission when we first saw the rockets, but on that day none of them came close to us.

The FW-190's and ME-109's finally hit us from every direction. The yelling on the intercom was intense but determined and reflected how this once rookie crew had become veterans of these raids.

Al, Smitty, there's a 190 at 9 O'clock low! Ted, 12 O'clock level, get him! Tex, he's head on but he'll be coming your way, watch your left. Eddie got one, he's smoking and spinning. I got one, I got one! That's confirmed Carl, I saw it--

There was still excitement in everyone's voices, but not panic like there was over Schweinfurt, and Roger didn't have to smack Ted anymore to make him set down his rosary beads and remind him to shoot back. Then, as fast as the Jerries were on us, they were gone. Approaching the IP the flak started exploding all around us and was especially thick. So thick you could walk on it, we would all say. Deadly puffs of black were all over the sky. They contained shards of metal fragments. Shrapnel that could tear through a human like a hot knife through butter. So far so good, but bumpy as hell. You could hear the shrapnel bouncing off the plane or scraping down the sides of the fuselage as we flew through it. If a shell exploded under us the ship would lurch up violently from the shock wave.

"Bomb bay doors open," Ted announced.

We had our eyes fixated on Baltrusaitis' plane as we made the run into the target. It only took a few minutes, but it seemed like an eternity when death was exploding all around us. A short time later Ted said,

"Bombs away."

As the lead ship dropped its bombs, Ted dropped ours and the "Feather Merchant" lurched upward from her sudden loss of 6,000 pounds. We started a slow turn to the southwest with the formation. Everything was looking good and it appeared as though we may just get lucky again. Our thoughts turned to the Jerry fighters that would be waiting for us on the other side of the flack field. We were just about through our turn when we saw Lt. Arthur Sample's plane, our old ship, "Ole Flak Sack," get hit. He was still flying with us, but it looked bad. She was smoking heavily out of her open bomb bay doors and waist windows. The bomb bay doors must have been knocked from their mechanism because they were flapping in the wind as the ship rocked back and forth. Art wasn't going to be able to keep up with the formation and he'd be a sitting duck after he dropped out. Then, a deafening explosion rocked our own "Feather Merchant." Had it not been for my belt I may have been knocked on top of Jack. It threw me sideways, to my right. The noise and concussion brought my attention back inside our own cockpit and away from Art. The controls were nearly torn from my hands. There wasn't time to worry about Art anymore. I scanned the engines in the direction the noise came from and I could see that we took a direct hit on our number two engine. The number two engine was right next to my seat and there were holes in the side of the cockpit now, with cold air whistling through. There was a burning and tearing pain in my leg. Some red hot shrapnel went into my lower right leg just above the ankle. I felt it travel upward and settle just below my knee. It was a tearing, burning pain, like I'd never experienced before. Man, I couldn't imagine taking something like that in the gut instead of the leg. I yelled at Jack that I'd been hit. He asked how bad it was as he took control of the ship. I said it's my lower leg and it felt like blood was running down inside my trousers. I could still feel everything and move everything. It hurt like hell but I didn't have time to worry anymore about it. The good news was that the freezing air would go through the same hole on my trousers that the shrapnel made, and it would stop the bleeding, hopefully.

There was oil flying everywhere out of the number 2 engine cowling and splattering over the wing. I told Eddie, our flight engineer and top turret gunner, to check for fire and other damage. It was smoking, but at least there wasn't any fire showing. It was imperative now to get the prop feathered. Feathering turns the edge of the prop into the wind so the wind won't catch the blades and make them turn. That would cause drag on the ship, slowing us down. It could also cause the engine to windmill out of control and could even take us down. I tried feathering the prop and all was going well as I watched the rotation slow and the blades turn a little, but then our fear was realized as it began to windmill. The oil pressure must have run out from the damage right before it completed feathering. Instead of a safe low drag prop we had a prop that caught the wind and spun the engine faster and faster. I couldn't help but think this was the same engine that quit on Jack just four days ago. I could feel the vibration getting worse. This was a bad situation. Jack and I were both swearing and tried again to feather it but we knew it wasn't going to happen, it was just too late. This was the beginning of the end for our "Feather Merchant." The high pitched whine that was coming from those blades hurt our ears, even over the other sounds of the engines, exploding flak, and Eddie's twin .50 caliber machine guns that were now blasting away again right behind and over our heads. The vibration was shaking the hell out of us and our ship-our ride home! Then the inevitable happened. The engine flew apart, tearing itself from the mounts as it separated from the aircraft. Pieces of the disintegrating engine hit the side of the plane and tore through the fuselage. The propeller flew up and backward, over the wing. We lost contact with Ted and Roger in the nose. Jack called them over and over on the intercom, but there was no answer.

"Pilot to Navigator, pilot to bombardier, check in! Roger, Ted, come in!"

God, I hoped they were alright. The shrapnel flew right into their compartment. I yelled at Eddie to get down there and see if they were alright, but then there was another flak hit and explosion right underneath and behind my position that rocked us upward so hard it jarred my back, knocked the wind out of me and knocked Eddie off his feet. My head was pounding like I had an ice cream headache, and then everything went suddenly quiet. I remember looking out the top Plexiglas window at the sky, and then there was nothing.

"Quinn! Quinn! God damn it Quinn! Wake up! Eddie! Get up here and give me a hand with Lt. Quinley! Quinn! Cec! Cec!"

Everything was surreal and dream like. Things weren't noisy anymore. I could still hear the explosions and the guns firing, but it seemed far off. My mind drifted back to Sacramento and my wife. We were walking by the lake in the park. Everything there was so colorful. Was that Jack's voice telling me to wake up? Why is he telling me to wake up, and why is he in Sacramento?

"Quinn! Snap out of it! Cecil! Look at me!"

He sounded like he was a block away. I felt a pressure on my face and it felt like I couldn't breathe. As I began to snap out of it and my senses slowly returned I could hear Jack telling me that I was unconscious because my oxygen was shot out. That's a bad thing at 26,000 feet. Jack noticed my head dangling backwards with a blank smile on my face looking out the top Plexiglas. He thought I'd been hit again and was dying but when he checked me out looking for injuries he found that my oxygen tube had been severed by shrapnel at the control valve. He put his oxygen mask on me while he was yelling until I woke up. I could see, hear, and think, but my body wouldn't do what I was trying to make it do. I could still hear Jack telling me to get myself on oxygen, over and over. Finally, I found a spare emergency oxygen tube that was working and put the tube between my teeth to hold it there.

We slid out of formation and things were looking pretty grim. A lone B-17 was a sitting duck and a golden invitation for the Jerry fighters to cut to pieces. We were being shot all to hell as those fighters were coming at us in swarms and from every direction. They knew we were hurt, and they were like sharks after blood. It all seemed like an eternity, but was only a matter of minutes. Our friend Art Sample in "Ole Flak Sack" was hurt too, so he slid down next to us to make a two ship formation to double our firepower. Good old Art. A gentlemanly southerner you could always count on. A couple big ole lumbering injured bombers must be quite a temptation to a fighter pilot, even if those bombers are shooting back. Smitty, our ball turret gunner, wasn't answering his com anymore and we assumed he was dead because he was no longer firing his guns. We'd been raked by 20mm fire from an FW-190 all along the bottom of the plane. One round went right between Jack's legs and turned his face white as a ghost, a close call. Also, the waist gunners told us that a rocket had hit us and exploded right near the ball turret. Our last communication with Smitty was right after the bomb run and before we were hit. Normally, we'd have the radio man, Sgt. Russ "Frenchy" Frautschi, check on Smitty, but he was busy firing his guns. Everyone was busy firing their guns-except Smitty.

Chapter 3
Fur Sie ist der Krieg uber

How's my man this very warm evening? We have had two very hot days this week. Our new office is in room 907 and the telephone number is 3-8747, in case you get a chance to call while I'm at work. We certainly drew the sevens, didn't we dear? Here's hoping they will be always lucky for both of us. I have been preparing some candied figs for you the last three days, it takes four days to make them. They are for your Christmas package. I didn't get a letter from my darling today but I reread the three that came yesterday so that is almost like getting new ones. They are swell letters, honey, all of them, so keep them coming. There was a nice letter from Polly today, and she is as excited as ever over 'junior's' arrival, which may be any day now. She hears from Jack quite regularly, and that makes her happy.

You know honey, I have been having nightmares about you! For about the past week it seems like I dream every night about you, and you're stepping out on me a-plenty! Sunday morning I woke myself up crying like a baby! I dreamed that you came home (I always dream that part) but just long enough to tell me you wanted a divorce and were going back to England to marry some RAF flying gal! Gee whiz it was so real! Don't do that to me darling. Then there have been blondes and brunettes and redheads just about every night, so you've got me worried. I won't think too much about it, though, darling. I really trust you, honest!

I see where you boys haven't been out on a raid since last Thursday, on account of weather I suppose. Bob Metcalf, a little short guy who used to be at C.W.S.L. when I was there, is now a bombardier on a Fortress over there, was awarded the DFC recently, and also was promoted to 1ˢᵗ lieutenant. I imagine he's okay because he was a pretty nice kid in the old days. Maybe you've seen him there. Guess I'd better be signing off, dear. I love you 'muchly' as always, and hope this old war will end soon so that you can come home. I miss you heaps, but I know you'll be flying home very-very soon, so I'll be waiting patiently but anxiously. Until then, and always, May God bless you and watch over you. Goodnight honey. I'll be seeing you soon 'in all the old familiar places.' All my love and kisses. Margaret.

We were all fighting for our lives and the gunners were shooting non-stop. We'd loaded extra ammunition because of our destination today, and that was proving to be very fortunate indeed, because there were no ammunition conserving short bursts now. No worries about damaging the barrels. Things were looking pretty bleak as we took one hit after another. It was all about survival now. The ship filled with the smell of acrid gun smoke and empty brass casings were raining down onto the floor. The gun barrels steamed in the iced air as the boy's valiantly tried to save our "Feather Merchant" from her inevitable fate, and ours. The Jerries were on us thick and the gunners were blazing away as much as they could, it was our only hope. Our old gal was taking a beating, her worst one yet. Al, on the left waist gun, was yelling over his intercom,

"I got one, I got one. That bastard won't be bothering us anymore!"

All of the gunners were shooting with deadly accuracy today. The Jerries were going to get as much as they gave. I heard no fewer than twelve shouts of "I got one!" But our girl was coming apart piece by piece. Jack was having trouble keeping her level as she shuddered all over the sky. Finally, it was time. Jack sounded the bail-out bell and yelled at me to prepare to get out. I got up and was behind the cockpit seats trying to get my parachute buckled onto my harness rings but I kept getting knocked to the floor by explosions and turbulence. Eddie shouted that another rocket strike just blew off half our vertical stabilizer and rudder. Soon after that, part of the right horizontal stabilizer was hit and separated from the ship. Another rocket hit the left wing and everything outboard of the number one engine exploded and fell away from the plane. Somehow, the number one engine kept running, even with fifteen feet of wing missing. How the "Feather Merchant" stayed in the sky was something only God could answer, I was sure of it. It had to be like balancing a diner plate on the tip of a pencil. Our guardian angels must have been holding her up with their wings so we could get out, for surely our girl's wings couldn't be holding us up on their own, it had to be impossible. Jack again ordered us to abandon ship and said he'd try to hold her steady while we all got out and then he would follow us. Art's ship had been dropping out with us the whole time and she didn't look long for this world either. "Ole Flak Sack" was still smoking badly and now had two engines on fire. Art was our roommate in the Nissen hut back at Ridgewell. He had been Baltrusaitis' co-pilot but was just promoted to first pilot in early September. This was his sixth mission as first pilot over-all, but his very first mission with his newly assigned crew, his 24th overall. He only needed one more to go home! Jack thought I'd already bailed out but I was sitting on the floor behind my seat still trying to strap on my parachute. I was having a hell of a time trying to get it buckled to my harness as the ship bounced violently with each explosion. Plus, I was still a little rum dumb from the lack of oxygen and the injury to my leg made it hard to move around. When Jack noticed me still there he yelled,

"Hurry up and get the hell out of here!"

I saw that some of the shrapnel had hit my parachute from one of the direct hits. That's not the kind of thing you want to see just before jumping out of a plane. I didn't know how much altitude we'd lost but we started at 26,000 feet. It scared the hell out of me, but the alternative was to stay in the plane and die. Stay and die for sure, or jump and maybe die, maybe live. I know it doesn't sound like there's anything, really, to consider. But, when you have very little oxygen in your brain, your reasoning powers get a little mixed up.

Eddie LaPointe came down out of the top turret right when I finally got my parachute buckled on. He checked his chute and started toward the bomb bay. I guess that was just the wake-up call I needed, to see someone else doing it, so I followed him. When we got to the bomb bay Eddie tried to open the doors by pulling the emergency release, but the doors were stuck. Great, I thought, Art can't close his bomb bay doors and we can't open ours. We were getting thrown all over the place by the turbulence while standing on the slim catwalk in the bomb bay. God, what else could go wrong? I was feeling okay now after having moved around some, and getting my blood circulating in the -30 degree temperature. After trying the emergency release handle without the doors opening a few times Eddie gave up on it and headed on through the bomb bay toward the rear of the plane. It's a good thing he did because he found Carl, the right waist gunner, injured and having a hard time getting his parachute secured good. The gunners wore their parachutes loose so they could move around while firing their guns. Carl had taken a shrapnel hit in his groin and was hurt pretty bad. He was pretty miserable with pain so Eddie helped him get his chute fixed right. They were yelling and screaming back there. I tried to follow Eddie through the bomb bay but something was wrong. No matter how hard I tried I couldn't get going and something kept pulling me back. I finally noticed that I still had that damn oxygen tube clamped between my teeth so hard that it kept pulling me back when it stretched to its limit. If it weren't for the circumstances it would be funny. Jack would shake his head think me an idiot but Roger and Ted would get a great laugh out of it, I'm glad no one saw that. I took the tube out of my mouth and was going to get a portable walk around tank for bail out. We were still at about 22,000 feet, I guessed, and that's way too high to go without oxygen. I figured I'd get one on the way to the rear hatch, but right when I was going through the bomb bay the number one engine took a hit from a rocket and it was knocked clear off the wing. The shock from that hit threw me to the catwalk in the bomb bay. The jarring also shook the bomb bay doors open. Without thinking, and without a portable oxygen tank, I got up and dove head first through the opening and into the ice cold rush of air.

As soon as I cleared the bottom of our ship I saw "Ole Flak Sack" explode in a huge fireball. I could feel the heat and concussion of the blast. She just disintegrated right in front of my eyes, there was nothing left as the flaming pieces fell to earth! My god, I thought, Art is gone! As sudden as that, Art is gone! I wanted to vomit but I just kept falling and tumbling through the cold air. I remember thinking, holy shit! I hope that plane doesn't fall on me! The panic I felt just isn't describable. Eventually I regained enough of my senses to start thinking again and I made a decision not to open my parachute right away. We'd all heard about some German fighter pilots shooting at our guys in their chutes. Plus, somewhere up here with me is a crap load of debris that used to be "Ole Flak Sack" and I didn't want any of those pieces hitting my silk canopy and ripping it up. Falling was the most peaceful, yet eerie feeling I'd ever known. Being without oxygen was undoubtedly contributing to my euphoria, but what a feeling it was. Fortunately, the lower I got, the more I woke up. I remembered this guy in our outfit that used to test parachutes. He would tell us about how you could use your arms in free fall to help steer yourself. I tried doing what he said and, to my surprise, it worked. It was almost like flying, but in those brief glimpses of clarity that interrupted my euphoria there was the realization that I was flying-straight down! I'm glad that getting lower meant more oxygen and better thinking ability. The euphoria I was experiencing could easily take hold of a man too strongly. Oh how easy it would be to just forget the situation and keep falling, until it was too late. I could see the ground below me and it was getting closer. I also saw some clouds below and I just kept falling toward them. Then, before I knew it, I got into one of those clouds and lost sight of the ground. It startled me, because I didn't know how high I was at that point, so I pulled the rip cord. I never did see any German fighters, or debris, or any survivors from Art's ship. Now I was descending much slower, hanging under my silk parachute, and I remember thinking how lonely it was. One moment you're part of a team of ten men, friends who all count on each other, and the next you're all alone in the sky. I'd survived so many other missions already, including Schweinfurt and Stuttgart, but now I'm all alone, falling through the sky and only two minutes ago I was standing in the "Feather Merchant." Fifteen minutes ago we hadn't even been hit yet. Where's the rest of the guys? Did Roger and Ted make it out, or were they killed when the engine flew apart? Did Jack get out or did he stay too long to save the rest of us? Then, I was awakened from my self-pity by the realization that I was beginning to swing back and forth pretty violently. I pulled the shroud lines to stop the swinging and it worked just like it was supposed to. It straightened me right out. It must have been pretty windy, though, because I started swinging again. As I pulled the shroud line a second time to stop it I looked up and I noticed that the damaged canopy was trying to curl over on itself and I could see that it was full of holes from the flak, so I didn't do that anymore. I would just have to deal with the swinging. I was getting close to the ground as I continued to swing back and forth and was coming down toward what looked like a barbed wire fence just before a ditch, and I was falling fast. I pulled my legs up underneath me as high as I could and just missed the fence, but I hit the ditch bank with my legs still tucked up underneath me and bounced several feet in the air, then flew down into the ditch landing on my head. The impact knocked the air out of me and everything went black for a while. I don't know how long I was out. I just remember laying there trying to regain my senses and catch my breath. Eventually, I climbed up out of the ditch and saw a huge pile of brush and slash from where it looked like someone had cut down some trees. I hobbled over to it and buried my chute there.

"So this is Germany, huh? Shit!" I said.

I could see two men in the distance walking toward me. I tried to stand up and run away, but the pain in my leg and back was overwhelming and there was no getting away, so I just sat down and waited. Like the Germans were fond of saying:

"Fur Sie ist der Krieg uber! For you, the war is over!"

I'm glad I mailed that letter yesterday. It's going to be a while before Margaret gets another.

Chapter 4
The Beginning

How'd my little Tootsie Wootsie make out? I hope you got there O.K. How's the weather up on your hill top? How's everything going by this time, okay? When seven P.M. came around tonight, I was so used to reaching for the telephone I couldn't hardly keep my hands off of it. Well, another day another dollar (for somebody). Nothing new in Sacramento. Boy, I sure had a swell steak for dinner tonight at the Rosemount on 9th street. Best I've tasted in years I think. It was about two inches thick and a foot in diameter, with nice crisp French fried potatoes. There's a skirt orchestra coming to the Rainbow next week, not a man in the whole bunch, oh boy! Hold me back!

I made a bet on the fight between Joe Louis and James Braddock today. I bet a guy five simoleons that Braddock would lick Louis. If he doesn't, I'm afraid he'll have another licking coming if I ever get near him. I haven't got much to do without my little darling around. Went to the show last night 'I Met Him in Paris.' Pretty good show and she married Melvyn Douglas instead of Robert Young, but Robert Young says, let her marry him and then when she finds out how bad a guy he is, then I can step in and things will be just right. I saw a preview of 'A Day at the Races' with the Marx Brothers. Boy I'll bet that will be a riot. I almost fell out of my seat laughing at the preview. One of them has a dame up in his room and she keeps saying, 'Hold me closer,' and finally he says, 'If I hold you any closer I'll be around in back of you.' They are just playing 'Hot Lips' over the radio, oh boy, wish you were here! I haven't drunk your little present you gave me yet. I'll save it for some night when I feel in the dumps. Well, I think that you ought to be tired trying to read this by this time, so I'll make my mark and sign off. This is Cecil signing off for tonight. Goodbye now.

Cecil Woodrow Quinley.

"Good morning Cec. How are you this fine day?" Clayton asked.

"Doing swell Clayton, thanks for asking. How things with you?" I said.

Clayton Cash was a salesman for a Coast radio store. It was September 9th, 1936, and I hadn't been living in Sacramento, California, for very long. I moved up the road from Ceres, which was about 80 miles south. The depression was moving across the country and, even though it hadn't hit my family very hard, I wanted to live in a place that had more opportunities, and there were more opportunities in Sacramento. Ceres was a small farming community and I was the youngest in a family of twelve children. I had five brothers and six sisters. My brother in law Jim called me when I was in my second year at Modesto Junior College. He asked me if I wanted to move to Sacramento and work in a garage. I was bored and it sounded good to me, so I hopped on a Greyhound bus and headed up the road on my twenty-first birthday. When I got to town I went over to the Elm Garage at 815 9th street for an interview. They hired me on the spot and told me to be back at 7 O'clock that night for my first shift. That happened so fast that I wasn't really ready for it. I didn't have any work clothes yet, so I made a beeline downtown to buy some. The boss at the garage told me I could find work clothes at the stores down around "Two" street. The big city was something I wasn't used to seeing. When I got downtown I went walking on "Two" Street and couldn't believe my eyes. Every ten feet, it seemed like, there was a drunk sleeping on the sidewalk. People were just stepping over them as they went about their business. I thought, Good Lord, what have I gotten myself into this time? I was a long way from the farm in Ceres! Even the police just stepped over the drunks. I guess they had no place to put them. I asked the cops why they just stepped over them and left them there. They said they just keep an eye on them and make sure no one rolls them over and takes their money or other possessions.

Clayton came back a couple hours later and told me he was taking his girlfriend, Virginia Spilles, to the state fair and asked if I wanted to go too. He said that Virginia had a friend with her and he asked if I would consider being her date to make it a double date night. I said I guess that would be alright. I was kind of shy but that sounded fun to me. By this time I'd been in town at my new job for about a month and a half. I hadn't really had time to meet any girls, although I did explore Sacramento a bit in my spare time. I didn't have a car yet either so Clayton did all the driving for our double date. We went to Virginia's and picked the girls up. That was the first time that I met Margaret Farley. Clayton and Virginia introduced us and we headed off to the state fair down on Folsom Boulevard. I thought that Margaret was beautiful and we just hit it off from the start.

Margaret Marie Farley.

In 1936 I was a student at Sacramento Junior College and was studying to be a teacher. I had many fond memories of my teachers as I was growing up and they always made a positive impact on me when I was younger, so that's what I wanted to be. I'd been living in Ft. Bragg, California, and intended to go to either Stanford or California and had already been accepted at both of those universities. In 1934 I applied to Montgomery Ward for a scholarship and was selected to receive 10% of certain catalog sales for tuition and expenses. By the time school was getting ready to start there was $500.00 in the fund, and that was no small amount. I met a girl named Anne Dimmick at Dimmick Park and camp ground in Mendocino County. The name was a coincidence, as there was no relation between Anne and the park namesake. We struck up a conversation about school. She was going to be starting her second year at Sacramento Junior College. She told me it made more sense to complete at least my freshman and possibly my sophomore years at Sacramento. That's what she was doing, and then transfer to the larger university. I told her I'd already thought of that and was looking at Santa Rosa Junior College. It was a natural step from there to Cal or Stanford. A lot of students used it as a stepping stone to the larger universities just down the road. She said that housing was less expensive and easier to find in Sacramento and there were more job opportunities there to help with expenses. So, when the time was right, we went to Sacramento and she showed me around the school and the town. It was Anne's hometown and I really liked what I saw, so I went and talked with the counselors at the college, then I decided I would attend there.

"Hey Maggie," Virginia said, "That was Clayton on the phone. He wants me to go to the state fair with him tonight. I told him I wasn't sure if I was up to it, but if he could bring a date for you I'd consider all four of us going, what do you think? Do you want to go have some fun? Are you up for a blind date? He's going to call back soon."

"Oh yes, that sounds like fun. I really don't want to go back to the Green's, they'll just put me to work, and it's my day off."

Virginia would often invite me over on Sunday so the Green's couldn't put me to work. Sunday was supposed to be my day off but if I was around the residence the Green's would keep me busy, so Virginia and I usually found something to do. It was 1936 and the day before the first day of my second year at Sacramento Junior College. I wanted to have some fun before the classes started. I was going to go to California beginning in my second year but that fell through. My counselor, Mr. Brickley, found a job for me as a receptionist at the International House in Berkley. The girl who held that position was graduating and they said they would hold the job for me. She decided, however, to enter into the Master's Program and asked to keep her position as the receptionist since she was remaining in school there. They agreed since she already held the position. Mr. Brickley said he could get me work in Sacramento under a new Government program designed to help kids pay for school by working at the college through the National Youth Authority. I got $20 per month working in the registrar's office at the college. I was also working for, and living with, the Green's. They owned a grocery store on "K" Street. I received another $20 per month for that plus room and board. Mrs. Green was the daughter of the Sacramento County Sheriff. They had three children; an eight year old boy, a five year old girl, and a baby boy. I was supposed to work four hours on Saturday and two hours per day during the week. Weekday duty was one hour at breakfast and be home in time for dinner and dishwashing. I had no room of my own and slept in the little girl's room. I could study at a card table in the living room if the family wasn't out there. Eventually they let me move into the guest room. They were real nice people, but if I was there they would put me to work even if it wasn't within the hours I was supposed to work. I didn't usually mind because I loved the children, but as I made friends throughout my first year I began to want to socialize a little more. Anne was right, I loved Sacramento. It was a lovely, lovely community. I lived with her and her family until the college placed me with a room and board job for my first year. That job didn't work out, so the college placed me with the Green's. About a half hour later the phone rang again and Virginia answered. After a few seconds she said goodbye and hung up.

"Clayton will be here at 7 O'clock to pick us up. He's bringing a friend of his named Cecil who works at the Elm Garage. He's twenty-one years old."

At 7 O'clock sharp the boys pulled up in front of Virginia's house, parked, and walked to the door. They were both dressed nicely in sharp white shirts. Clayton had on dark pants and Cecil was wearing tan pants. He stood about five foot eight, had dark well groomed hair and was very handsome. He was soft spoken as he introduced himself to me. Cecil

Quinley was his name, from Ceres, California. We went out and got in the car, boys in front and girls in back. When we got to the fair we parked and walked in. The fair was huge. I'd been there before. But the size, smells, and sounds always made me feel like I was in a storybook. The first thing we did was find a place to eat. I had a corn dog, lemonade and a cotton candy. A girl always has to have cotton candy you know. The boys were perfect gentlemen the whole night. We walked along the promenade and played games of chance. Cecil was good at the game where you throw a ball at some heavy bottles. If you knock them all over you win a prize. He won me a brown Teddy Bear. There was a platform set up as a dance floor and there was a "big band" playing. We stopped and danced for a while. Cecil was a magnificent dancer, very gentle and always smiling, although he did step on my toes a few times. He would apologize every time and turn beet red with embarrassment. After a while we made our way over to the rides. We rode the Ferris wheel a few times and it was very romantic. We were able to talk some on the Ferris wheel and get to know each other better. There was a large Merry Go Round and we sat on the bench together for a ride on that. We even went on the Loop-A-Plane. When we were at the top of the Loop-A-Plane, and upside down, the ride stopped. What little money the boys had left fell out of their pockets. We felt terrible about that, although the ride was still a lot of fun. We girls were screaming our heads off at being suspended upside down. The boys were just laughing so hard they almost cried. After the ride we walked around the fair more and looked at the exhibits and the animals. I loved petting the horses that would come to the stall door. It began to get late so we told the boys that we needed to get going because tomorrow was the first day of school. We made our way back to the car and headed home. This time, though, Virginia sat up front with Clayton, and I sat in back with Cecil. I think Virginia and Clayton planned that while Cecil and I were on the Ferris wheel. Clayton dropped me and Cecil off at the Green's so we could talk and say goodnight while he drove Virginia home. There were stoops on each side of the steps and we sat on those across from each other as we talked. He told me again how his family did some farming in Ceres, how he was the youngest of a family of twelve, that he hadn't lived in Sacramento very long. He said although he didn't attend church very much he was a Baptist because that's what most of his family was. He wanted to fly airplanes and I thought that was so romantic. He had already told me some of that, but I think he was a bit nervous and didn't know what else to say. It was cute. I told him I was from Iowa, but we moved to Ft. Bragg because of the depression. We drove out to

California when I was a kid and we would just stop on the side of the road, throw a blanket out, and sleep wherever we stopped. My dad would build a camp fire that mom would cook something over. I had two older brothers. One of them, Kenny, thank God, wasn't here because he treated my dates horribly. He would question them until they wanted to run away. I would get so mad at him, but he would always say that he's my big brother and it's his job to take care of me.

Chapter 5
Stan Kenton

For the rest of 1936 Cecil and I were pretty busy, but we tried to make as much time for each other as we could. I had school and my two jobs and he was quite busy at the Elm Garage on 9th street. Virginia and I felt real bad about the boys losing their money on the Loop-A-Plane at the state fair. A month after our blind date there was going to be a concert at the Senator Hotel. Stan Kenton was coming to town. I had already discovered that Cecil and I shared a liking for this kind of music when we danced at the fair and talked later that night at Virginia's house. I asked Virginia if it would be considered inappropriate for us to ask the boys to the concert.

"That's a good question," she said, "let's ask my sister."

Her sister was older and wiser in these things, so we trusted her judgment. She said it was a wonderful idea and although, normally, the men paid for the date, she didn't think it would be inappropriate to take them to the dance. I asked Cecil and Virginia asked Clayton and both were excited about it. We had to start saving right away. The cost was $5 per couple, but it would be a team effort. Virginia and I would pay for the dance, but Clayton was the only one with a car, so he would provide the car and Cecil would provide the gas. It was a date! I was already at Virginia's chit-chatting our excitement about the upcoming evening:

"So, what do you think about Cecil?" Virginia asked.

"I like him," I said, "is it too soon to like someone after only one date?"

"No, I don't think so. Not as long as you don't get too carried away. It's okay to like him, just keep taking it slow and get to know him," Virginia said.

"How about you two?" I asked. "How are things going with you? Have you gotten serious enough with Clayton to talk about marriage?"

"Yes, it's serious. We've talked a little about it. We're trying to be practical though. I have to finish school and Clayton needs a career that's a little more steady and with less travel. But yes, I'm head over heels in love with him, that's for sure."

"That is so sweet. You guys make a beautiful couple too."

"Thank you Mags," Virginia said.

"I'm so glad you asked me to the fair with Cecil. I think he's swell and I hope we get to know each other more over the summer."

"That's so wonderful. I'm glad you feel that way. You guys are cute together too. It seems like you have so much in common. It's pretty obvious that he really likes you too."

At 6 P.M. the boys pulled up outside. They were both dressed handsomely in dark grey suits. The concert was wonderful and Stan Kenton played a mix of swing and jazz that made the night magical. Cecil didn't disappoint with his gentlemanly demeanor and soft spoken way about him and his dancing skills. We talked, laughed, and danced the night away. I don't remember ever having this much fun or feeling this close to a man before. We waltzed divinely, 1-2-3, 1-2-3. I had been on some dates before, but those were teenager type dates in Ft. Bragg. Here I was, all grown up and sipping Champaign between dances with a handsome man in a suit. Talking about our history, our present, and our possible future. I already felt like I'd known Cecil my whole life. We made plans to do this as often as possible and to get together as much as our schedules would allow. After the concert was over Clayton dropped us off at the Green's again while he took Virginia home. Again, Cecil and I sat across from each other on the stoops by the steps to the porch and talked more about family, interests, us. Sometimes nervously repeating things we'd already said, but that was O.K. This time, as Clayton pulled up in front of the house, Cecil came over to me and told me he had a wonderful night. He leaned over and kissed me on the cheek. I stood up and we looked at each other for a moment and we kissed each other softly on the lips. After that I found myself in the house, not remembering exactly how I got there. Is this what it feels like to fall in love?

For the rest of 1936 we made as much time for each other as we could. We played tennis on Sundays. Cecil was quite good at it. He beat me as much as I beat him and we grew even closer the more we were together. I got to meet one of Cecil's sisters, Milly. It was Milly's house that he was living at. I got along swell with Milly and her husband Jim. For the rest of 1936 and into 1937 those scenes just repeated themselves. School, work, and we played when we could. Cecil was busy at the Elm Garage too. He worked long hours changing tires, greasing and tuning up cars and filling gas tanks when people pulled in. As the summer approached I made plans to go with several of my classmates to work at Fallen Leaf Lodge by Lake Tahoe for the summer. It was decent pay and the splendor of living in the cool pine trees by Fallen Leaf Lake was too irresistible. They provided the lodging and the meals too. We were allowed to use everything there if it wasn't reserved or in use by the paying guests. We had boats to row in the lake, and we could swim, but the water was quite cold. There was ping pong, dancing, and hiking. Stateline, Nevada, was not far away and there was always something going on there. Then, too, there was the beauty and majesty of Lake Tahoe. What a miracle of nature. It's something that has to be experienced. Words alone can't paint a good enough picture for someone to (feel) what you're trying to explain to them. Lake Tahoe is indeed heavenly. Part of it is in California and part is in Nevada. The town of South Lake Tahoe wasn't very far away from where I was staying, and right across the state line was, named appropriately enough, Stateline. While I was at Fallen Leaf Lodge Cecil and I would write to each other every day and he would come up to visit once a month, twice near the end of summer as we fell more deeply in love. We would drive to the south shore and see movies or go dancing. Other times we would do outdoor things. I cherished our time together when he came. We were in love alright, and the more we were together I could just tell that he was the one for me.

Hello my darling. Here I am, safe, all in one piece. Having fun already and meeting many nice people. The trip was grand and I enjoyed it immensely. The scenery is superb. Gee, it's perfectly heavenly up here! Everyone is grand and I've met lots of the kids. It's going to be loads of fun but I wish you were around to enjoy it too. The lake is scrumptious. So far the altitude hasn't administered any serious ill effects and I don't believe it will. The food here is fantastic. Am I ever eating like a horse! It's terrible! Seconds of every course including desert and coffee! By the time I see you again, soon I hope, I'll be able to drink you under the table, as far as the coffee is concerned of course.

My lonesomeness for you is registering itself in the music of the typewriter. Pauline and a couple of the boys are playing cards, but I didn't feel in a gambling mood. Mrs. Rehm, a very nice Swedish lady from Sacramento, gets the Bee and through her kind consideration has consented to drop it by my door in the evening when she finishes it. She's awfully nice, and what a charming accent. Thanks to her I will be able to keep up with all the daily gossip in Sacramento. Did I tell you that all of us girls in the 'Hen

House' (our quarters, ahem!) brought our tennis racquets up with us? Boy, are we going to have fun. Pauline, Mary, Peggy, and I have already agreed to a doubles match the first chance we get to play!

Hello again on this Sunday night, although it doesn't really seem like Sunday. Two very nice letters arrived from my sweet little Cecil today. One of your letters, as well as my report card, was miss-sent to Fallon, Nevada. Please excuse me for falsely reprimanding you for not writing. Today we rowed across the lake and hiked to the top of the Angora Lookout Mountain along a line of new telephone poles that had just been planted. I made it to the top in only 40 minutes. The view was gorgeous from there. We gazed through one of those glasses which brings things near in focus and looked at all the mountains around here. The man in the moon had just set out his lantern when we started back. How I wished you were there to enjoy it, but then it probably would have been much later when we got to the bottom. Uh hum!

We work with a fellow named Dick. He is working his way through Stanford for an MD degree. Brilliant as heck, is employed here as a porter, but does all kinds of work. I'm sure you'd like him! Tall and blonde. Everybody around here thinks he's tops. Is my darling jealous? Please don't be, after all, with a big 'skirt' orchestra on the way to Sacramento I'm almost tempted to return! You deserved that! Gee, I nearly hit the sky today when I read your letter! To think there is the slightest possible chance that I may see my darling over this weekend! Sweetheart, my joy knows no bounds! Gosh, I hope you'll be able to make it! But don't drive recklessly! I'll be raring to go any time after five O'clock, so come on Cecil, let's go to town in a big way! Jean Englander and his orchestra are playing at the Bal-Bijou. There's always a swell orchestra at State Line and also an equally fine floor show.

Did I tell you a lady tipped me a whole dollar yesterday? She'd been here a whole week. With your two lovely letters also came invitations to three U.C. sorority teas. Sigma Kappa, Mu Delta Zeta, and Alpha Theta Upsilon. Pretty nice, huh? However, I'm still not going to be sap enough to try and go to Cal – at least not this fall. After dinner four of us went down to the social hall where we played ping pong for a while, then danced to the Lucky Strike orchestra on the radio for about fifteen minutes. Then we hiked up to see the Glen Alpine Falls and on to Lily Lake. When we got back, Dick Jürgen's came on the radio and we danced for another half hour. Then George Hamilton's Music Box Orchestra came on and we danced to that. It was as grand as ever I thought it was, but I wish you had been here to dance with me. A few nights ago we heard both the Showboat and Bob Burns. They were good; did you hear them as well? Jack Haley is swell! Did you hear him sing 'The love bug will bite you?' It was cute.

Lois asked me how I felt to know I was in love. She wants to know what tells you you're in love with a certain person. I just said that that person means more to you than anyone else, and you think about him all the time and stuff! Anyway, I don't suppose there's any need to tell you again that I love you, and always will. You're my every thought, my every song etc. In fact 'All I do is dream of you,' always. I should say 'think' I guess, or is it a 'dream?' 'Are you a vision? A vision or no, I adore you, wonderful you.' I just thought of another adjective to describe you. You're enchanting, divine, and mine, all mine, for life everlasting, I hope. I must say good night and be good, write soon, and 'love me forever.' Margaret.

Chapter 6
Fallen Leaf Lodge

"How many eggs you want this morning?" Milly asked.

"Two," I said, "thanks."

"How'd your date go last night? Margaret seems like a wonderful girl. Do you like her? What does she do? Is she from Sacramento? I'll bet--"

"Well if you'll slow down for just a minute maybe I could answer some of your questions," I broke in with a giant grin on my face. "It was a fantastic night. We danced the night away and talked a lot, I really like her. I hope we get to see more of each other."

"Did you kiss her?"

"Milly!" I said.

"Okay, okay! Well, did you?"

"Milly! That's none of your business!"

"You did, didn't you? I can tell. I haven't seen you this peppy in a long time."

"Yes, we kissed, now can we talk about something else? Please?"

My sister was nosey about my encounters with Margaret. I guess she just wanted to see her little brother happy. She must have noticed that all I've done since arriving in Sacramento is work and wander around town looking for something to do. I'd even gone to some speakeasy establishments in the downtown area. They were called speakeasy because of a little sliding window that they had on the door. A big guy usually would open the little window upon hearing a knock and he would decide if you got in or not. They started in the prohibition days. While prohibition was over, the custom kind of held on and was used, I guess, to limit access to who they wanted in there. It never dawned on me that there were bars that didn't do that anymore. That maybe I shouldn't be going into a place that has a big roughneck peeking through a hole in the door, but I was young and naive. You never knew who you'd run across. One time I went in to find something to do and found the Sheriff, Chief of Police, and the Fire Chief all involved in a poker game. I got a beer, lit a cigarette and sat down to watch the game. I could tell that the two lawmen weren't too comfortable with me being there, but the Fire Chief told them I was alright. He recognized me because he came into the Elm Garage a lot. I didn't have money to gamble but it was fun to watch, and there was a dame singing that sounded just like Billie Holliday. She only had a piano backing her up instead of a whole band, but the guy could really play, and she could really sing. I could have stayed there all night and listened to her. It was relaxing. That was about the extent of my excitement before I met Margaret. Other than that I went to as many movies as I could afford. I got to liking movies during the depression. My family farmed and grew a lot of our own food, and California had good soil and water so the depression didn't hurt us too bad. We had to grow food because of having twelve kids around. I mean, things got a little tough, don't get me wrong, but we had it a lot better than many families did. Especially the families that migrated from the Midwest. Me and my brother George and Milly would go to the movies as much as we could. If we couldn't afford it we might just sneak in. After finally getting caught the owner made us a deal that he would let us come in for free if we stayed around to help him clean up the place.

The Stan Kenton dance was fantastic. Margaret was a very good dancer and she loves dancing. The smell of her perfume captivated me the whole night. A couple times I caught myself just going through the motions on the dance floor. I'd lose track of the music as it kind of faded into the distance. The result of my getting lost staring into Margaret's eyes. When the night was over we found ourselves on the same step abutments staring at each other, and giggling. We decided to date more and spend as much time together as we could. It'd be hard, because of our busy schedules, especially Margaret's, but we decided to have some outings together. I was working up the courage all night to try to kiss her and my shyness was winning the fight, and I had not done so yet. When I saw Clayton pulling around the corner it was just the push I needed. I couldn't look afraid in front of him. I went over and gave her a kiss on the cheek, just like she gave me after the fair. Then, all of a sudden, she stood up and we were staring into each other's eyes for a moment and it just happened. We were kissing! On the lips! It only lasted a few seconds but it seemed like forever. We played a lot of tennis through the rest of 1936 and into 1937. I was surprised at how good she was. One of my favorite things to do was to simply go to a park and have a nice picnic and throw bread to the ducks and geese. We named all the ducks. Margaret got a kick out of some of the language I used. I didn't swear or anything like that, but when I would say dame, or skirt, I got that look. I think she understood that it was just habit from growing up with five brothers. After all, she had two brothers of her own. In the summer of 1937 she went off to Fallen Leaf

Lodge at Lake Tahoe to work there and earn money for college. A lot of Stanford people worked there too. I missed her terribly. By then we had developed a deep love for each other and that absence just made the heart grow fonder. It had its drawbacks too. I was stuck in the one hundred degree weather in Sacramento while she was up having fun in the pine trees and cool mountain air. We wrote to each other every night. I know she worked hard, but I couldn't help but be a little jealous sometimes when I read about her dancing and having fun, and there were other guys there. I knew that she was devoted to me by this time, as I was to her, but the thoughts could drive a man to drink. Occasionally, I was able to drive up and spend some time with her on her days off. We were growing closer and closer and I could tell that she was the girl for me.

Dear Margaret.

How are you anyway? Fit as a fiddle and ready for love, or has your fiddle got a broken string? I hope not. It hasn't been so awfully hot here today, not much more than a hundred even, pretty good for this old dump eh what? Bob Burns is on the radio now. Some dame was just singing some opera stuff. When she got all through Bob asked her 'are you through now?' He doesn't seem to mind what he says to embarrass his entertainers. Jack Haley is on the showboat and he was just telling someone that he wrote funny verses on his checks, but the bank must not think they are so funny because they keep sending them back marked 'no funds.' Good pun huh?

I just heard over the radio that Amelia Earhart's plane was believed to be down in the ocean someplace or another. It said that the last radio report they got from her she had gas enough to last her for about half an hour, but they said that her plane was constructed so that if the plane went down with all the gas tanks empty it could float on top of the water for a number of days. More power to her.

I guess I'd better tell you that I'll be up to see you Sunday or Monday. I think Monday. The boss told me today, before I ever got a chance to ask him, that I could have Sunday and Monday both off and then he asked me where I was going and I said 'that all depends on whether I can find somebody with a car going the same direction as I

33

want to go.' So my boss says; 'well, I think that you might just as well use one of mine if you wish.' And so I didn't refuse. You can be thinking of something nice to do with your little darling Cecil while he is there. I wish I was getting a couple weeks off so I could see my darling every night, but maybe someday (if she is willing) I can see her every night of the year. In other words - I love you very much darling, very, very much. So until I see you, be good and don't do anything I wouldn't, or maybe I shouldn't say that, but anyway, be careful and furthermore I love you my sweetheart.

Hello again, this is Cecil Quinley and his bit of scribbling coming to you through the courtesy of the U.S. Mail Department. And how's my exquisitely delightful little darling this very lovely evening? I am practically in the pink again, about one more night and I'll have caught up on all my lost sleep. I went to the show last night and saw 'Parnell.' It sure was good. All the fellow Irishmen and stuff. Boy that guy Clark Gable sure is good and I don't mean maybe. If I was a woman I think I'd go for him too, maybe. Myrna Loy was good also, not bad anyway. Damn these people who keep wanting gas while I'm trying to write to you.

I see by the evening paper that they are about to give up finding poor Amelia. It's too bad, but she shouldn't get lost where people can't find her. I should be ashamed of me for talking like that, huh? Anyway, I feel sorry for her and wish that they would find her, but she'd probably go right out and do it again. How are you coming with your play these days? Getting enough of it? I hope so, but don't do any of the wrong kind of playing is all I ask of my darling. If you catch what I mean, because I love you very much.

Variety is the spice of life, they say, except where you're concerned. One is just right. I love you as much, if not more than ever, and I think you're just right for me and you're adorable and every nice thing there is.

This is yours truly signing off for tonight, and I shall come to you again tomorrow evening at the same hour through the courtesy of love and so forth. So until later, be good and have a good, good night. Sleep well and dream nice dreams about me. I do about you. Goodbye now. Love Cecil.

Chapter 7
Endless Summer

    I continued to drive up to Fallen Leaf Lodge as much as I could. It was hard getting time off sometimes, or finding a car to drive, or having enough money to go. I missed Margaret dearly and thought about her all the time. Sometimes it made it real hard to do my work at the garage. I spent most of my days changing or repairing tires and doing lube jobs on cars and trucks. They started training me a little to do minor tune ups but there were the gas pumps to man every time that darn bell would ding when someone pulled up to the pumps. When I wasn't thinking about Margaret I was thinking about flying. I still wanted to join the Army Air Corps, but that would require going back to school and finishing my degree. You had to have at least a two year degree to become a pilot in the Air Corps. It was still in my plans and I dreamed about it out loud when we were together. Toward the end of July and into August it was getting easier to find a car to get up to the lake. My boss figured out that I worked harder and was much happier when I had trips to see my honey to look forward to. He had plenty of cars and began letting me use one to go see Margaret. It helped also, I guess, that he was a hopeless romantic at heart. When we got together up in the pine trees and the fresh mountain air it was like heaven on earth. Sometimes we would boat on the lake and Margaret would show me all the sites she'd discovered on her previous outings. We hiked to the tops of mountains. Sometimes we went over to Stateline at the south shore of Lake Tahoe to go dancing at the Bijou. Every once in a while they'd have a nice band playing there. Dancing was probably our number one romantic thing to do, besides necking in the car and wearing our lips raw trying to get enough kissing in to last until our next rendezvous.

    At the Bijou we found a table near the dance floor. Dick Jurgens and his swing orchestra was playing. A waitress came by and offered us drinks. Margaret had a glass of red wine and I had a beer. Neither one of us drank very much, so a couple drinks would last us the whole evening. We usually ended the night with coffee and tea. I'd have a cigarette every once in a while, but I tried to cut back when I was with Margaret because I didn't want to smell like an ash tray. We danced the Jitterbug to the swing music and the waltz to slower songs. I was getting better at not stepping on her toes. Margaret would complement me all the time on my dancing, but it was her who was the expert. I loved to dance because it meant we were close, and doing things together. We could see into each other's eyes and I'd get lost in her perfume. It was an all-around swell time. After the dance we drove back toward Fallen Leaf Lake and I stopped and parked by Taylor Creek on the west shore of Lake Tahoe. I didn't have to say anything, Margaret and I were on the same page by now. We kissed for about an hour and rubbed up against each other as lovers do. It was very romantic. We could smell the pine trees and hear the running creek water. The forest animals and birds made noises. We'd neck as often as we could, which sometimes was problematic because we were both determined to save ourselves for marriage. It left me often with the need to take a cold shower, but we knew it would be worth it in the end. We were both raised that way. It was about midnight when we finally rolled into the parking area next to the lodge. I bid goodnight to Margaret and she retired to her room. There were no men allowed in the ladies rooms, and since she was an employee of the lodge, she was not allowed to come to mine either. It was a long night that began with another cold shower.

I was pretty disappointed when Margaret was asked to stay on for another month to help out. We'd talked it over and she agreed to do so since she wasn't going to be able to afford to attend U.C. yet. At least I was able to see her more often now since my boss was letting me use his car. We always had my weekends to look forward to. I usually had Monday and Tuesday off. It was still pretty hot in Sacramento. Usually at least one hundred degrees or more and it didn't really cool off much at night. It seems like it just got muggier and made it hard to sleep, so I was going up to the lake as much as I could. On one occasion, in August, I was able to get a Sunday off too, giving us three days together. I decided to take her over to Silver Lake, which was a little south west of Lake Tahoe and about fifty miles from the little town of Jackson, California. My brothers, Lester and John, ran a boys camp there in the summer. Lester had spotted Silver Lake one day, I think around 1933, while he was driving past it. He'd always wanted to start a camp for boys to give them something to do and to mentor them. He saw an island of about 40 acres out on the lake and thought that it would make the perfect site. He drummed up investors to get the ball rolling and when it was done he named it Camp Treasure Island. It would accommodate boys ages nine to sixteen. Later, he would add a camp on the mainland of the lake for girls. Lester recruited John and me to help build the cabins. Being the youngest, I would be the fortunate brother who got to do the roofing. John owned a ski lodge on leased land that he ran in the winter called Donner Trail Ski Lodge. This time of year, though, would find him at Silver Lake.

It was time for Margaret to meet Lester and John. It was a real long day for me. I drove all the way from Sacramento up to Fallen Leaf Lodge, picked up Margaret, and headed down the road to Silver Lake. I left at the crack of dawn so we'd have some time to spend with my brothers before bed time. Of course, once we got there, we still had to take a boat out to the island where the camp was, but it was a great visit. Women weren't normally allowed on the island, but they made an exception and made sure the boys remained covered up during their open air showers and such. It was somewhat hectic because of all the campers running around, but we had time for a nice visit all day Monday. John grilled up some delicious steaks over wood and pine cones for Monday night and later we sat around a campfire roasting marshmallows. In the morning, Lester, John and I got up early and ran down to the water. We rowed a short distance out on the lake and caught some rainbow trout. Then, we hurried back to camp and cooked the trout on the grill with sage and garlic, along with some fresh eggs. We surprised Margaret with the morning feast and fresh brewed campfire coffee. I could tell that she loved every minute of it, and so far I think she loved all three of my siblings that she'd met (Lester, John and Milly). Things couldn't be going any better. After breakfast we helped clean up the dishes, said our farewells and headed back to Fallen Leaf Lodge. I dropped Margaret off with a hardy kiss and raced the sun westward. I got into Sacramento somewhat late at around 9 O'clock, but I'd gotten home to Milly's much later than that before. It was a very satisfying trip and, although exhausted, I went about my nightly routine of taking a bath and reading the letters that came from Margaret today while I was gone, and sitting down to write to her.

> Hello again my most adorable darling. And how are you feeling by this time? You should be right in the pink after your days off. I guess I must be in love, writing so much, but I just finished reading your most lovely letters and I enjoyed them immensely & tremendously & even more.
>
> I'm glad that you liked the lip balm and I hope it keeps your lips in very good shape and all nice and pretty and stuff – just as I have always found them to be, because I just thrill with the thought of them in contact with mine. I agree

with you that you should go to J.C. cause then I will say goody-goody and then I can see you very often. Of course your studies would interfere considerably with my visits with you. Ha-Ha. But I could at least be with you much more of the time than I am now or I would be if you were in Oakland or San Francisco.

Milly was just wondering how you managed to read these letters. She made me sit up straight. I had my feet parked up on the back of another chair and my elbow hanging over the back of the one I am sitting in, to keep from falling out, and my fanny out in space with my head resting on the corner of the table. Boy what a position, But at least I was comfortable until she came along and spoiled my comfort. I'll get her for that. I'll have to duel with her. Tooth picks at fifty paces or maybe something a little less dangerous.

Boy, if I had a car like my friend Mr. Rich has I could make it up there in nothing flat on Mondays. He has a great big new Studebaker. He left Meeks Bay for Sacramento this morning and made it to his home here in Sacramento in two hours and fifteen minutes. Boy, that's really moving. He said he took in the whole road, detours and all. I asked him if it would do a hundred and he said he didn't know but he was hitting above the ninety mark this morning.

My very sweet, sweet darling I shall have to say good night about now and get to bed. It is about 11:30 and I should by all means get my beauty sleep. I need plenty of it. Ouch! The chair just fell out from under me and I hit the floor. Guess I'll sit up straight now. Glad Milly didn't see that! Until tomorrow remember that I love you and adore you and think that you are the tops etc. So now to bed, and sweet dreams of you, and I hope I may kiss you in my dreams. Lots and lots of love and kisses. Cecil.

Chapter 8
High Sierra Rendezvous'

Fallen Leaf Lodge had a nice western style rustic chapel but they also conducted services out in the open air. Lois and I just attended one.

"I just love having services outside like that, surrounded by the pine trees with the lake right over there," Lois said.

"Me too," I said, "I've been to Sunday church services my whole life, but this is the first place that I've seen like this. I just love it too. Do you want to go get some hotcakes before we have to start work?"

"Oh yes! Let's do that, I'm pretty hungry this morning. Is Cecil coming up to visit tomorrow?"

"He's planning on it. We're going to go to the Bijou again. Last time he was up Dick Jurgens was playing and we had a swell time. We danced all night. Cecil's a wonderful dancer, and just my size. I trust him. We always have a great time together."

"I noticed you came in pretty late that night, I know the dance didn't last that long. Have car trouble?"

"Ha-ha, I'll never tell. Let's just say we're in love and leave it at that. It's not like you're thinking though. We're both waiting for marriage for that."

I just gave Lois a look when I responded to her question as we both sat down with our short stack of hotcakes. Outdoor church services in the fresh mountain morning air, and now hotcakes with hot butter and hot maple syrup and a hot cup of coffee. This is the life. I may not be making much money here, but oh my how the living conditions are dreamy. I only wished Cecil were here to share it with me. I suppose I might not be feeling this way if it were January. But right now, it doesn't get much better than this.

"Has he asked you yet?" Lois kept prodding.

"Not in so many words, but we banter back and forth about the subject, in a round-about way in our letters. He knows I have to have more school first. Plus, he's nowhere near being able to support a wife and family yet. He has a good steady job, but it doesn't pay much and there's no room for advancement there. He keeps talking about joining the Air Corps and flying. I'd support that completely but he'd have to go back to college and finish if he wants that. There's just a lot of stuff to consider before we take the big plunge."

"Have you met his family yet? Has he met yours?"

"I've met his sister and two of his brothers. They're just wonderful people. Right away they made me feel like I'd known them forever. He hasn't met my family yet. My mom went over to Detroit so my step dad could find work in journalism. My brothers are still over on the coast. I've told everyone all about him, but they haven't seen him yet. How about you?"

"How about me what?" Lois asked, caught off guard.

"Have you and Mark talked about marriage?"

"Yes, as a matter of fact, we have. He's getting a promotion at the Southern Pacific yard. He's working inside right now, calling in the train crews. He likes it alright, but he'd rather be on the trains. They said he would be within the year. Then he'd be making good money with room for advancement. I'll be finishing up school about then and looking for a teaching job. Everything is headed in that direction and we, I think, both assume the same thing, but he hasn't actually asked me yet. I know he will though. He'd better!"

We wrapped up our breakfast and went off to our assignments for the day. I had several cabins to clean. I always hoped that someone would leave a nice tip to supplement my pay. It was always a nice surprise when they did. Later, I settled into my room and began to write Cecil my nightly letter. It was always a nice escape and a way to keep him close. I always looked forward to reading his letters. As usual, though, Lois wanted to get to bed, but we agreed on an hour before lights out. I turned on the radio and listened to some shows and music. It was relaxing. I read Cecil's last letter with a grin on my face, and then began to write. I told him of all the things I'd been doing throughout the week. That is, if I hadn't already done so in a previous letter. The season was winding down now, but I'd be staying on an extra couple weeks since I wouldn't be going to Cal this year. I'd decided to stay at SJC to take more classes, simply due to the cost. I just couldn't afford Cal yet, but maybe next year. I wondered in private how my relationship with Cecil would affect that decision, and if we married how that may change my plans. I suppose that's something we'd have to talk about. I think he'd be supportive about my education. He struck me as a very understanding and selfless man. As I finished the letter I folded the pages and placed them in the envelope. I didn't seal it because I'd add more in the morning before heading off to work. As my work day tomorrow would be winding down, my love would be arriving to sweep me off my feet again.

The morning came early and the air was brisk, even for this time of year. I washed my face and shook the cobwebs from my eyes and set pen to paper again. I don't know how I always found more to say in the morning. I hadn't done anything but sleep since I finished the letter last night. I guess I just felt like I had to talk to him whenever I could, and since he isn't here I'd do it by writing. I finished the letter, sealed it up, stamped it and went down to breakfast. I'd drop the letter in the mail on the way to the cabins. Breakfast this day was bacon and eggs with oatmeal. I put a slice of butter and a tablespoon of maple syrup on the oatmeal. Not healthy, I know, but darn good. A nice cup of coffee would get my blood pumping. Then, after stopping by the post office, I headed down toward the cabins to begin cleaning. It was tough keeping my mind on my work today knowing that Cecil would be here later. To try and take my mind off of it I'd hum and sing while cleaning. Its effectiveness was questionable because I found myself singing and humming songs that we danced to. I guess it made things better, though, because it made me happy singing and it helped the day pass more quickly.

And a good, good evening to you my darling. I hope this finds you feeling well. Captain Henry's Showboat is on, featuring Mary Boland. She's a scream! You're probably listening to it also so I won't go into any details. Garwood Vann and his orchestra are playing 'Yours and mine' and 'Where or when.' I like both particularly well. Here's hoping they play 'My cabin of dreams.' I like 'There's a sailboat in the moonlight,' 'If I can count on you,' 'Can I forget you?' I'm having fun catching up with popular songs. Holy Mike! I don't believe it! He's playing 'My cabin of dreams!' Am I lucky? Pardon me while I dance with your shadow my dear. Hmm! That was swell!

I'm trying your method of writing, but instead of risking falling out of a chair I'm stretched out on my bed. It would be fine if my neck wouldn't get stiff and my left arm wouldn't go to sleep holding up the rest of my big fat self. It has really been warm here today! This evening it was too hot to remain in our rooms, so Lola May and I took the boat

43

out for a ride. It was about 8:30 when we left and almost 10:00 when we returned. The lake was calm and placid and there was a full moon, almost full, it will be full on July 23rd. It was hanging just over the Angora Lakes side of the lookout. It was heavenly out there! We sat out in the middle of the lake and wished that both you and Johnny could have been there with us. No such luck, alas!

Yesterday, my day off, I went to Camp Richardson with the mail truck and got a hair-cut. I had lots of time because the mail was an hour late due to the fact that the Oakland train was derailed just outside Oakland and the mail left there two hours late. However, the Tahoe mail boat made up the time in one hour. Not bad huh? It certainly is nice over there at Camp Rich! Swell beach etc.

Earlier in the week, us outside girls went on a picnic to Mr. Hansen's home over at the 'Y'. We had the best steaks you ever ate! Boy, they were good! Plus, an equally grand raspberry shortcake with whipped cream and all kinds of other good things. Combination vegetable salad, sandwiches, hot coffee, chocolate cake, and white cake, etc. It certainly was fun! We went in the little Ford V-8 pick-up, or mail truck, and did we have fun in the moonlight coming home! Mr. Hansen drove us over to see the moonlight over on Lake Tahoe. It was glorious!

A bunch of the kids are having a wienie roast up at Lily Lake tomorrow. I wish I were able to go, in a way, because I'm hungry for a nice hot dog. But maybe my sweet Cecil will buy me one at the fair if he takes me, which I hope he will. Speaking of the fair, we must celebrate the anniversary of our first date, September 9th, 1936. Remember way back then? Virginia and Clayton were merely sweethearts and now look at them! She didn't know him as long as I have you before she married him, but we haven't taken the final leap as yet, not that I don't often wish we had, but then such is life I suppose. I made another $1.00 tip today. Three days in a row! More fun! My total is now $16.25 (tips and otherwise). Nice going for a while.

Mr. Craven came up over the week and he and the Mrs. went over to Silver Lake to see Billy, their son, who is staying at Lester's camp. Mrs. Craven was saying how good it made her feel to see all those kids having so much fun, so many advantages, and under such grand supervision! Nice boasting for Lester, huh? She was really very enthusiastic about all she'd seen. But then, why shouldn't she be? Look whose camp it is!

Have I told you I love you, my sweetest sweetheart? If not, remember I always shall, and I shall ever rejoice in the ecstasy of being loved by so noble a person as you. How am I doing? Anyway, I do love you and I can't help it but I still have to close for tonight. So once more, be good, be careful, and love me always. Please God take care of him (you) for me and his mommy! Good night most precious one. Love Margaret.

Chapter 9
Thanksgiving in Ceres

My! Oh! My! And was I surprised to get a letter from you tonight. Thank you my darling. It was sweet of you to write to me like that and I love you for it. I guess you didn't get tired of seeing me if you write so soon afterwards, and that is so nice. Your friend Lucille Murphy just came in after her car. Boy, when she got back from vacation last Saturday night she looked like she had lost about ten pounds. Mostly, I guess, from being drunk for about two weeks straight. In fact, she was still kind of drunk when she got here. She sure must be able to soak plenty of that stuff up. I don't hardly think that you will ever get that way. Will you my sweet?

About next Tuesday, I don't know anything definite yet, and won't until about Friday or Saturday, but you just start praying for me and maybe it will help me get there. A chance to find out if it does any good to pray. I sure hope so. Of course I will be so very, very disappointed if I don't get to do so. You certainly must have felt funny when you got out in the boat the other day and lost your oars. I should have liked to have seen that. Pardon me but I'm afraid I would have laughed very hard. Maybe you should get a strap and strap yourself in your seat. Next time you might fall in the lake instead of the bottom of the boat, so be careful my darling because I wouldn't want you getting yourself all wet. Make sure you stay within hollering distance or you might end up swimming back, or tearing up a seat to use it as a paddle, or using your shirt for a sail.

In case you haven't heard about it we had a nice murder last night in Sacramento, William Land Park to be exact. That place is getting terrible. Some man shot his ex-wife who was picnicking with some other guy. I heard about it last night right after it happened. I certainly was surprised today when I found out that I knew the guy's sister. I don't know her exactly, but I see her all the time.

47

She works in the engineering department in the federal building. Boy, she sure was feeling terrible today. She was over at the garage looking for Mr. Rich to try to get him to get his brother, an attorney (Senator Rich), to defend her brother, but he didn't seem to think much of the idea. I feel sorry for her because she is a nice kid.

The fair starts again pretty soon here in Sacramento. Maybe we can go and celebrate once more again. Sort of an anniversary, don't-ya-know. Remember? Do ya think that we could have as much fun once again as we had that first time? At least I sure had a swell time. I hadn't had so much fun since the cow kicked my old grandmother through the side of the barn.

Its sure been a long time since I saw our old friends Virginia and Clayton. I just happened to think of them because Clayton's old boss, Mr. Levitt from the radio store, was asking me about him today. He wanted to know how he was getting along and if he was still working at Sears and Roebuck, and all I could say was I guess so. I drove out by Virginia's mother's place the other day, Sunday, and thought maybe I'd see them, but I didn't see Clayton's car around. I supposed they were gone someplace and so I didn't stop to find out. Maybe they aren't there now, but probably so.

Do you still love me my darling? You had better, because you will be coming home in just six more days, and then I'll be so happy. Because then I can see you at least once or twice a week, I hope, and won't that be sumpin? Once again, before I go, I love you and think that you're the sweetest and bestest girl in the whole big universe. I guess that takes em all in. Be sure and be good and take care of yourself until you get back to Sacramento and then I can help you be good. It's so-long now, as ever, with Love and kisses. Cecil.

Margaret came home from the lake the last week of August. Just in time for the state fair. Just as we had planned, we attended as kind of our first year anniversary. Just like last year, we rode the Ferris wheel, the Merry-Go-Round, and of course the Loop-A-Plane. But this time I made sure my money wouldn't fall out. There were other differences this year too. This time we didn't go as a double date. And this year we held hands all night as we walked around to all the attractions, except of course when we were eating cotton candy or hot dogs with lots of mustard. I won her another Teddy Bear throwing the ball at the heavy bottles. There was a swell band playing again this year and we danced for a couple of hours. At about 11:00 we were both feeling pretty tired so we called it a night. I drove her home as she sat right beside me in the car with her head resting on my shoulder. When we got there we kissed for a while in the car and as she was getting ready to get out I said,

"What would you think about having thanksgiving with my family down in Ceres? After all, your mom is still up in Michigan. I think it would be fun."

"Oh, I'd love to have thanksgiving there. I've been dying to meet the rest of the Quinley clan. I'm so very fond of Lester, Milly, and John. I'd just love to meet the rest," she said.

And so it was a date. For the next month and a half I saw Margaret about twice a week. She was busy with school and I was busy at the garage. On our days off we'd picnic at William Land Park and play tennis on the courts there. One time we went with Milly and her husband Jim to see a Sacramento Solons baseball game. They were a minor league baseball team affiliated with the St. Louis Cardinals. I wasn't much of a fan, but over time I found myself liking baseball more and more. Milly and Jim went to games a lot. There were only a couple more games to play this year and they were going to finish in first place.

My boss at the garage got his hands on a car that he accepted as payment on a debt. It was a tan 1931 Chevrolet coupe with one bench seat and a six cylinder engine. He knew I was still hoofing it everywhere so he offered to sell it to me for a great price. I bought it from him for $75 and never looked back again. Wow, my first car! There'd be no stopping me now! About the time thanksgiving rolled around I made sure that the Chevy was ready to go. Thursday, November 25th, 1937, I picked up Margaret early, about 8 O'clock in the morning, at the apartment she was now sharing with three other girls. She was dressed in a mid-shin chiffon dress and some sort of a little hat. I wasn't exactly a fashion expert, but it looked great on her. We settled in for the 85 mile ride to Ceres. During the ride I took the time to instruct her on the names and occupations of my parents and many siblings. She already knew about John, Lester, and Milly, and that my parents, Cora Belle and John Winson, were retired farmers. We took the next nearly hour and a half talking about the rest of my sisters and brothers. The closest brother to me in age is George. He's an electrician by trade. Then followed in order by ascending age are John and Lester. Clarence, who's the head of the irrigation district in Oakdale, California. The oldest boy is Ormal. He's a mechanic. My sisters are, from youngest to oldest, Rebecca, a switchboard operator at the telephone company. Corabelle, who works at the fruit cannery. Then there's Milly, who Margaret was already friends with. Milly is a clerk at JC Penney in Sacramento. Then comes Martha, who works as a secretary at a local feed store. Viola helps her husband run their hardware, plumbing, and electrical business. The oldest sister is Ester, who volunteers for the American Red Cross.

"Boy, that's a lot of Quinley's to keep track of," Margaret said.

"You bet! When you have the ingredients right you don't break the mold, you just keep using it," I chuckled.

"I don't know if I'm going to remember all that."

"You'd better. My mom gets really mad when my dates don't know the family ahead of time. She expects them to study up on this."

"Really? Oh my God, I don't think I'm ready for this today."

"No, I'm just kidding. No one expects you to know anything at all about the family. In fact, you're the first girl I've ever brought home to meet everyone. They'll take you as you are and love you because I love you. That's the way we all are, and that's the only thing they'll expect of you."

"You brat! You had me going there for a minute. You know I'll get even for that, don't you?"

"Oh, I'm sure I'll pay for that one, but it was worth it to see you squirm a little." I said, chuckling again.

When we arrived at the house we could hear the chatter and laughter from outside. John and Lester were sitting outside having a smoke when we pulled up and they walked over to the car to greet us. They were more excited about Margaret being there than I was, and I was pretty excited. They stomped out their cigarettes, helped Margaret out of the car and hustled her into the house to meet everyone. I'm sure she was overwhelmed, but you couldn't tell by looking at her. She was grinning from ear to ear. We visited for a couple hours, then wandered around the property. I showed Margaret where we kept the dogs, which reminded me of a funny story. Well, it's funny now, but I didn't think it was so funny when it happened.

Lester, John, George, and I were coming back to the house from working out on the property. I guess I was about twelve at the time, maybe thirteen. It sounds silly now, but we were using an old fashioned horse drawn buckboard wagon. When we got close to the house a bunch of coyotes surrounded us. They were yelping and hollering at the horses. It was unusual behavior for the coyotes. They'd never been that aggressive before. There was no one else home at the time so we took a vote, a vote that wasn't my idea and where my vote didn't count. Lester's idea was to have me jump down off the wagon, run to the gate, jump over, and go release our four hound dogs so they could run off the coyotes. I wasn't very happy with the idea, but they somehow talked me into it. The plan worked like they said it would, but it took me a couple hours to stop shaking. At about 3 P.M. we were called back inside to prepare for the feast. My mom and older sisters always did thanksgiving up real nice. The younger sisters would help set the tables and we had smaller tables set up in the living room for the kids. Mom cooked two turkeys, two hams, string beans, mashed potatoes, candied yams with marshmallows on top, and of course, cranberry. Everything was all set by 4 O'clock and we all took our assigned places. As we all held hands, dad, seated at the head of the table, began.

"Bless us Oh Lord, and these thy gifts, which we are about to receive, from thy bounty, through Christ our Lord, Amen."

Chapter 10
Ft. Bragg

Dear Mom

It was a wonderful thanksgiving! I got to meet the rest of Cecil's family. I wish you were here to share it with us too. It was a grand feast of turkey and ham and all the extras. I don't think I talked as much ever. Cecil's brothers and sisters swooned over me all day. I think they like the idea that there may be someone in his future to look after him.

It's the first day of December now and Christmas is right around the corner. I hope all is well up there in the big city of Detroit. I sure do miss you mom. Cecil wants to know if you've been to any Lions or Tigers games (Oh my!). I guess that's football and baseball. How's the job going up there? Cecil and I are going to bring in the New Year dancing the night away at the Senator Hotel. He is a swell swing dancer and not bad at the waltz either. On the morning of the 1st we're going to drive over to Ft. Bragg and I'm going to show him around and introduce him to Ken and Ray. So far they only know him through the letters I've written them. I guess they're getting a little huffy about not having met him yet, especially Ken, and you know how he is.

I'll be starting a new job at the California State Life Insurance Company. I'll be a clerk typist. I hope to make enough money to go back to school next year. I'm still more fond of Stanford, and I have a lot of friends from there that worked at the Fallen Leaf Lodge with me, but Cal always seems to be more attainable. I guess we'll see when the time comes. I have some chores to do for a little while but I'll write more later.

Well, the afternoon is upon me and I must get ready for Cecil's arrival. He has his own car now, which he bought from his boss. We're going to go play some tennis if the

53

weather cooperates. It's a little chilly, but there's no wind to speak of, so we should be okay. If it gets too bad we'll probably go see a movie. I'm so looking forward to seeing you again, whenever that may be. Your last letter was heartwarming and made me miss you all the more. I love the way you described the lake there. It sounds like an ocean. Time for me to skedaddle. Until next time mom. I'll love you as always. Margaret.

Cecil arrived right on time after I sealed the envelope of the letter I'd just written to my mom. I was still feeling overwhelmed from our visit to Ceres. Perhaps overwhelmed isn't the right word. His family had accepted me so totally that all I could feel was warmth inside me and that I'd found a place that I really belonged. I hoped and prayed in private that this thing we had would work out. I had no reason to doubt that it would. It's just one of those things where you feel like something's too good to be true. How could this feel so perfect? How is it that life has shined such a nice light on little old me? Cecil just seemed like the perfect guy for me. We still had our busy schedules to contend with and I was still committed to completing school. In the back of my mind I was always wondering if Cecil was okay with that. He said he was, but you never really know. I want to believe that he is.

"Hey good looking," I said to him, as he walked up the steps to the door.

"Hi, are you ready for some fun tennis playing today down at the park?" Cecil asked.

"You bet I am mister, and this time I'm going to beat you soundly. You better watch out. Would it be okay if we drove by the post office? I just finished a letter to my mom and I'd like to get it in the box, even though it won't go out until tomorrow."

"Of course that's okay. We'll head straight there, and then on to the park."

I was glad to be back from Fallen Leaf Lodge. It was so beautiful and peaceful up there, but it's nice to now be able to spend more time with my honey. We headed on down the road and dropped my letter in the mail. From there we drove straight to William Land Park and found a place to park the car. I loved Cecil's new car. The tan color was kind of drab, but just having the car gave us a new sense of freedom that we hadn't known before. After the match, which by the way I won, we sat by the lake and watched the ducks and geese. We didn't bring anything to feed them this time and they were visibly upset about that. Cecil and I talked about the upcoming year and what we wanted to do. He still had no real ambition outside of the garage, except to fly airplanes in the Army Air Corps. He had to finish his schooling first, but he didn't seem to have any urgency to do that. The thought was constantly in my mind that maybe I was holding him back because he was so smitten with me that he would put everything else on hold to be with me, even if it meant losing his dream of flying. I don't think he was doing it on purpose, but every day that went by made it less likely that he would be able to accomplish his dream. I worried about that a lot. What if, twenty years from now, he regrets not following his dream and our marriage suffers from that decision that he made in haste because of his new found love for me? I wasn't sure what to do, or say, if anything. Mom always told me that if it's meant to be, then it will be. That if two people really love each other they will wait and still be there for the other when the time is right.

January 1st, 1938. Cecil picked me up at 8 A.M and we drove over to Ft. Bragg. On the way there I gave him the same instruction that he gave me when we were going to his family's house. My mom and step dad (Don) wouldn't be there of course, and he knew that. My brother Ken was living there now. He'd been in Epworth, Iowa, in the mid 1930's, attending a seminary. He'd changed his mind about entering the priesthood. Now he's married and lives in Ft. Bragg. He married a nice girl named Zelma Dunn from Utah. Ken works for the local drug store and for the ambulance and mortuary. He has to go with the firemen to pick up the dead bodies out of the surf. The people who overestimated their ability to swim in the cold Pacific Ocean currents, or got stuck in the kelp fields. Ray was still there too. He ran the movie theater. He bought a nice house a couple miles inland, right up from Ft. Bragg and out of the fog zone. It seemed like it was always sunny there, but still cool. Ray married his school sweetheart. Her name is Dolores Salvador. She's of Portuguese, American Indian, and Spanish lineage and a very lovely girl. They were both looking forward to our arrival and had planned a great sea food feast. Abalone, muscles, crab, and black sea bass. Yum! They even promised some oysters that they had some fishermen friends send down from Eureka. Grilled oysters are to die for, if you do it right. I loved the abalone too, as long as it was cooked right. You had to cut the meat the right way and then pound the heck out of it to tenderize it, and when I say pound, I mean pound. The boy's would lay the slices on a thick wood table in the yard and pound it so hard it sounded like they were building a house out there. Then, and only then, did you use whatever batter you decided on and fried it to perfection, and even then it could still be a bit chewy.

We got into Ft. Bragg at about noon. The fog had receded off shore, but you could see it hanging around out there just waiting to come back in. I hated driving in it but I loved watching it roll in and move ever so silently up the streets. When it enveloped you it was like being placed into a silent room. Things just get quiet and a little spooky. When the fog came in at Ft. Bragg you would hear the moan of the fog horns along the coast telling the mariners where the shore was. It was one of the things I liked about the coastal areas. I used to live in an apartment above the Ft. Bragg Advocate newspaper. My step dad, Donald H. Phillips, who was not married to my mother Ella yet, leased, managed, and published the paper. We drove directly to Ray's house and found him out mowing his yard. When he saw us he grinned from ear to ear and came running over to the driveway to give me a big hug. I introduced him to Cecil and the two of them hit it off right away. The subject of fishing came up, as it always did, and Cecil told him that he liked to trout fish on the mountain lakes and streams, but he'd never been fishing at the ocean. Ray insisted that they would have a future date to do just that. Zelma and Dolores were inside and came out when they heard the commotion. Gosh it was so swell to see everyone again. My school, jobs, and new relationship had taken up so much of my time that I forgot how long it had been since I was in Ft. Bragg. Ken had run to the store to get some beer and a few ingredients to go in his secret fish batter. If you ask me, it's the beer that's the secret, but I'm not telling. Ken got back in a half hour and he hugged me so hard I thought I heard ribs cracking. He was pretty strong for a little guy. Ken was a soft spoken man about five foot eight. His soft careful speech came from his years at the seminary and his job at the mortuary, but he could use his scary voice when he needed to. The one he used when he was out rescuing people. He looked right at Cecil with a stoic face and said,

"So, this is the guy, huh?"

"Cut it out Kenny, now you be nice!" I said.

"I'm only kidding," Ken said as he held out his hand, "welcome to the family Cecil, nice to see that she managed to find a fellow Irishman."

I'm glad that was over. We all sat on the porch while the weather was nice and talked about the last year in review. The subject of politics came up, so us girls wandered off to do our own things and get ready for the feast.

I could hear the men talking every once in a while as they sat there smoking their cigarettes and sipping Pabst Blue Ribbon beer. Their thoughts echoed the general public sentiment of people who paid attention to such things. It was starting to get a little scary over in Europe with the new Nazi party having seized power. Japan was making war already but there really wasn't much news on their activities. Most of the news was following the situation in Europe. I tried not to pay attention to such things, but the men were chatting away about it between smokes and beer. It's a good thing it's a Saturday and we're spending the night here. We'll be in separate rooms, of course, because I was still being a good girl and I'm sure the brothers would see to that also.

Chapter 11
Mo Ghrá Eternal

Dear Ray.

Another letter from your most wonderful little sister. Well, it's Saturday, April 15th and tomorrow is the big day. Your little sister will be an old married woman by the time you get this. You'd better not ever call me that or I'll find you and make you pay for it (ha ha). I'm so glad that you and Cecil hit it off good. He likes you too, and also wishes you were here to celebrate this day with us. There won't be a reception after the service. As you know, money is tight and we want to save as much of it as possible to take on our honeymoon. Not only that, but we'll be moving into a new flat when we return from Los Angeles. It would be nice to have the memories of a reception, but we just can't have everything I guess.

Everyone's happy that we have an Irish Priest to perform the wedding. Not meaning to sound odd, but it just fits with the history of the families and it makes everyone feel like they're back in the old country, even if they've never actually been. I don't know any other way to explain it. Getting in touch with our roots I guess. It just fits, that's all, and the wedding will kind of be themed that way. We decided on April because of an old Irish proverb, of course, that says 'Marry in May and rue the day, marry in April if you can, joy for maiden and for man.' And, we'll have an old Irish blessing said by the priest after the vows. It's kind of exciting.

Ken and Zelma will be bringing mom. She got in by train from Detroit the other day. It's going to be great to see her again. All of Cecil's family are here. Boy, what a crowd that is, but I love them all. They've all been so wonderful to me. I haven't done much since I last saw you, other than work, work, work, and take more classes. We had thanksgiving at Cecil's parent's house again last year. As it was the year before, we had a wonderful time and more food than we could eat. Christmas was a nice quiet break from school, but the job was still there to go to almost every day. It's not hard work, just time consuming and monotonous with no perks like I had up at the lake. Everyone is real nice but boy did it sure spoil me to have that lake, those mountains, all the perks of the lodge for when I got off duty. Who knows what the future holds here?

Well, it's beginning to get late. I'm already packed and we'll be leaving directly after the service. I'd better get a nice soak in tonight, I think by candle light, to calm my nerves a bit and relax, then it's off to bed. I sure miss you Ray and wish you could be here. We'll take pictures for you. Love you as always big brother. Margaret.

I folded the letter and placed it in an envelope and sealed it, then retired to the bathroom and ran a nice hot bubble bath while lighting some candles. I put on a Stan Kenton record to listen to. After the tub filled I slipped carefully into its inviting depths. As I lay there my thoughts drifted back to that Thanksgiving Day last November in Ceres at Cecil's parents. Before dinner we went for a nice walk, just as we'd done the year before. We strolled past the barn, being followed by the dogs, and walked out across a field to where a big old oak tree stood with my initials carved in it from last year. It was a heart with the names Cecil and Marg in the middle. I thought that was so sweet. I didn't see him do the carving because he did it on one of his trips home leading up to thanksgiving, to surprise me. He walked me out there on purpose and waited to see how long it would take me to notice it. It didn't take me long, and when I did notice it I jumped into his arms and gave him a great big kiss. This last Thanksgiving we walked out there holding hands and talking and when we got there he looked at me, cleared his throat a little and said,

"Mo grá síoraí. Beidh tú ag pósadh liom?"

"What?" I said.

He was expecting that response from me, but he wanted to be original, and he certainly was. As his grin got bigger he pulled something from his pocket and said,

"It's Irish. It means my eternal love, will you marry me?"

I was stunned at first, but then lunged into his arms and kissed him all over his face and said over and over again,

"Yes-yes-yes-yes?"

After, I cried a little, and finally noticed that what he took out of his pocket was a very nice diamond engagement ring. He held my hand up and slid it on my finger and I cried more. After I was able to compose myself we walked back to the house. Milly could see the blush on my face and she knew that Cecil had asked me. She already knew he was going to, but she kept it a secret from me and the rest of the family. She raised her voice and said,

"Everyone! It looks like Cecil has something to say."

Cecil then told everyone that we were engaged and the whole house lit up with applause. All the women rushed over and hugged me and all the men shook Cecil's hand. That was my extra special thanksgiving of 1938. Now here I am on the eve of my wedding.

Our wedding was scheduled for the Cathedral of the Blessed Sacrament in Sacramento by Father Renwald. Since Cecil wasn't Catholic he had to attend some meetings with the good father, as well as the classes we had to attend as a couple that prepared us for a marriage in the Catholic Church. In the morning I got dressed and went over to the Cathedral where I met Zelma, my maid of honor. My mother Ella, Milly, and Zelma helped me get dressed in my mother's nice white wedding gown. It was beautiful. As is the Irish tradition, a happily married woman must place the veil on me. I can't do it myself. Milly had that honor and placed it on me. As she began to cry. I said,

"Now stop that Milly, you're going to make me start if you're not careful."

My mom and Milly went to take their seats and Zelma escorted me to the entrance of the Cathedral. There were about fifty people in attendance. Zelma handed me off to my brother Ken, who would be walking me down the aisle and giving me away. Zelma went up front toward the altar to take her place as the pipe organ began to play "Wagner's Bridal Chorus" (here comes the bride). I held onto Ken's left arm and we strolled down the aisle very slowly. I was shaking all over as I felt every eye in the church staring at me, but I began to calm down when I got close enough to see Cecil's face and see how handsome he looked in his suit, standing next to his best man, his brother John. Ken identified himself as the man giving me away when prompted to do so. Cecil accepted my hand. We turned to face the altar and knelt down for the mass. When the time came, we recited the vows as stated by Father Renwald, and when we were done he said,

"You may now kiss the bride."

There were some cheers and whistles from our friends and family. When we were done, Father Renwald instructed us to turn and face the congregation. When we did, he offered us this traditional Irish blessing in his rich Dublin accent.

> May God be with you and bless you. May you see your
> children's children. May you be poor in misfortune, but rich
> in blessings. May you know nothing but happiness from this
> day forward. Ladies and gentlemen gathered here today.
> May I introduce you to Mr. and Mrs. Cecil Quinley.

The church reverberated with applause and the organist belted out one last song, "Mendelssohn's Wedding March." As the pipe organ played we exited out the doors and waited for everyone else to come out so we cold thank them all for coming, since there wouldn't be a reception. We mingled for quite a while in an open area of the church before we both retreated to our separate changing areas and got ready to hit the road.

When we came out to get in the car we found it to have "Just Married" written on the rear window and long strings of Blue Ribbon beer cans tied to the rear bumper. It made quite a sound as we drove off down "K" Street. After we got out of sight Cecil pulled over and took the cans off, but then we got right back on the road. We headed over to highway 99 and pointed the car south toward Los Angeles and our first night as a married couple. We started looking for motels at Modesto but all the places we saw looked too secluded and too far from the road. It made me nervous, so we just kept going until we got to Fresno. There, we found a nice place we could afford and we checked in for the night. Fresno, California, our first night together as husband and wife. Since neither one of us was experienced in these matters it was quite awkward, but we managed, since we were so deeply in love with each other. Waiting is hard, but that first night together after getting married makes it all worth it. The expectations, the mystique, the clumsiness. The romance and closeness just can't be replaced. It's all new and exciting. In the morning we got up early and showered. Well, tried to shower, but things got romantic again. Eventually, we worked up the willpower to get showered and dressed and we meandered off to breakfast. Biscuits and gravy were the specialty, and boy were they ever good. We even had some pancakes and coffee with them. After breakfast we hit the road again and finished our trek to Los Angeles. When we got there we stopped by to visit with Maude, Henry, and Beverly, not intending to stay there. But they insisted that we stay for the night. They wanted us to visit with them more and look up some friends that lived there too before heading farther south. It wasn't what we'd planned, but how could we say no to such an invitation. It did, though, kind of put a damper on our new togetherness. We visited most of the day, went around and saw some old friends, and found out purely by accident that Les Brown and his Orchestra was playing Tuesday night at the Biltmore Bowl in Hollywood. That's just too good to pass up, so we got some tickets. I put on my best dress and Cecil donned his suit, so we were a sharp dressed couple that night. Once again we hit the dance floor for a waltz, but this time it was as Mr. and Mrs. Quinley at the Biltmore Bowl. The evening was splendid and magical, just as it's supposed to be in Hollywood.

Mo Ghrá Eternal – My Eternal Love.

Chapter 12
Biltmore Bowl

Our honeymoon was a wonderful adventure. It was the first time we'd gotten away for a trip together, other than our little jaunt to Ft. Bragg or our drives to Lake Tahoe. It was nice to get out of town with Margaret, if even for only a few days. Our budget wouldn't support much more than that since we had to move into a new flat when we got back. Margaret's mother, Ella, decided she wanted to stay longer and not go back to Michigan right away, so we offered to let her stay with us. She helped get everything moved into the new flat at 2626 "Q" Street while we were gone on our honeymoon. There wasn't much to move since we didn't own much. Plus the flat was only a one room place with a fold down Murphy bed. I suspect she wouldn't be there very long, so I didn't mind. We stopped in Long Beach to see some friends of Margaret's from her childhood. Maude and Beverly Beach had been Margaret's neighbors when she was growing up in Waterloo, Iowa. Beverly was Margaret's age. Beverly had been adopted at around four years of age by Maude and her husband Al Haldum. Her parents were tragically killed in an accident. Al worked at the railroad with Margaret's father and had later also been killed in an accident. Sometime later Maude had married Henry. Margaret and Beverly became close throughout their childhood. Margaret told me stories of her and Beverly skating together on the frozen ponds of Waterloo in the winter and running through the corn fields chasing butterflies during times of good weather. I could just picture that in my mind as she told me the stories.

Fate carried the two families in separate directions, but they kept in touch. We also visited with Maude's first daughter, Juanita, and her husband Joe. Our visit with them was an expected stop along our route and we would be staying with them for a couple days. While we were there we discovered that Les Brown was playing at the Hollywood Biltmore so we made a night of it with Juanita and Joe. Dancing the night away at such a famous venue with a famous band playing, dressed to the hilt, not a care in the world except what the next song was going to be. It doesn't get any better than that. The room was large and there were a lot of people there, all dressed nicely. There were murals on every wall and a lot of mirrors that reflected light throughout the huge space. The stage was a beautiful wood shade with short brass railings and a large canopy covering part of it. The band

65

members were all dressed in dark suits and they played magnificently. We dined on steak and drank from crystal glasses. The champagne tickled Margaret's nose and made her giggle. We danced the night away on the huge dance floor that was dizzy with the smell of expensive perfumes. Les Brown performed all the popular songs of the day and I don't think I stepped on Margaret's toes once. It was the perfect evening. At around midnight we all decided to head back to Maude's house because Joe had to work the next day. What a night to remember!

Dear John.

I can't believe it's already Wednesday. The honeymoon is just a blur so far. It's passing way too quickly and I expect we'll be back in the real world soon enough. Just a quick letter to thank you for all you've done for us and for being my best man at the wedding. Whose idea was it to put the Blue Ribbon cans on my car anyway? Nice touch though! It sure surprised Margaret. From here we leave after breakfast for San Diego to do some sightseeing down there. We're going to go to the zoo and also see some of the old missions. I'm thinking of driving into Mexico to look around a bit but I haven't decided yet. Let mom and dad know that the car is running fine and all is well. Oh ya, I almost forgot to tell you. Yesterday, we got over to the beach and did some swimming in the ocean at Long Beach. Well, not really swimming, but playing in the surf and getting knocked over by the waves. The water there isn't nearly as cold as it is at Ft. Bragg. We had a lot of fun playing in the waves. They were about three feet tall is all, but it was a blast.

I heard on the radio yesterday that the New York World's Fair is opening tomorrow. Wow, I'll bet that's better than the state fair that we like to go to. As much fun as we have at the state fair it sure would be swell to be able to go to a world's fair. We decided that if we can afford it we'll go to the brand new San Francisco World's Fair. I think we're going to try and go for my birthday.

Well, I'd better wrap this up so we can get some breakfast and hit the road. Tell everyone we said hello and that we're having a blast. Your younger (and better looking brother-ha ha), Cecil.

We got into San Diego a little before noon and found a hotel with a pool. After check in we had some lunch and went to Balboa Park to look around. A trip to the zoo took up the rest of our afternoon. My favorite part of the zoo was the elephants. They took peanuts right out of our hands. It was exciting watching the nervous look on Margaret's face turn to joy as the elephant ever so gently took the peanut with its trunk and placed it in its mouth. I'm from the country and I'm used to animals, but something like an elephant is new and exciting. We didn't have any elephants back on the farm in Ceres. The big cats were up and around because it wasn't very hot. I really didn't care for the way they paced back and forth and stared at the little kids that were there with their parents. After we left the zoo we decided to go for a little drive. I drove down into Tijuana to look around. Not for any specific reason. Perhaps just to say we got to Mexico. We didn't stop for any shopping, but I heard that there was a bull fighting ring near there. I'd never seen a bull fighting ring so I just thought that would be something to see. We found it alright, it's called El Torero De Tijuana. It just looked kind of like a round football stadium from the outside with a round dirt center. It was neat seeing it, but afterwards you say to yourself Okay, well, I guess I saw something new and that's done with now, let's go. We got back in the car and headed back to the hotel for some dinner and rest.

After breakfast we packed up the car and went over to old San Diego to look around. Margaret wanted to see as many old Spanish missions as we could on our trip and, I have to admit, it sounded interesting to me as well. After stopping to look at a small adobe chapel in old San Diego we stopped at the Mission Basilica San Diego de Alcala. Now that was an interesting stop and full of fun things to look at. After snooping around the mission we headed back toward San Diego and then turned north. Our plan was to drive from mission to mission until we got home. Our next stop would be Mission San Luis Rey de Francia in Oceanside, then on to Mission San Juan de Capistrano. We bypassed a few and then stopped again at Mission Santa Barbara before heading to Maude and Henry's house for the night. After a nice night of sleep we all went to the beach for more romping in the surf. Henry had to work, but Joe took the day off, so Maude, Beverly, Juanita and Joe went with us. It was a little chilly with the breeze blowing in. The temperature was only about sixty degrees but we braved the conditions and splashed right into the Pacific Ocean. Margaret, Beverly, and Maude chased the water back to the ocean, and then they'd run like mad to escape the returning waves. It was a blast to watch them all have so much fun, and Joe and I could hardly contain our laughter. After a while Margaret and I waded into the waves to see how far we could get. The water was chilly but not near as cold as it was in Ft. Bragg. We managed to get the water about a foot above our waistline before a big wave took us off our feet and sent us back to shore. That scene was repeated several times as we learned to ride the waves. What an amazing day we had with our friends! Later in the afternoon we packed up the cars and drove for home. When we got there we found that Henry had a barbecue started and he threw on some hamburgers and hot dogs shortly after we all climbed out of the cars. He also had some beer on ice and we all sat in the yard and praised his thoughtfulness and planning expertise. What a trip it'd been so far, and what a day we'd all just had. It seemed like we were a lifetime away from Sacramento, but we'd soon be returning to reality there. Back to the grind and the real world. The morning found us climbing back in the Chevy and heading north again. Once again we'd stop at some missions along the way. We wouldn't have time to see them all. We stopped at the Missions San Luis Obispo de Tolosa, San Juan Bautista, and Santa Cruz. Our last stop was the Mission Santa Clara de Asis as we headed back inland and toward home. We spent the night in Santa Clara and back tracked to that mission in the morning where we attended mass and toured the grounds before reluctantly leaving for home.

As we got home to our new flat on "Q" Street we found Ella dusting and getting everything ready for us. What a nice surprise that was. Since we had nothing planned, the three of us went out for a nice return dinner. We were all hungry and I'd been just itching to go there again so I loaded up the ladies and drove over to 9th street and the Rosemount. Before leaving I called Milly and she and Jim met us there too. It was just as I remembered, the biggest steak I'd ever seen, and char broiled to perfection. Nicely charred on the edges, perfect marbling, pink in the middle, and as big as the plate. There was hardly room for a potato, but they managed to slip one onto the plate, barely, and it was loaded with butter and sour cream. After dinner we all sat and talked about the honeymoon over coffee. Everyone loved to hear of our great adventure but there would be some news forthcoming that I hadn't planned on. I soon found out from Ella and Milly that I'd have no job to go to in the morning. Ella had received the news during the week, but didn't want to ruin our trip. The Elm Garage changed one of their contracts with some government services. The government vehicles that I'd been attending to would be serviced by their own people now instead of them contracting with the garage. That meant that I'd be without a job. Jim had been talking with my old boss, though, and he lined up a new job for me at a Goodyear Tire shop. I guess I'd be interviewing for a new position in the morning. Welcome back to Sacramento. Boy, what timing!

Chapter 13
San Francisco World's Fair

It was April 24th, 1939. I walked out the door of our new Quinley homestead on "Q" Street in Sacramento to go find a new job. I got hired on the spot by the Goodyear Tire shop. It was nice of my old boss to set it up for me while I was gone, but it didn't take me long to decide that the new job wasn't for me. They had me changing tires for huge tractors. The tires were taller than me for crying out loud. At my size I couldn't even begin to move them around or work on them. On my lunch hour I stopped by Miller's Standard Oil Station and applied for a position there. It was probably the busiest service station in Sacramento because it was near the capitol building. They did a lot of business with the coming and going politicians and so forth. Gasoline, tires, batteries and what not. They hired me on the spot and told me I could start right away, but I asked if tomorrow would be fine so I could finish out my day over at Goodyear. They said that was fine, so I went back to Goodyear and thanked them for giving me a chance. I explained to them that the job was just too much for me and I didn't think it would work out. They were very understanding and we parted ways on good terms.

For the rest of the year I worked at the service station. It indeed was the busiest station in town and we were always running wild there trying to keep up. We pumped the most gas of any station in the city. The country was trying to stay out of all the stuff happening in Europe but the war drums kept beating louder and louder. California, of course, wasn't directly involved in the decisions in Washington regarding foreign wars, but our Senators and Congressmen came and went and the state had to come up with contingency plans just in case. After all, California possessed much of the country's resources and economy and had a lot of military bases. These things assured that there were always people coming to the capital, and all those people stopped at Miller's. Margaret and I talked a lot about the possibility of war and what we would do if it happened. It was all over the news. The Germans were spreading their influence out again. The Japanese were running amok in China, and we didn't seem to be getting along with them very well. Our thought was that I should enlist in the Army Air Corps before something happened, because I certainly didn't want to get drafted. They still required a college degree, though, and I needed to go back and finish. I started out my new job at Miller's Standard Oil for $25 a week and quickly worked my way up to $40 per week. Margaret was still working at Cal-Western Insurance Company and making $70 per month. Our plan was to save some money, move into a larger flat, and then I would go back to college to finish up my degree. After that I could get into cadet school.

Dear Mom and Dad.

How are things down there on the farm? We're doing great here. I can't wait to see John and Lester again. Starting next weekend we're going to spend some weekends up at the camp helping out. I heard Lester is going to have a great turnout this year with a lot of kids. A nice mountain trip sounds like just what the doctor ordered, even if there is work involved. I heard on the radio tonight that Lou Gehrig retired from baseball. Wow, that's hard to believe. They also said that Teddy Roosevelt got his face on Mt. Rushmore. I guess there's a lot of things happening everywhere this year.

Have you heard about that new movie that's coming out; 'The Wizard of Oz?' Margaret and I are going to go see it next month when it's showing here. We both read the book, but you know how that is. It probably won't be anything like it. Hey, did you hear that Joe Louis won again? That will teach me to ever bet against him. Braddock lost me five simoleons when he lost to Louis! Margaret and I are going to try and get to the San Francisco World's Fair while it's still open too. It probably won't be until after the summer since we'll be busy up at the camp. Okay, time for me to get cleaned up and help with supper. I'm getting that look that says, why aren't you helping me with this? Love you always and so forth, your best son, Cecil.

July 8th we packed up the Chevy and climbed the hill to Camp Treasure Island at Silver Lake. We were looking forward to the clean mountain air. When we got there we parked the car and loaded up a boat for the trip to the island. At the island, Lester greeted us with a nice cold soda. By the time we got there on Saturday most of the morning activities were winding down. Lester announced to the kids that there was a woman on deck and they needed to stay covered and act appropriately. As far as I know Margaret was the only woman he ever made an exception for being on the island. The kids were busy getting ready for lunch with their counselors. Lester recruited a lot of counselors from Stanford to come up for the summer and help out. It must have been some sort of program that they had. We dined on barbecue hot dogs and chips. It really hits the spot when you're hungry. Toward the evening Lester was teaching some kids how to fish, and boy could Lester fish. He sure was a real pro at that. John took some kids out on the lake to row around and other counselors were supervising hikes around the island. You could get a decent hike in on a 40 acre island. After dinner we sat around the fire and roasted marshmallows again. In the morning was when the hatchet finally fell. A load of groceries came in and I was informed by Lester that I volunteered to bring most of it up to the cabins. I liked to call that "voluntold." Always the little brother I guess. Low man on the totem pole. It was quite a hill to climb when carrying bags and bags of potatoes. I finished up my "voluntold" chore at about 10:00 and went for a swim with Margaret to get cleaned up. John barbecued up some trout that Lester had caught and we ate that for lunch. I think he was just trying to be nice to his little brother since I carried all those potatoes up the hill. After lunch it was time to head for home, beginning with the boat trip back to the parking area. After loading up the car we headed out and stopped in Jackson for gas before the drive to Sacramento. This would be a scene repeated many times in July and August and I wouldn't have missed it for the world.

On September 9th we made our trip to the World's Fair. It was also called the Golden Gate International Exposition in celebration of the Golden Gate Bridge and the new San Francisco Bay Bridge. They built a whole island out in the bay and called it Treasure Island. That's where they were holding the fair. We drove out across the Bay Bridge and man oh man was that a big bridge. It made me a little nervous driving out across it. A little more than halfway across is Yerba Buena Island and that's where we exited the bridge. Attached to Yerba Buena is the new man made Treasure Island. As we pulled closer to the island the magnificent buildings came into view. We parked the car and started walking around. We walked and we walked and we walked. There were several attractions there to see. We saw an old western type show and a show with dancing girls. I'm not too sure if Margaret liked that one, but I did. There were exhibits that showed modern living at its best with gadgets we would never be able to afford. I got a kick out of watching a Pan American Clipper airplane take off. I'd never seen a flying boat type of plane take off before and it just made me want to fly even more. The fair had enormous buildings everywhere and a tall statue they called the Tower of the Sun. It was a statue of the Goddess of the

Pacific Ocean. There were colorful flowers and trees everywhere. We rode on a giant ride called the Octopus and a giant Ferris wheel. I looked for a Loop-A-Plane for old time sake, but if there was one there, I didn't find it. After so much walking we realized that we hadn't eaten lunch yet so we sat down at about 3:00 and ate a nice seafood dinner. They served crab to order right there on the sidewalk just like they did down at Fisherman's Warf in San Francisco. Along with the crab came some of the best clam chowder I'd ever tasted and, of course, some famous San Francisco sour dough bread. We ate outdoors with a nice cool breeze blowing to break up the heat. There were no insects to speak of but we had to occasionally chase away a seagull that got too bold. After our meal, exhausted and full, we found our car and started back for Sacramento. The closer we got to Sacramento the hotter it got. August was behind us, but it was still quite warm. At home we carefully hung up our nice clothes that we wore because we would need them the next day. Then it was taking turns in the tub and off to bed. I didn't remember much about getting into bed. The last thing I remembered was turning off the lights and then my alarm going off. I guess I was pretty tired from all that walking around.

On the morning of the 10th we -donned our nice clothes again and drove the Chevy to mass at the Cathedral of the Blessed Sacrament. Margaret didn't miss many Sunday masses and I usually went with her, even though I still wasn't Catholic. She'd been trying to convert me, and I probably would do it someday, I just wasn't in a hurry to change. I really liked Father Renwald. He was a funny guy and really cracked me up with some of his talk about Ireland. Almost every time I saw him he would say,

"Quinley eh! That's a good Irish name don't-ya-know? What happened back in Ireland that you're no longer Catholic?"

I would just have to chuckle and say I didn't know, because I didn't know. On this day I had a surprise for Margaret. After mass I took her to the theater to see "The Wizard of Oz." Boy did she get excited when I told her where we were going. As we sat there eating our popcorn we watched some of the recent news reel footage about the politics and fighting overseas. I guess it was time to talk again about it. That past week England had declared war on Germany. A German submarine had sunk a British Cruise Liner killing a lot of people. President Roosevelt still wanted to remain neutral but the way things were heating up over there it was only a matter of time. Much of the country wanted to get involved already. Margaret and I both felt that we couldn't allow our friends to stand alone. The isolationists had some valid points, but those points were near sighted and somewhat naive. The world was a big place, true, but its modernization was shrinking it more every year. Soon, there would be no hiding from the consequences of world affairs. We would have to join the fight while there were still allies for us to help and, in turn, help us. Waiting for their defeat would mean we'd have to fight on our own, on our enemies terms, after they have grown too strong from plundering the resources of their captured lands. The United States would have to join the fight sooner or later. None of those recent events was on the news reel that we watched, but we listened to it on the radio last week and the news reel made us think about it again. I was wondering if the Air Corps would drop the college graduate requirement if we entered the war. I couldn't count on that to happen, though, so I guessed I'd better hurry up and get back to school. The problem was finding the time to go to school and hold my job. I didn't want to leave Margaret as the sole bread winner while I went to school. Anyway, the movie was excellent, even if we dampened the experience by talking about such a serious subject. My favorite character was the Cowardly Lion. He made me laugh. This would definitely be a film we would have to see again.

A letter found on the sink after my bath:

"My Dearest Cec. Thank you for going to mass with me today, and always. The Wizard of Oz was a magnificent addition to a wonderful weekend. Come to bed."

Chapter 14
It Begins

Dear Mom.

Happy new year from California! I hope all is well in Michigan and the newspaper business is doing well too. It should be, there has been plenty of news to print, hasn't there? Cec and I have been talking about what he should do. We're worried that he may get drafted before he's able to enlist in the Air Corps Cadet Pilot Program. We're hoping that they'll relax some of their college requirements soon so he can get in. We've been trying to find the time for him to get back to college so he can finish up, but it's been tough. We're both working all the time just trying to make a living. I know I'm preaching to the choir here, as you've been wrestling with that your whole life. I guess this is the part where you get to enjoy watching the kids go through what we didn't understand as we were moving around the country following your work. Now listen to me, I'm sounding like I'm griping, but the truth of the matter is that we're very happy indeed. All good things come to those who wait, I guess. It's just that the waiting can be hard sometimes. It isn't the present that we worry about. In the present we both have jobs, we make enough to pay the bills and have some fun and we love each other as much as two people can. It's just the uncertainty of the unknown future with all the fighting escalating all over the world that is worrisome. We know that sooner or later the Unites States will have to get involved.

Enough of the doom and gloom talk. Have you seen 'Gone with the Wind' yet? Oh my, what a beautiful movie that is. It left me in tears though. It's a really long movie at four hours, but we had several intermissions to stretch our legs. We enjoyed a nice Christmas at Cecil's parents in Ceres. We went to mass on Sunday morning at the cathedral and then drove down to their house and stayed the night. It was wonderful waking up on Christmas morning with children in the house all clamoring for their gifts. We walked out to that tree where Cecil carved our names and sat there for a while reminiscing on our time together so far. Man did I get lucky. This is the perfect guy for me! Well mom, I'd better be signing off now. I sure do hope we can see each other again soon. I love and miss you a bunch. Your daughter, Margaret.

Margaret.

1939 ended on a nice note for us, but September 25th was the beginning of a stressful few days because there was a cyclone that came ashore in Long Beach and we were worried sick for our friends. We heard that there were a lot of people killed because of the flooding, but two days later we heard from Maude that everyone was well. The eventual news was good, but the two day wait had me tied up in knots inside. I was worried sick for my friends. My job was going well at the insurance company. I was only the fifth person hired for that department so I gained a lot of seniority in no time at all. In April we took time off to head up to John's Donner Trail Ski Lodge in the sierra. We'd go up there to help him when we could and we got to ski for free. It was just like going to the summer camp that Lester had. There's no doubt that John would let us ski for free anyway, but we're family, and we all help out where and when we can. On this particular trip the new lodge that was close by was having a race. The lodge was named Sugar Bowl and it was started by a man named Hannes Schroll. His nickname was the Madman of the Alps. He was a magnificent skier who came here from Austria and won some championships. The unusual thing about him was that he would yodel as he came down the hill, almost appearing out of control, but he won a lot. Cecil and I loved skiing and we really wanted to see this man race. This was their inaugural race and it was called the Silver Belt Race. They called it that because the winner got a big silver studded belt with a big silver buckle. All the lodges were packed full of people to see the spectacle. The Olympics that were supposed to be held in Germany in February were canceled because of the war, so all the best skiers from around the world came to Hannes' new hill to race.

We helped out at Sugar Bowl as much as our legs would hold out. John liked to show off for his little brother's wife. He would come down the hill real fast, doing slalom type skiing. I loved it when he would go flying over jumps and spread his skis and arms way out in a spread eagle type of pose and then bring them back together just before hitting the snow again. He was real good at it. He tried to get Cecil to do it too, but Cecil knew his limitations. Cec could do the slalom real good, but he drew the line at jumping. We drove our car up to the lodge and John saved a good spot for us. I'm glad he did, because the place soon become jam packed with cars stuck in every nook and cranny. That wasn't the only way people got up there, though. The railroad had special trains that hauled skiers up to Norden. From there they could be taken by horse or tractor drawn sleds to different lodges. The day of the race Cecil and I got a good spot just a little way up the hill from the finish line. We stood there on the hill for hours watching the different men's and women's racers come racing by us. It was quite thrilling. Cecil had a thermos of coffee and I had one of cocoa, so we were all set for the day. John brought us some tomato soup at noon. We didn't want to lose our spot on the hill and he was worried we would get hungry. Cecil is lucky to have such a caring brother as John. Finally the last racers finished and the winners were announced. The men's winner was a man named Friedl Pfeifer. He too was an Austrian that had moved to the United States. The women's winner was Gretchen Fraser. She was an American of Norwegian descent. That night found everyone drinking and partying around the lodge. The place was so crowded that people were sleeping on the floor in extra rooms. John let us sleep in his room. After drinking too many hot buttered rum drinks by the fire we retired for some much needed sleep. The last thing I remembered was falling asleep with my head nuzzled up under Cecil's arm, resting on the side of his chest. We kept each other warm all night. It was a good thing we had those hot buttered rums because the place stayed noisy all night. The drinks, I think, helped us to sleep through it.

The rest of 1940 was business as usual. Cecil and I went to our jobs and we'd meet as much as we could for lunch. Sometimes we'd have a picnic on the lawn of the state capital. It was close by, and we could get back to work easily. In the summer we'd again go up to Lester's camp and help out. I loved being around Cecil's family. Camping, fishing, eating outside by a fire and drinking coffee under the stars. It was over way too soon as we got back to the hustle and bustle of working in the city. The war was heating up and it made us pretty nervous to hear of everything that was happening. Paris fell to the Germans, so we knew for sure at that point that we would be going to war soon enough. They were attacking England now. How long would our president wait before entering the war? It wasn't that Cecil wanted a war to start, and God knows I didn't want anything to happen to him, but if we waited for all of our friends to be defeated we'd then have to face the enemy all alone and probably at our doorstep. President Roosevelt was becoming very unpopular in our circles. At least he was sending money and supplies to England and Russia to help out a little. April 1941 saw our second anniversary come and go. We went back up to John's ski lodge and visited with him for a few days. Skiing, laughing, and having a grand time. We went over to Sugar Bowl and watched the Silver Belt Race again. We had a lot of fun, but still couldn't shake that daunting feeling that time was going to catch up with us soon because of all the events going on around the world.

Cecil.

It was December 7th, 1941. Margaret and I went to mass at the Cathedral on Sunday morning. I still hadn't converted to being a Catholic yet, but I enjoyed going with her. I also enjoyed talking with Father Renwald after mass. His Irish accent intrigued me and for some reason it just kept my attention focused on our conversations. At around 11:00 we made our way over to Milly and Jim's house to spend the day with them and my parents, who were up visiting from Ceres. We had the stand-up Philco console radio on in the living room while we were sitting at the dining room table playing rummy. We were listening to the Lawrence Welk show on the radio. I liked his music well enough, but I was hoping I'd get to hear some Glenn Miller. I was really liking some of the music that Miller was putting out like, "In the Mood," "Chattanooga Choo Choo," and "Pennsylvania 6-5000." We were all chatting and getting louder, so we couldn't really hear the radio very well. Milly's kids were in the radio room and they were probably trying to find a mystery show or something to listen to. At about 11:30 the boys came running into the dining room shouting about something. Jim told them to slow down and speak normal so we could understand them. They were both talking at the same time and seemed like they were out of breath, but it was clear what they were saying.

"You have to come listen! Come quick, the Japanese are bombing Pearl Harbor! It's on the radio right now! Hurry!"

All of us went into the living room and listened to the report on the radio. Jim turned up the volume. From what we were hearing it sounded horrible. We knew this would mean war for sure. There were police sirens going up and down the streets in Sacramento. I don't know what they thought they were accomplishing by driving back and forth in Sacramento with their sirens on. Maybe they were just trying to get people to turn on their radios so they could hear what was happening too. Someone in Hawaii was reporting on the bombing and he said there were still Japanese planes all over the sky. It took our breath away. We knew we would have to get into the war someday, but we never dreamed it would be like this. Those poor people in Hawaii, and their families. It was horrible, just horrible. My mother was the first to say it. She told me I'd better get down to the enlistment office and sign up for the Air Corps if I wanted to fly. Otherwise, I would be drafted for sure now. The draft had passed me by twice already, it wouldn't happen a third time, not now, I was sure of that. This would mean more than war with Japan. We would be fighting all over the world. The hair was standing up on the back of my neck as I thought about it. Ready or not, we're going to war. I was going to war.

Chapter 15
Santa Ana

How you doing by now anyway? We finally got down here at about 11:30 last night. We left San Francisco by bus about 8 A.M. and went over to Oakland to the train and left there about 9 A.M. We got two of the oldest cars the Santa Fe Railroad had. All the cars on the train were air conditioned except ours, and it sure was hot all the way down. After we got in about 11:30 we had to sign up and fill out a lot of papers. We finally got to bed about 2:30 in the morning. They let us sleep until 6:30. Generous huh? It's swell here though. I guess they'll make us work like the devil from the looks of things. But I think I'll like it. They put some of the guys into one squadron to finish filling it up and about 30 of us started a new one. About 40 more guys came in today. A bunch of them were from Pittsburg and another bunch from New York. We have to get about 180 in the squadron before we start anything. Until then – we drill.

They issued us our coveralls and ball caps today. We don't get any more clothes until we get classified, which will be about 14 days. There's about 5 guys came down yesterday who were from the Bronx. All of them get to talking some of that Bronx double talk and stuff and it sure is a kick. They're all from the 69th infantry. You should hear all the guys in the barracks around here every time a new bunch of recruits come in. They all hang their heads out their windows and beg for eats and smokes, and holler 'you'll be sorry, you'll be sorry,' and then you come to the next barracks and a bunch of the guys start screaming and hollering 'don't beat me mister, I'll be a bombardier!' I guess it used to be worse. They put out orders to stop it. The second night we were here the guys in the barracks right in back of our tent were watching and hollering at a bunch of guys that just got in from Boston, when all of a sudden one guy came screaming out the door with a bunch of red streaks all over his back and another guy right behind him with a strap. The first guy was hollering 'don't beat me anymore mister, I'll be a bombardier.'

I'll be here for about 38 more days before I can get a 25 hour pass. We're allowed to go to Los Angeles if we want. Be thinking what you want to do. In a way it's swell to be here and in a way I sure wish I wasn't. I love you and miss you and dream about you every night. So long now honey. Love, Cecil.

After the Japanese attack on Pearl Harbor, Margaret and I spent some time getting our finances in order because I knew that I'd be leaving, in one branch of service or another. I figured the best thing I could do was take charge of my own fate and enlist in the Air Corps, which is where I wanted to be anyway. My mom told me I'd better go do it before my draft number comes up again. They already passed me over twice and there undoubtedly wouldn't be a third time since we were at war now. I went down to the recruitment office almost every day on my lunch hour but the line was always too long and I had to get back to work. Finally, around mid-March, I was able to get signed up. Me and a bunch of other guys took a test that lasted about three hours. They tested us on a lot of different things. A friend of mine that was already in the Air Corps told me to make sure that I didn't score tops on the math part. They took all the top math guys and made them navigators. I must have done alright because they signed me up for the aviation cadet training program, but all the bases were full, so in the mean time they swore me in as a private. I was a little worried that they were going to pull something on me but they said I'd get $30 a month as a private until a base opened up that I could go to. They said they'd notify me when to report. The next stop for the bunch of us after the swearing in was the courthouse. We had to fill out some paperwork so the war department knew not to draft us, since we were signed up in the Air Corps already.

Margaret and I went about our normal business for the next few months and I finally received notice that I was supposed to report to Oakland for my physical on Monday, August 3rd. Things were looking pretty bleak in the war. It seemed like the Germans and Japs were unstoppable. Even General McArthur had to be evacuated to Australia. The United States managed to bomb Japan once, but it didn't slow them down. I thought for sure that I would be shipping out to the Pacific somewhere when my training was through. The United States finally won a major battle by beating the Japs at Midway and the morale around Sacramento rose a lot when we got that news. Dad was starting to get sick a lot and I began to worry about him quite a bit, even though mom told me not to and that I should concentrate on what I needed to do. He had a lot of stomach problems and pain all the time. When it was time for me to report I took Margaret with me and we went to Oakland early so we could visit my Aunt Becky and Uncle Will on Saturday, August 1st. They lived between Oakland and Berkley. It was nice to get out of the heat. It's close to the bay, so it's much cooler than Sacramento is in August. We had a nice visit. I hadn't seen them in a while. We took the ferry over to San Francisco to do some sightseeing and we had a great dinner at a classy steakhouse. Monday morning I reported as I was told and was introduced to my first ever military hurry up and wait routine. It certainly wouldn't be my last. They had us sign papers, and turn in papers, and they talked to us more. They gave us some meal tickets and a lodging ticket and told us to come back at 6:30 Tuesday morning. By the time I got out of there I tried to find Margaret, but she had already gone home. Some of us recruits took the bus over to San Francisco to the beach for a while and then out to a show. There were a bunch of us who couldn't get rooms at the YMCA Hotel, which is where our lodging tickets were for, so we had to go out and find another place. Three of us went up to the Stanford Hotel and got two double beds for five dollars. The next day, on the morning of the 5th, we again took the bus back to Oakland, but this time it was to the train station and they shipped us down to Santa Ana, California.

Santa Ana is where we got indoctrinated. The first thing I noticed was how crowded it was. All the barracks were full, so I got stuck in a tent with a lot of other guys. Also, there were some guys that had been there for a while who tried to scare the daylights out of all us new guys. They did a good job of it too. Some of the things we did there was physical fitness testing. I did the most chin ups in my group and it wasn't easy. The bar was pretty high and we had to jump up to it. Each chin up had to be done without kicking our legs, and then we had to go all the way down until our arms were straight. I managed to do 13. There were the usual pushups and sit ups too. They did more medical screening on us. The Wassermann test, a urinalysis, chest x-rays, and the Schneider test. The longer we were there the more clothes they gave us, but we had to pay for all the clothes ourselves. I thought that was odd. We all had to take our turn at the unpleasant duties of the base. I had to be a fire guard while we were still housed in the tent. All that means is that I was the night watchman and had to stay up at night. We all had our turn at KP duty and that was probably the hardest thing I had to do there. I was plenty sore the next day after that. Doing a rotation on the phone switch board was a heck of a job. There were plenty of phones to answer and we had to then figure out where the recruit was so we could transfer the call over. The most interesting thing we did was get briefings on high altitude flying and then we went in the pressure chamber.

They took twenty of us fellows and we went into a room and they numbered us. Then, they took our temperature and pulse and put us in the pressure chamber in seats corresponding to our numbers. They gave everyone oxygen masks and hooked them up with the oxygen lines, which you start using at eighteen thousand feet. They shot us up to 5,000 feet and held it there for a minute and then came back down. They looked to see if everybody's ears were all clear. After that, they shot us back up to 5,000 feet and stayed there for a couple minutes, then shot us clear up to 18,000 feet. When they stopped there we all had to take our pulse and respiratory count and we stayed at that altitude for about five minutes. We had to put on our oxygen masks and take our pulse and respiratory rate again. Then, they picked out one person to take off his mask and we went up to 24,000 thousand feet. I was hoping I'd get to do so, but they picked another fellow to do it. It was Dick Noah, who is in our tent. When we got to 24,000 thousand we stopped for a while and took our pulses and respiratory again and then they had Dick multiply 895x87. It took him a while but he finally made it. After that, he had to write Mary had a little lamb. He wrote it, but you couldn't read his writing, and he looked like he was intoxicated. He then got to put his oxygen mask back on and they took us up to 28,000 thousand feet and we checked ourselves again. When we started down was when all the fun began. Everybody blows and swallows as they try to keep their ears open. We came down at about 3,500 feet per minute. No one hollered until we got down to about 17,000 feet and then one fellow couldn't stand it any longer so they stopped and went back up 500 feet and gave him some stuff to clear his head, then we started on down again. Somebody else hollered at about 13,000 feet, so they had to do it for him too. They had to stop it for that fellow three or four times. I almost had them stop it for me, but I made it. Boy, it sure makes your ear drums feel like they have a knife stuck in them!

How ya all today? Just swell I'll betchya. Well, we got classified today. I got classified as a pilot. Hoorah! Hoorah!! We sure got classified in a big hurry. Today is only the eleventh day since we arrived. They didn't take any navigators out of our squadron at all. There were about 40-

50 bombardiers and about 30 fellows who were not classified yet. I was afraid that maybe I would be a bombardier when they said that over 50 were going to be. It would have been okay because I put that down as my second choice. But as you know, I've always wanted to fly. Looks like I'm finally getting my chance! Love, Cecil.

Chapter 16
Aviation Cadet

Here it is another Sunday morning in the army, with lots of time to write a letter to my honey. How are you this lovely A.M? I suppose that you have just gone to church or are preparing to do so. I didn't get there again today, the last mass was at 7:30 and we had to attend reveille (as usual). They had a couple weddings in the chapel yesterday afternoon. I saw them coming out and it looked real pretty, all the swords in an arch and the guys wearing white gloves.

We had our immunization shots today. It doesn't hurt you any while you're getting them, but I don't feel so good at present. We got them at about 9:30 this morning and its 3:30 P.M. now and my left arm is good and sore. We got three shots, one for tetanus, one for typhoid, and one for small pox. The one for tetanus made my arm feel just like someone gave me a good solid punch in the shoulder. It goes away in about 30 minutes and then the shots in the other arm start to hurt.

We're now settled in squadron 47 and I hope that we stay here for a while. We got our rifles, not that I know how to use one, but I guess that I'll soon learn, I'm afraid. We drilled with our rifles all morning. I guess I'll learn how to go through all the maneuvers one of these days. We learned the manual of arms this morning.

I don't know whether I'll have much to say from now on or not. They gave us definite instruction not to say anything about what goes on here at the post, as the mail is now subject to inspection. So if we go someplace else we're not supposed to say so until after we get where we're going. We're not supposed to say how many people are here or what they teach us or when. In other words, shut up! We had the articles of war read to us this afternoon. So now, if we do anything wrong, we can be punished accordingly.

I got a letter from Esther today. She says that dad keeps dropping off more and more. He only gets up for a little while every afternoon and mom has to help him up. She also said that he kind of drifts off into semi-consciousness for a few seconds now and then. She says he wants to see me and I should get some kind of furlough so I can come. I just don't see how that's possible though. Well honey, I'm running out of paper and words all at the same time, so I'd better sign off until tomorrow. So adieu and God bless you darling. Love and kisses, Cecil.

Life in the Army, or Air Corps, wasn't that bad, or even hard. Yes, there was the physical fitness stuff and the shots, but you get used to that pretty quick. Probably the hardest part is being away from the people you love. It was hard for me to be away from Margaret. When she was at Fallen Leaf Lake I could go see her as much as I was able. In the Army we're at the mercy of what they'll let us do. I have to admit, they try their best to find stuff for us to do on our off time and they really do try to accommodate us when our wives come to town. My thoughts were with my dad too. It was killing me not being able to be with him. His health was failing and he was getting worse. One of the reasons we moved to Ceres was to get him out of the dust of the fields. It didn't seem to be working very well. I think the doctors didn't diagnose him correctly. He was in a lot of pain, but mom has been keeping him medicated pretty good. We drilled, and drilled, and drilled. Our squadron was getting better at it and finally we won the best squadron award for drill. It was a long time coming, but it took us some time to get used to the routine.

They took us to the range once to watch a demonstration by a guy from the Remington Rifle Company. He was really good and he could sure shoot. He could shoot so fast it sounded like a machine gun. He could throw a lime up in the air and shoot a hole right through the middle of it. Then, he would throw about five eggs up in the air and shoot them one at a time before they hit the ground. He spent about an hour shooting things from different guns and angles. Once we'd been there for a while and assigned to a permanent squadron they would take one squadron into Santa Ana on Saturday for a short show. On one Saturday, however, they took a lot of us. We went to town in a convoy of Army trucks, about 400 guys. Everyone was hollering and singing all the way. I think it did everyone a lot of good. We had a military and police escort there and back. They gave us ten minutes off before the broadcast station opened. Everybody took off running up and down the street, in and out of stores, and going wild in general. Most of the guys went in the beer parlor across the street and had a bottle of beer. It was a swell show and a lot of fun. The program started at 5 P.M. and was a half an hour long. They had the west coast Army Air Corps band and it sure was a good one. Most of them came from famous orchestras and bands from before they were in the Air Corps. At this point the war effort was an all-out effort by the entire country. Even famous people put their careers aside and supported the effort one hundred percent. There was no selfishness in 1942. The Master of ceremonies was a corporal who used to be an announcer. First we did a lot of hollering and then sang the Air Corps song. Then, George Murphy came to the microphone and talked and joked with the MC for a while. He looked just exactly like he did in pictures, a swell guy. Then he called up Jackie Coogan, who was a glider pilot, and they talked together for a while and made more wise cracks as usual. After a while Connie Haines came out, who sang with Harry James and Tommy Dorsey before. She sang three songs during the program. She was a cute little trick and got lots of cheers and applause from everyone. Someone named Brenda and Cobina came out and did a couple numbers. After that, the major general, who is in charge of the west coast Air Corps training, came out and made a short but effective speech. There were about three major generals and a bunch of colonels there. The major generals came in the rear door and someone called us all to attention. They sauntered down the aisle in their Palm Beach uniforms and one of them held his hand up in a little gesture and said,

"At ease men."

What a life. They ended the show with the Army Air Corps song by the cadets again, and there was lots of cheering. It was all really a lot of fun. When I got back to the post I saw a lot of visitors sitting around waiting for their loved ones to get back from town. I should have been really happy after a show like that, but I just kind of fell into a state of the blues because seeing those people made me think of Margaret and all the fun times we had together, but she wasn't there. I knew I'd see her again soon, but at that moment in time it wasn't a consolation. I had to buck up. Flying is what I wanted, and here I was. I needed to toughen up and get over it, but it was hard because it was our first separation since being married.

We weren't getting much sleep because of all the extra duties. Cleaning every morning, fire guard, KP, guard duty, phone duty, you name it. They told me that it would make it easier on me when I got to my next post. They told me that when I get to my primary school I'll have to get up at 5 A.M. every day and go like the devil until 9:30 every night. They say that you get so tired there that if you get through at any earlier time you just collapse in your bunk. It sounded good to me, though, if I could just get there. They said there are four fellows to a room there, and only two rooms to a barracks. Each room has a shower and a bathtub and dressers. Our officers said that the cadets there even have better quarters than the officers at the bachelors quarters do. I was getting along fine in training and in the classroom. The junior college time that I had helped me out pretty good. I was getting good scores on pretty much everything. Even my math scores were always between 98 and 100. I was looking forward to getting on to my next phase of training. The phase that included airplanes. There was a lot of learning to do in Santa Ana in a short amount of time. I had a guy in my physics class say that if he dropped his pencil it would take him two weeks to catch up on what he missed while he was picking it up. Sounded somewhat ridiculous, but it was prophetically true.

Margaret had been planning her vacation for quite some time. We were talking about it in a lot of our letters to each other. She went to San Francisco to get a physical for the Army to see if she could enlist as an officer. She planned it so she would get her vacation before there was a possibility of being called up. When she finally got the chance to come visit me, though, it wasn't to have fun and lock ourselves in a hotel for the weekend as we'd planned. It was to escort me up to Ceres for my father's funeral. Dad died in his sleep and was found that way in the morning by my mother. The base chaplain was kind enough to arrange an emergency furlough for me to attend the funeral. Margaret and I rode the train north to Ceres and attended the funeral on a weekend. The whole family was there. I was pretty upset about the whole affair. I'd been getting letters that said dad was doing better. Then, I'd get letters saying he was worse. There was nothing I could do. Toward the end mom had a nurse come to the house to help her with him. We found out that it wasn't allergies that he was suffering from. He had rectal cancer. There wouldn't have been anything they could have done for him, but it still upset me that the doctors didn't know what was wrong with him and they misdiagnosed him. It was a sad weekend, but there was no time to sit around and sulk. I had to get back to the post in Santa Ana and finish up my studies so I could move on to primary training. There was a war on, and personal problems had to wait. Even if it did mean that it would be harder to concentrate on things from now on. My dad and I were very close, and I would miss him more than I could imagine. I carried some guilt about not going to see him when he was asking for me. I figured I could make him proud by finishing up my studies and getting my wings. I took the train back to southern California and checked in-in time to not lose any ground. I ended up graduating on time with excellent marks and found out that my next post would be Tucson, Arizona, at the Ryan School of Aeronautics, flying the Ryan PT-22.

I finally made it dad!

Chapter 17
Ryan School of Aeronautics

So sorry if you got yourself worried over me not phoning you or anything. But my darling, it's not that I didn't want to, but just that it's impossible to do so from this place, so I know that you will forgive me. We left Santa Ana about 4:30 on Tuesday and arrived here about 3 P.M. Wednesday. It was a nice trip. It was a troop train. No civilians. We left a bunch of the fellows in Phoenix. A couple hundred of us came on to Tucson. We're about 16 miles out of town, and there's nothing but desert all around. It's quite nice here though, not a very big place. At least compared to Santa Ana. But it's much better than Santa Ana, as far as the officers and the general feelings of everyone are concerned. The only scenery around is a few hills here and there and a lot of cactus, but they have lots of airplanes here, and that makes everyone feel better.

We were assigned to flying instructors this morning. Five of us to each instructor. I think I managed to get a pretty good instructor, at least he certainly appears to be so. The group I'm in has a 2nd lieutenant in it, but he's just a student like any of the rest of us. We're going up in a ship in the morning. I imagine it will be for about a half an hour apiece. The instructor said he would let us handle the controls while in the air. I guess I can remember what they are all for without too much trouble. The airfield here is built and run by Ryan. The government pays them for teaching us to fly. Of course, we have Army officers around and the whole thing is supervised by the Army, but the buildings and everything belong to Ryan. All the planes here are built and owned by Ryan too. They call the plane a P.T. 22, which means primary trainer and the 22 is the model number or something. We'll only be here for nine weeks, which I hope will not seem too awfully long. Of course, some of us won't be here that long, but we won't know who until after the first two or three weeks. It takes that long to tell whether you can fly or not. They give you from nine to fourteen hours in which to solo.

I'm back to pen and paper honey. I went up for my first airplane ride. We had to be out on the flight line at 7:15 A.M but I didn't get to go up until 11:00. I was up for fifty minutes, and I must say that it was quite a thrill. I handled the controls most of the time, after we got in the air of course, but with considerable assistance from my instructor. But anyway, it was a lot of fun, at least until we started down, at which time the air was rather rough and I went and got sick. But I only heaved once and was alright after that. I hope that it doesn't affect me that way anymore. A lot of the fellows were in the same fix. Good-bye for now my darling and May God bless you and keep you just for me. Love and kisses, Cecil.

Ryan Field was a much nicer post than Santa Ana was. I guess they were trying to weed some of us out back in California, or welcome us to Army life anyway. I got the blues almost as soon as I got to Tucson, though, and I missed my wife terribly. The combination of the enormity of a whole new life style, worried about making the grade, missing Margaret, not being able to phone her before leaving Santa Ana, and my dad dying was beginning to build up in me. They only paid me $8.29 when I left Santa Ana, and that was a bit stressful. We all got $50, but they took out what we owed for uniforms. Now, to all of a sudden find out that flying makes me vomit, well, I really began to wonder if I would make it all the way through my training. Having to go through this really gave me a new respect for the officers I saw every day that already had the silver wings on their chest. They'd already made the grade. As far as Ryan Field goes, I knew I'd like my time here. Most of the time the weather was tolerable, but once in a while the wind would kick up, blow the sand around, and you couldn't see twenty feet in front of your face. One time, not long after my arrival, there was such a bad wind storm that they called all of the cadets out to the flight line to hold down the planes. By the time we got there some were already damaged, but we were able to save the rest. It wasn't an easy task because it took several of us to hold on to one plane and we had to stand there and take the blowing sand in our faces and on our exposed skin and it hurt like hell. The best a fellow could do was just stand there with his eyes shut, hold on, and listen for instructions. When it was finally all over I thought I'd never get all that sand off of me. The weekends weren't as busy as my last post and we had time to get out and do things. My first weekend in Tucson, me and four other married fellows went into town and we saw a football game. The University of Arizona played Utah. The game wasn't much good. Arizona won 14 to 0, but they weren't much good either. All four of us slept in the same room at a hotel. We had two single beds and a double bed in the room. It only cost each of us a dollar and a half, so that wasn't bad. The next day, after a late breakfast, I was able to get Margaret on the phone and I began to feel a little better about everything. It was pretty funny in town, because there were a lot of officers around from the east coast. I don't think they'd ever seen a cadet uniform before, plus many of them were just pressed into service and were doctors or something just a couple weeks ago. They were confused and they kept saluting us as though we outranked them, one was even a major, so we got a pretty big kick out of that.

The drinking water at Ryan field was put into barrels outside the barracks. They fill the barrels and put in a chunk of ice, and everyone has a glass which they keep in their locker. We didn't have footlockers there like we had at Santa Ana. We each had a wooden locker in back of our bunk. There was room to hang everything on hangers and there were shelves on which to put our other stuff. There was a nice big mess hall and all the meals were pretty good. They served them cafeteria style, which I imagine cut down considerably on the amount of work for each meal. The barracks all have several cooling systems in them. They are all one story and very wide. Unlike what we were told by that guy at our last post, we didn't get rooms. We had tables and chairs down through the middle of the barracks, and there were about fifty or sixty fellows. The fellows in the class who had been there for about six weeks were called upper classmen, not that we had to look up to them or anything. They mixed all of us new fellows up amongst them in the different barracks. I didn't get my second flight as scheduled. It didn't bother me once I found out about my instructor. He was an older fellow who had flown in the Canadian Air Force. He'd already flown in combat in England and flew cover for an evacuation out of France to England. He came back to Canada but got bored, so he came down to the United States and went to work for Ryan as an instructor. He had a history of having the first student to solo in the squadron, and I was hoping it would be me. I also heard that he had a method of getting his students to pay attention and get things right. I was told that he would slam the stick back and forth between your legs if he didn't like something. His students all had black and blue marks between their legs. Not to mention that he would holler at us if he felt like it. I missed my second flight because he'd take a student up for fifty minutes to an hour instead of the half hour that the other instructors did.

Dear Margaret

I finally wrote a letter to mom today. I think it was about time. I was ashamed of myself for not doing so sooner, but you know how it is in a new place and busy and you're kept on edge all the time and never know what's coming next. Now that we have our schedules arranged and we know when we do what, it will make it a lot easier to do things. I went up for my second hour of instruction in an airplane today. I did a little better than I did the first day, at least I didn't lose my lunch this time. After we got off the ground I did a lot of climbing turns and then more climbing turns until we got up to about 8,500 feet. Then, I flew it around for a while, with the instructors help now and then. After that he did a couple of stalls, which consists of shutting off the gas and gliding with the nose pointed up until the plane almost stalls, then the nose starts to drop and you push down the stick and kick the rudder back and forth to keep the plane straight, then you dive for a while to pick up speed, turn the gas on, the engine kicks on, and you level off. More darn fun, huh? They call that a power off stall. Then, we did a power on stall, in which you leave the power on and nose the ship up until it starts to stall. Then, you dive it, just the same as the other, except that the power is on all the time. It's a little easier, I did about three or four of each after he did a couple to show me how to do it. I did alright on a couple of them. After our stalls he took the plane into a spin. Boy, your stomach comes up in your mouth on the first one! He did two more of them and was going to have me do one, but he asked me how I felt and I mentioned that my stomach was starting to go around, so he started back down again. At least I kept my lunch down today, and I imagine that by tomorrow it shouldn't bother me anymore. Of course, it will be another week after this one before I know whether I'll be able to be a pilot or not. And even then, you can't be too sure. We get our first flight check at ten hours. We're supposed to be able to do spins and stalls and climbing turns and such on our first check flight. We're supposed to be able to solo in from nine to fourteen hours. I guess maybe I can do so. It's like the instructor says; either you learn how, or else. That's what keeps everybody on edge. I think, or rather, I know, it's going to get powerful lonesome around these parts before I get out of here. Remember that I love you and think of you always. You're the sweetest girl and wife in the whole wide world. Bye now. Cecil.

Chapter 18
Short Snorter Club

Hello Sweetheart!

Thanks for the two nice letters which arrived today. They were dated last Sunday and Monday, so you see, it takes a little longer for them to come to me from Arizona. You keep them coming, though, my dearest, as often as possible. I always feel much better after reading even a short letter from you. It sounds as though Ryan Field is pretty swell. But don't you talk about being a wash-out this early in the game. If anyone should earn his wings you should, sweetheart, so don't even think about flunking out as a pilot. Time enough if such an absurd thing happens. You just keep plugging along, applying yourself to everything, and don't let any little things bother you. You'll come out on top, among the finest and best, I just know it.

Gee, that storm must have been something! I can vaguely remember a few similar ones when I lived in Yuma. That old sand really flies, huh? I was glad to hear that your planes weren't too badly damaged. It's nice that you have such a generous instructor. You just grin and bear it when he takes you through those spins and loops. Pretend you're on the Loop-A-Plane. Remember our first date and our ride on that contraption? That was really a thrill, but I like skiing better. Anyway, just swallow hard and your food will probably stay where it belongs. Yes, I think the fellows earn their wings these days. They have to be good to survive the rigid training they get in the short amount of time allowed. I'm proud of all of our boys, especially you, my darling.

Please excuse the short letter, dearest, I'll write a long one tomorrow, I promise. Good night again, good luck, and God bless you and keep you safe for just me, because I love you so much and hope for the time to come soon when we can always be together. All my love and kisses, Margaret.

101

The weather was pretty windy quite a bit at Ryan Field. It made it difficult for us new guys to learn the type of precision flying that the Army wanted us to learn. I could fly alright, but when I would have to follow the instructors directions about precision climbing turns, "S" turns, and doing those types of maneuvers without losing altitude or keeping on a desired ascent while doing it, well, that wasn't so easy. I got my turn cancelled a few times because the afternoon wind would pick up and make it too dangerous to fly. There was a lot of sitting around time. We all had to be out at the flight line waiting for our turn, even if it was going to be hours before we could climb into the cockpit. When our plane landed we would have to go out and hold on to the wings as it taxied into a parking place. I guess that was so no one could walk into a prop and the pilot and instructor could easily see all of us. About mid-October my rotation was switched to morning and my flight time increased. I got pretty good at the stalls, climbing turns and spins, and I wasn't getting sick anymore. My confidence was beginning to improve that I might actually pass and get my wings after all. On the anniversary of my first date with Margaret I was the first to go up in the morning. By this time I'd been taking the plane off several times and I even landed a few times, although I still wasn't very good at the landings. We flew around for a while and my instructor had me fly out to an auxiliary field where we practiced a few landings and take-offs, and then he had me land and stop. When we stopped he got out and said,

"Well, you're now over the minimum hours needed to solo. As you know, my students are the first to solo in every class. Are you ready to take the controls?"

I nervously said yes and he told me to take off and fly around for a while. I taxied down to the end of the runway, pointed the ship straight, shoved the throttle forward and raised the tail. Then, I pulled back on the stick and raised her off the ground. It was quite a thrill. I went around the field three times and started to land each time and then decided I wasn't just right about the time I was going to hit the ground, so I gave it the gun, pulled it up and went around again. The fourth time around I put it down and bounced it quite a bit when I hit, but I kept it under control and came to a halt. The instructor came over and grinned and asked me how I liked it. I told him that I loved it but that I bounced it quite a bit. He said,

"Well, you got it down didn't you?" Then he said, "Congratulations."

He shook my hand. I took it off again by myself and landed it the first time around. That landing wasn't anything to brag about either, but it was much better than the first one. It really felt swell to get up there all by myself. When I got back to the barracks I got a new nickname. They called me HP Quinley, for (hot pilot), for being the first guy in the class to solo. I really wasn't, strictly speaking, the first to solo. I was the first to solo of everyone in the class that wasn't already a pilot. There were a few guys that were civilian pilots already who had a hundred hours flight time before they joined up. Those guys soloed pretty quickly after being checked out by their instructors and being shown the maneuvers they had to practice. My confidence level was growing every day after soloing. My instructor had the second and third guys to solo also. It was a shock to learn that we'd be losing him before we graduated because he got a promotion. Back at the barracks I was in for a big surprise. I belonged to a new organization called the "Short Snorter" club. I don't know where it got the name, but you had to solo to belong to it. When you get down from your first solo the first guy to find it out, who already belongs to the club, grabs you and signs his name on a dollar bill (one of mine of course). You have to write your name across the edge, and the time and place of your solo flight. Also, they write the "Short Snorter Club" across the top. You have to pay the first two guys a dollar each who signs your dollar. But, if there are more in the group that catches you the first time, you have to pay them all. I was lucky, there had only been a couple guys, the guys that were already pilots, so I was only out two dollars. Everyone who soloed after that would sneak around and get two signatures before announcing that they'd soloed. After the initial (catching), you just exchanged signatures with the other members, but that didn't end it. You had to always carry that bill with you from then on. If another member ever asked to see it you'd better have it on you. If you don't have it you have to pay him a dollar. If you're in a bar you have to buy him or them a drink. On the other hand, if you do have it when they ask, they have to do the same for you. It was a silly game, but a lot of fun, and it was swell to feel like I belonged to something special. As more of the guys got to solo, more and more accidents happened. No one got killed, but a lot of planes got wrecked. One guy flipped over frontwards when he landed, and several guys did ground loops when they landed because of the screwy winds here. Out of the five of us that were assigned to our instructor, two would wash out.

The longer I was at Ryan Field the more I got comfortable going to town. There was quite a bit of entertainment in Tucson and there was almost always a dance going on somewhere. I found a few other married guys to hang out with. They were all good Catholic boys from Pittsburg. We began to hang out together and do things like go to see films, or go to the USO to play pool and have a few drinks. We didn't want to do the things that the single fellows wanted to do. Chase skirts all over town. Sometimes we had to go to the dances because it was required. I guess it made it easier for them to keep track of us all. One weekend we underclassmen weren't allowed to go to the dance at the hotel in town because a few guys had been caught drunk the week before. In mid to late October the Navy arrived in Tucson. I don't know what they were doing there, some kind of training at one of the other posts. They were a long way from the ocean if you ask me. There were so many officers in town between the Navy and Army that a guy would wear his arm out saluting the whole time he was in town. Around the first of November they moved us to a new barracks. There were only about five of us left in that barracks by then anyway. That made it hard to clean, because there were only five of us to share the work. They made us move because they had an outbreak of Scarlet Fever at Santa Ana and they wanted to keep all the incoming new underclassmen together just in case any of them had it. They had to do everything by themselves until the doctors were sure it was okay.

After my instructor left I continued to solo until the new instructor arrived. I guess I developed some bad habits while I was doing that. I was flying just fine, but all that technical Army stuff had been getting rusty without an instructor to keep me in line. When I went up with the new instructor I got real nervous. My old instructor would holler and swear and bang that stick back and forth. The new guy didn't say a thing, and that was what made me nervous. I never knew how I was doing. After flying around for a day, we landed, taxied over to the flight line and he just said,

"You soloed?"

Well, that brought my confidence down a few notches. He got what was coming to him on our next flight, though, when he had me do a roll. The PT-22 is an open cockpit monoplane. We were flying along straight and level and he told me to go ahead and do a slow roll. About the time we were inverted he began hollering at the top of his lungs,

"Kick it over! Kick it over!"

He forgot to fasten his belt and parachute harness. That made my day, but it was still hard getting back into the habit of flying by the numbers because I never knew while we were in the air if I was satisfying him or not. At least back at the barracks we all got a great laugh when I told everyone about the slow roll incident

Hello darling! Here it is another day, and the first of another month. I sure can't imagine it being the first of December already. Maybe if I get back to California it will seem more like that time of year. I only had to fly for 35 minutes today and all the other fellows only had about that long to go, so we got through early. I finally had my Army check ride too and managed to pass it, not with flying colors or anything, but the lieutenant was a very nice fellow. He was the one in the plane number 97 picture that I sent you. That was the plane that I took my check ride in. We had our graduation party last night. I sat at my instructors table and had a couple of drinks with him and his wife. Well, I'm all finished with primary now. We turned in all our equipment and then packed our barracks bags and put tags on them, but they didn't tell us where to address them. I guess I'm getting a little excited now that we're about to move on to Basic. It will be an Army post, so there will be a lot more drilling and so forth, but the ships will be bigger and faster. Goodbye now darling. For the last time from Tucson I hope? Love, Cecil

Chapter 19
Gardner Army Airfield

Hello tonight my darling!

I certainly am a much happier man tonight than I was last night. Because last night I wasn't so sure that I was going to see you or not. I guess that is one time when I can be thankful for the rain. Of course, I would have certainly been happy to have been able to stay all day with you and see you into Bakersfield. But at least I got to see you once more before leaving our fair state for another spell. We had a couple hours lecture this morning, that's all we had to do all day. We would have gone on our cross country tonight if it would have cleared up, but it didn't. I went to see the Lum and Abner Show this afternoon. It was exceptionally good. Lum and Abner were only on for a couple of minutes, but they were pretty good. Abner was reading a letter to Lum from his cousin and she was telling about her friend having triplets, and how rare it was because it only happens in one out of 89,000 chances. Lum says gosh, when did she ever find time to do her house work? The Merry Macs were there and they were really good. There was also some gal who was doing imitations of people. The post orchestra played for the show and the master of ceremonies said that it was the best he'd heard in all the Air Corps.

Here I am back again. Thank you for such a nice big letter today. I enjoyed it very much indeed. Your mother sounded very good in her letter also. I'm glad that she's happy and settled down in Long Beach. Here it is Saturday night and I sure am missing you tonight.

Honey, we had something very sad happen here. My instructor and one of my fellow students were killed in a crack-up today. The cadet's name was Joe Almond. I don't believe that you ever met him. He was a real swell fellow and was married for about six months. Nobody knows just what did happen for sure. They were flying in formation with two other instructors and their students. They were just finishing making their last turn into the field to land when the plane went on its side. They had it straightened out just before they crashed and it looked like they were going to make it, but they didn't have quite enough altitude. The plane burned after it hit, but they couldn't have been alive. You met Lieutenant Markham, my instructor, over in Bakersfield at the bus depot. I feel plenty bad about it, you kind of feel it when it hits so close to home. But I will promise you that I won't let it bother me. It's just one of those things that you can't do anything about. The weather was too rough to be flying formation today, but it was even worse for anything else. Don't let something like this worry you about me, though, because as long as I'm not scared or worried, you shouldn't be either.

I sure wish that I was sitting at home in front of the fire by the side of you tonight. It's still dreary and gloomy outside. I always seem to miss you and home the most on these kinds of nights. I guess it's because I love you so much and need you to love me. Good night my darling, and May God bless you and bring you safely to see me soon. Love and Kisses, Cecil.

I arrived at Gardner Field in Taft California on December 4th, 1942. I was ecstatic to be going back to California. It would make it so much easier for Margaret and me to see each other once in a while. It was a long train ride from Tucson, but for our last leg we left Los Angeles on the 3rd at about 7 P.M. They put our Pullman cars on a side track in Bakersfield and let us sleep on them until 6 A.M. on the 4th. I didn't know about that until the morning of the 4th, though, because I went to bed as we were passing through Mojave. There isn't much to see out in the Mojave Desert. But at night there was just pitch darkness all around. We played cards, talked, and drank coffee until I just had to lie down and get some sleep. Gardner Field was a fairly new post and was even nicer than Ryan Field. There was green grass everywhere and cream colored barracks. The barracks weren't open bay. They actually had rooms in them. I shared a room with a fellow who came in from King City Primary School. Most of the rooms were shared by four people, but ours was a two person room. We had steel lockers and a very nice desk with a black top and a couple of fancy desk lamps. There were about 300 of us new cadets that came in. 110 of us from Tucson and

180 from King City. On December 6th they hauled us all out to the flight line and we were assigned our planes and an instructor. My instructor was Lieutenant Markham. He told us we'd be flying the BT-13 trainer. Here I thought I knew a little bit about flying, but boy was I wrong. Lieutenant Markham told us that at primary school all they taught us how to do was to get a plane off the ground and keep it off until you wanted to bring it down. I guess he was right when you stop to think about it. Here, we'd be learning how to fly in formation, instrument flying, land navigation and cross country flights both in day and night. We'd also get some introductory aerobatic flying. We'd be spending a lot of time in the Link Trainer learning instrument flying before they let us try it in the BT-13. The BT-13 seemed like it had a lot of instruments and levers compared to what we'd been flying in Tucson. One nice thing about it was that we didn't have to turn the props to get it started. It took a little getting used to, but when you did it was easy. You had to hold down about three gadgets at the same time and then hit the start and it cranked right up. They let us all try the procedure out when they showed us the planes and gave us our instructors. The Link Trainer was a box that looked like a model or toy airplane. We'd climb in and they'd shut a lid on us. The box moved according to our control inputs and gave us a limited feeling of flight. Of course, since this was an Army Post, we would once again be drilling and having to do physical fitness training. I'll tell you one thing, though, the food at Gardner Field was the best I had in the Army. Our first night there they served us a huge steak that was the best I had since the Rosemount in Sacramento. They also gave us potatoes and gravy, corn, and real good milk. On new year's day they served us roast duck, dressing and gravy, mashed potatoes, salad, and topped it all off with cake and ice cream. They even gave us a package of cigarettes to go with it. Boy, once Margaret and I are able to be together all the time this Army life won't be too bad I think.

For about the first month and a half we didn't hardly get any flying time because of the weather at Gardner Field that time of year. It was almost always either too hazy, cloud cover too low, or just downright foggy. I started getting worried that we wouldn't get our flight time in by the time we were supposed to move on to our next base. On December 31st I was finally able to get in a full day of flying. Up until then it had been pretty sporadic. Even on that day we were fogged in for a few hours in the morning, but we stayed on the flight line until it burned off. Then we went up for 3 ½ hours. I got some instrument flight time under the (hood). The hood is a black canvas sheet that you pull over your head while you're flying. Your windows are blacked out too so it makes it so you can't see outside and there's no light except for the lighted instruments. Your instructor gives you headings to fly and has you make turns and banks. You have to rely on your instruments completely because you can really get disoriented under the hood. It feels like you're flying level, when in fact you're losing altitude or banking and so forth. I was real good at the instrument procedures. In fact, Lieutenant Markham told me that I did better when I couldn't see where I was going. I wasn't sure how to take that, but I guess I needed to use my instruments more to help me with my visual flying. We all got a good laugh out of it at my expense. That's okay though. When you do something that people laugh at all you have to do is wait for their turn and there will be something they've done to laugh at too. When we weren't flying with the instructor we could take the plane up and get some solo time shooting take offs and landings. I did that as much as I was able to get the plane.

About two thirds of the way through my training Lieutenant Markham didn't show up one day and we had a fill in instructor. A captain decided that he'd take us up since the lieutenant would be indisposed for a few days. Boy was he ever an ornery cuss. I was glad when we got to land and he got out so I could get up there solo. There was no pleasing that captain. We did everything the way the lieutenant told us, but everything had to be his way, even if we didn't know what his way was. I found out that the lieutenant had been grounded until he could go before a board of officers and explain why he and two other instructors buzzed the town of Visalia. We could hardly contain our laughter when we heard the news. Our only regret was that we weren't there for the buzzing. But I guess the brass doesn't take kindly to complaints from the town folk, war or no war.

January 4th, I got my first taste of formation flying. That was a kick and I enjoyed it a ton. Of course, for the first time, the instructors did the flying to show us how it's done. It keeps you on the edge of your seat at all times. They got so close that you couldn't slip a piece of paper between their wings. I was hoping that maybe someday I'd be that good too. It was tough having to hang out on the flight line all day just to get two hours of flying in, but the weather was still touch and go. They really turned us loose when it was clear though. I loved the night flying solo. It was usually nice smooth air. I'd go up until about 1 A.M. They had us fly in assigned zones. There were four zones that were divided into three altitudes (lower, middle, and upper). You just fly around in your zone until they call you in to land. The first time we did it they had flood lights on the runway. After that they used smudge pots to line the runway. It was a little harder to judge, but we got used to it. I was also getting about three separate hours per day in the Link trainer. Getting to do cross country flying was the best. It was more like you were going somewhere, instead of just flying around. I always wished we could fly up to McClellan Field in Sacramento and spend the night, but no such luck. On January 17th I went on a cross country flight north to Porterville, then we turned west to Coalinga and then a south easterly heading back home for about a 240 mile trip. On the same day we flew to Wheeler Ridge, which is just where you start over the grapevine toward Los Angeles, then north westerly to Fresno, then Lost Hills and back home for about 280 miles. It was all individual flying and we took off in thirty second intervals. No one got lost and everything went just as planned, imagine that!

There were two accidents while I was at Gardner Field. The first was a lower classman who hit the ground real hard. It was the first accident in a long time at the field. No one really knows what happened. The plane kind of pancaked onto the ground and there wasn't that much damage, but it killed him just the same. The worst was Lieutenant Markham and his student. I couldn't believe my eyes as I watched the whole thing happen in front of me. They looked like they were going way too slow for being in a turn in formation. All of a sudden the plane tipped on its side. The thought was that he lost lift and stalled, but it was pretty gusty that day too, he could have gotten a sudden draft, but it didn't seem to affect the other two planes, so we all figured he stalled. He almost pulled it out; he was just a little too low. Lieutenant Markham was a good pilot, but being too low to the ground sometimes that doesn't matter so much. To see the fireball was really shocking to all of us and it really made it hit home that we were in a dangerous profession. That day would be my first exposure to loss, other than my father's death. To witness a loss like that, especially someone you know, like, and respect, makes you reflect. Plus, there's always the thought in your mind that you could have been that student with him. Little did I know in January 1943 that this exposure to loss would only be my first. It would only be the tip of a very large iceberg of loss heading my way. The rest of my time at Gardner Field would go off without a hitch and I would graduate on time. Next stop, Luke Field, Phoenix, Arizona.

111

Chapter 20
American Red Cross

January 23, 1943.

Just received your telephone call and am still a little upset from the news of the accident today. I just can't believe it's true! Lieutenant Markham seemed like such a grand fellow. I really liked him, he was so clean-cut and polite. I guess we just can't tell what's coming next from one minute to another these days, can we dear? I know how badly, you especially, as well as all of his other students must feel. He was a very good man, I'm sure, because you said he was, and you liked him so very much. I surely wish I could be there with you this weekend, darling. But I guess I've just got to be patient and wait another long week. Do keep that brave chin of yours way out and don't let this unhappy day have too great an effect upon your future. I know it's hard to take, but we all just must keep going regardless of whatever happens.

Remember always that I love you and have you ever in my heart. I think you're the grandest and swellest little guy in the world too, and I always will. You are, you know, and I know so, because I'm the gal who married you and I'm pretty lucky to be your wife.

Here I am, back again to tell you hello and how much I love you, and miss you too. Gee, I wish you were here. You could even meet me after work maybe. Oh well, someday we'll be living together at home again and this old war will be just a bad memory that we won't even mention. Let's just keep on hoping and praying that that day will come real soon. Darling, just four more nights and I'll be leaving on my trip to visit you. That won't be so bad, will it? I mean the days and nights in between. I surely hope you can be on hand to meet my train at midnight Friday, but I won't feel too bad if you don't get off until Saturday night. If you don't meet me I shall come over to Taft Saturday morning unless I hear otherwise from you. My train leaves to come home from Bakersfield at 4:00 P.M. Sunday, which won't get me home too late, not that I'd care of course. The more time I'm able to spend with you the better and the happier I'll be. I love you sweetheart, just heaps and heaps, no fooling, and I'm anxiously awaiting our visit together. Confidentially, I'm hoping hard, and praying too, for you to be transferred nearer to home for advanced training. It would certainly be grand if you could come to Stockton, even better, Mather or Chico, or anyplace in California. I could still visit you once in a while.

There really isn't much news from yesterday, except that I love and miss you an awful lot. That's old stuff though, isn't it darling? I'm a little tired tonight and should get some sleep. Once again darling, I am so very sorry about Lieutenant Markham. Good night, my own dear sweetheart. God bless you and keep you safe and happy always. I'll be seeing you (in all the old familiar places) real soon! Love and kisses, from your Mrs. Margaret.

I couldn't help but take the news of the death of Cecil's friend and instructor hard. I worried about him, but I had to be strong for him. It was times like this that he needed encouragement, not to have to listen to me cry and worry about him. Lieutenant Markham wasn't the first crash. There'd been a student that Cecil didn't know who crashed also, but that is almost to be expected sometimes. It was more shocking to your psyche to know that an expert such as the lieutenant could fall too. We'd also gotten news that a high school friend of Cecil's had crashed and was killed in a bomber while practicing down in the south eastern tip of California. Cec was quick to quote statistics about how safe flying was compared to driving. He tried to convince himself he was doing the right thing, and he tried to convince me not to worry about him. I know those statistics weren't compiled using numbers from military training over the last year, as the United States was rushing to get pilots qualified to fight in the war. But even so, it made us feel better. The important thing was that he was following his dream, and he knew, and I knew, that he needed to follow through with it or he'd regret it for the rest of his life. Some high school friends of his had tried real hard to get him to join the Navy with them, but he isn't too fond of that big old ocean and the idea of something happening to the ship. No, flying has been his dream for as long as I've known him. This is what he wants to do and I support him all the way and am very proud of him. The only problem, as I see it, is that it doesn't look like we'll have a normal life as long as this war is going on. No stateside normal duty, coming home at night to me, telling me about his day, seeing him fly over our town with the rest of his squadron. As long as this war is going on there's no telling where he's going to end up. I pray about it every day and twice as hard on Sunday at mass.

I'd been keeping myself busy on the home front. My new job as assistant clerk typist in the Engineer Division at the War Department was quite literally driving me crazy. You never knew whether my boss was going to be nice, or a grump. I think he drank too much at times and took it out on us girls when he was hung over. He was always giving me a hard time for working too slow, when in fact I was the fastest worker in the office at getting accounts billed. One day he had the gall to yell at me,

"Margaret, if you were faster at your job, maybe the war would end sooner!"

My friend that sat at the desk behind me stood up and got in his face and told him that if he wasn't a draft dodger and would pick up his own rifle and get out there and join the Army, maybe the war would get over sooner too. I laughed so hard I began to cry a little. In fact, everyone in the office laughed at him. He yelled at us all to get back to work and he stomped out of the office with his old stinky cigar clenched in his teeth. His statement did start me to thinking later that night. I was working there simply for the money and wasn't happy there at all. He was, in fact, kind of right. I wasn't helping the war effort. I went out and got a paying position at the Red Cross and quit the War Department. At the Red Cross I put together a news bulletin, helped with accounts since I was already trained in that, and eventually I was elected president of our local chapter and oversaw incoming donations, the bookkeeping for it, and the deposit of the monies into the bank. We usually took in over $30,000 a day, all cash. When I was ready to take it to the bank I'd call the Sacramento Police Department and they'd send over two uniformed officers to escort me to the bank. Because of them I never felt worried and I was really proud of what I was doing. I finally felt connected, like I was contributing to the effort. I began to take nursing aide classes at Sutter Memorial Hospital so I could help medically also. In February I graduated from the program and worked as a nurse's aide in the labor and delivery department at Sutter Memorial. Believe me, there were a lot of babies born as a result of lovers being separated and then having brief encounters on visits or leaves. Helping an expectant mother to deliver is a beautiful and wonderful thing and I finally felt as needed and complete as I could with my own darling being gone. It sure beat working for old grumpy britches at the War Department! Many of the nurses, nurse's aides, and Red Cross people were married too, or in some other way related to a military man, so they had a lot more understanding for the trials of separation. We all leaned on each other for support and it was easier to get time off when the opportunity arose to visit with Cecil. I finally felt like I was where I was supposed to be. I was able to go down to Taft every two to three weeks to see him. One time he couldn't get off the base like he was expecting to, so it just turned into a nice relaxing long train ride and I got to see the post band play at the theater in town. They were very good. Cecil had told me that the base colonel was an old Army officer who'd served in the cavalry in the First World War. Cecil said he even still had a horse on the post and a sergeant was assigned full time to care for it. I thought that was quite interesting and humorous all at the same time. I could just picture that old colonel riding his horse around the post with airplanes flying over his head. He was stationed for many years before the war in the Los Angeles area somewhere and came to have a lot of contacts in the Hollywood scene. When he was putting together his post band he called some of his friends down there and got them to arrange for some of the guys who had gone in the service to be sent to Taft.

I did my best to hold things together on the home front. Mom moved to Long Beach and seemed much happier than when she was in Detroit. I was getting letters from her semi-regularly now. Since Cecil's father died, mother Quinley wasn't so tied to Ceres and she was able to get out and visit all her kids more. She came up to Sacramento a few times and I'd usually see her at Milly's house. We had some trouble setting up Cecil's allotment to me so he didn't have to send money all the time in the mail. It finally got taken care of at Taft, about midway through his training there. We got a lot of rain in January and I had a leaky roof that I couldn't get fixed. I kept telling my land lord, Mr. Busby, but he just wouldn't get it done. Cecil was about to leave his post and come up to Sacramento and take care of Mr. Busby, but I told him to keep his nose to the grindstone and I'd eventually get it done. Milly's husband, Jim, had words with Mr. Busby and the roof finally got fixed, for the second time, and stopped leaking. I was hoping against all odds that Cecil would go to advanced training somewhere in California so we could keep seeing each other. Alas, it wasn't to be. His orders came in at graduation for him to be sent to Luke Army Airfield in Phoenix, Arizona. Of course, as is the Army way, I wouldn't find this out until he was already at Luke Field. They weren't allowed to say ahead of time where there were going, but they could call or write after arriving at their destination. Arizona, again! I didn't have anything against Arizona; after all, I used to live in Yuma before moving to California. But it was a long way from Sacramento and I guess that would be the end of our visits for a while. I hoped that I'd be able to get down there, maybe once to see him, but it was just wishful thinking. It would take a whole week round trip on a train for a one day visit. It would be worth it, but not very practical. Our visits were quite special and kept us close emotionally and physically (wink). No, Phoenix was just too far, but thank God it would only be for two months and he would probably get a leave before moving on to fighter school.

Margaret's Sacramento Junior College Graduation Photo

Cecil's First Car-1931 Chevy

Margaret's Wedding Day Photo

Wedding Day-April 16, 1939

**The Mothers
Cora Belle McCoy-Quinley (left)
Ella Farley-Phillips (right)**

Cecil's Parents
Cora Belle and John Winson Quinley

Dancing at the Biltmore Bowl

The Honeymoon Chariot-1939

This Photo was sent to Stalag Luft III

Honeymoon-Balboa Park-San Diego, California

Margaret at John Quinley's Ski Hill

Margaret and Cecil at John Quinley's Ski Lodge

Margaret and Her New Clubs

Margaret Volunteered for the Red Cross

Brand New Air Cadet Quinley

Senior Air Cadet Quinley

Cecil in front of his AT-6 Texan

Margaret Wearing Cecil's Silver Wings

Cecil in Training

The Short Snorter Dollar

The New 2nd Lieutenant in Ceres, California

Ready to Take on the World

Daniel J. Quinley

Having Some Fun Before Shipping Out

Margaret Selling War Bonds
Sacramento, 1945

Cecil's Official Graduation Photo

Forever

**This beloved photo was later made into a large pencil drawing
by an artist and family friend-
C. Cook**

Daniel J. Quinley

**Cecil Carried this Photo with Him Throughout
Captivity and on the Death March**

The Pry-Quinley Crew

The Crew of the "Polly Jo." July, 1943. Left to Right.

Kneeling: Waist gunner Sgt. Al Johnson, Top Turret Gunner/Engineer Sgt Eddie LaPointe, Ball Turret Gunner Sgt. Irving "Smitty" Smith, Waist Gunner Sgt. Carl Baird, Radio Operator Sgt. Russ "Frenchy" Frautschi, Tail Gunner Sgt Martin "Tex" Brandt.

Standing: Pilot 2nd Lt. Jack Pry, Bombardier 2nd Lt. Ted Snyder, Navigator 2nd Lt. Roger Burwell, Co-Pilot 2nd Lt. Cecil Quinley

Chapter 21
Luke Army Airfield

February 7, 1943.

Hello again my darling! Here I is again. My only regret for coming here so far is that I'm so far away from you again. I was sure happy that I could see you for those couple of days anyway. I wish that it could have been for a couple of weeks. We had a good ride over on the train. It was a peaceful, quiet ride. We got into Glendale, which is about ten miles from Phoenix, at noon. We had to wait for a couple of hours for the trucks to come in after us. We're about twenty miles from Phoenix out here, not that it makes much difference I guess. They took a couple of pictures of us, one in which I had a sign under me saying 2nd Lt. Cecil W. Quinley! A little premature, but I guess they don't have to throw away very many of them, I hope. They gave us more tests here for Valley Fever. I guess it must be something worse than I thought it was. We get a lecture in a couple of hours from the post commander. I guess that will be our welcoming speech as we haven't had one yet. We haven't had any officers at all tell us anything here yet. The less they have to say, though, the better we'll be.

You should see all the 2nd Lieutenants around this place. They just graduated and not many have left yet. It's pretty easy to tell a new one from one who has been an officer very long though. The new ones give you a big grin when you salute them. The weather here is the same as it was when I was in Tucson. The sun is shining and the dirt is blowing all around. It isn't quite as baron here as it was in Tucson though. They have green fields and trees all around here, which is something, as the trees are orange groves. We're going to get several hours flying time in P-40's while we're here, which is pretty swell. They're fighters and they look pretty swell flying around up in the sky as they go whizzing by. I went up in the AT-6A for a half an hour this afternoon. I rode in the back seat and it was just more or less a ride to look over the country, except that my instructor did a loop. I didn't do a thing except just sit there. I guess the plane won't be too hard to fly. There are a lot more gadgets on it though.

February 11, 1943.

I flew for two hours yesterday afternoon with my instructor. It's quite a bit different than flying a BT. I guess it won't be too difficult though. He told me to do him a loop after we were up just a little while. I tried to do it about like he did and it wasn't too bad. This plane has quite a bit more power. I was supposed to solo today but I made a rather raunchy job of shooting landings so I'll have to make another try at it again tomorrow. I think I can do much better than I did today.

February 13, 1943.

I got to solo one of these AT's today which was very nice. I went over and shot one landing with my instructor, Lieutenant Dean, and then I made two landings solo. We came back to the main field then and I signed out a ship for an hour of solo flying. They sure do fly swell. They don't fly very much faster but they sure do have a lot more power, and it's a lot easier to do things in them. We have to learn gunnery while here in the next three weeks, because then we go to another field for a couple of weeks of practice. They say that the only reason they teach us to fly is so we can handle the plane well enough to shoot at something and hit it. It should be a lot more interesting than just plain flying. We'll have something else to concentrate on also. It's almost time for taps now darling, so I must be going. Good night now my darling. I love you very much and remember that I love you the most, first, and always, and don't ever think any differently, because you're the swellest gal in the world. May God bless you darling. Love and kisses, Cecil.

So much for staying in California for advanced training. Surprise, we were sent back to Arizona. Luke Field was a nice post, but I hated being so far away from Margaret. At least in California she could come see me sometimes. I shouldn't complain, though, many of our guys were a lot farther away from home than I was. They kept us pretty busy at Luke anyway. We had ground school both day and night when we weren't flying. On my flying days sometimes I'd fly for a few hours, go do Link training, then go back to the ship and fly more. There were two theaters on the post, but they both played the same film. We have two chaplains, a Catholic and a Protestant. There was no requirement to attend services, but it was encouraged. Margaret sent me homemade candy and cookies from time to time. My sisters, Milly and Esther, and my mother would also send cookies. It was tough keeping my weight down with all the goodies at my disposal. It was a good thing I was a small guy I guess. Anyway, just to be safe I shared my goodies with my barracks mates and it made me very popular, at least when they noticed that I got a package in the mail. The weather at Luke was interesting. It would get hot in the day and cold at night. I'd go to bed with hardly anything over me, then I'd have to pile as much on me as I could find throughout the night. Except for the temperature swings it was really quite tolerable. I couldn't imagine, though, what it would be like here in the summer.

We'd be learning more formation flying here and how to shoot things with the airplane guns. We'd also be learning more small arms marksmanship with the Thompson machine gun, or "Tommy Gun" like the old gangsters used to call them. We'd be firing shotguns, a Government model .45 pistol, and a .50 caliber machine gun. It was all a lot of fun. One of the more fun things that we got to do at Luke was to chase the instructor. In our second week my instructor began to accomplish two things at once with us while flying. We all had planes, so we could all fly at the same time. My instructor would have one of us flying instruments under the hood and the rest of the guys would have to fly formation on that ship. It really cut down on the training time and the waiting around time. Flying formation in the AT was a lot easier than it was in the BT. During our flights the instructor would do what he called a rat race. He'd get in the lead and then peel off. Each of us would in turn peel off too and try to follow him. It wasn't easy trying to keep up with him. He was a very good pilot. I got real good at the formation flying. My wingtip was almost touching my instructor's wingtip. It was only inches away, and that's the way he wanted it. Of course, that was only for training and control purposes. In combat formation we'd never fly that close. It would make us sitting ducks and too vulnerable to one mistake taking out several ships. Plus, you have no idea where you are when you're flying like that. All your concentration is on the lead ship and he's the only one paying attention to direction, speed, and altitude. But it was swell fun to do out at Luke, because that's what flying is all about. We were finally getting to the fun stuff. In only two weeks I had 18 hours of flight time. That would have taken over a month at Gardner Field. Getting to do high performance flying, formations, and shooting in a powerful plane was a blast. I could hardly wait to get into fighters. On the other side of the post there were some Chinese pilots being trained by American instructors and they were flying P-40 fighters. They were old worn out planes, but they were nice looking, sleek and powerful to us new guys. Every once in a while they'd fly over our side of the post and we'd just look up and stare at them going by. One day a couple of P-38 Lightning twin engine and twin tail boom fighters came flying low over our area and they did a slow roll right over top of us. Right then and there I knew that it was one of those that I wanted to fly when I graduated. Oh man was that a beautiful ship in the air. It looked kind of awkward on the ground, but sleek and fast in the air, and it seemed to glide by without effort as it rolled. That's what I wanted.

Getting into our third week of training we began cross country flights again. I had to plot the first one for our group. We went from Luke Field to Roosevelt Dam, to Wickenburg, to Salome, to Gila Bend, to Hester, and back to Luke. It was about 365 miles and took about two and a half hours. I'd just passed my navigation course test and it was pretty easy, so it wasn't too hard plotting the course we took. Of course (our) navigation school isn't as tough as a navigator's class, but it was enough for us. The country we flew over was pretty rugged, especially out around Roosevelt Dam. Following our course proved more difficult than I'd anticipated, because many of the towns that were listed on the map just weren't there anymore. I guess they blew away in a dust storm or something. Over the course of the next week we did two more trips. We all flew the same route, but solo. One of the trips was about 500 miles long and one of our guys got lost, being about 70 miles north of his planned route. He had to land in Prescott and refuel before coming back to Luke. In about three weeks we'd be heading out to Gila Bend for gunnery practice. It's forty miles west of Luke Field. In the mean time we did more cross country navigation and some high altitude flights on oxygen. We put on our oxygen as we climbed through 15,000 feet, then, weaving our way through the clouds we climbed to over 20,000 feet. Oh how beautiful it is to fly among the clouds. Even though the AT-6A was the most powerful plane we'd flown so far, it still took over an hour to weave our way over 20,000 feet and back down again. Our shotgun training consisted of shooting skeet with a 12 gauge. I'd shot one before, but it'd been a long time, and I'd never shot skeet. It was fun to give it a try. I wouldn't win any competitions, but my score was about average compared to everyone else. Boy was my arm and shoulder ever sore after going through fifty shells. Some of the guys looked like someone had taken a meat cleaver to their arms.

They sure kept us busy at Luke. Margaret was keeping busy back home too, but I could hear the loneliness in her voice when we were able to connect on the telephone, and I could see it in her letters too. It was difficult keeping up with some of the paperwork we were required to do, since they didn't really give us much time to accomplish it. It sometimes took a long time for things to be approved. I guess because of the sheer numbers of guys who'd gone into the service in a short amount of time. My pay allotment to Margaret took a long time to get started for some reason. That made it difficult for her to manage our finances and pay our taxes. Then, I had to get my life insurance policy set up properly because after graduation we had to start paying for it ourselves. It came out to about six dollars a month. It was frustrating at times, and we felt like no matter how hard we tried, we were beating our heads against a wall. But we eventually got it all squared away. Compounding our stress was the fact that they started rationing canned goods back home, among other things. I felt like I should be there to take care of her, especially when she was having trouble with the landlord over the leaky roof and the guy who bought our car not making his payments. Luckily, my old boss took care of that one for us. Her newsletter was a smash hit in Sacramento and she sent me news clippings with her picture in articles talking about her Red Cross job, the newsletter, and her getting her nurse's aide pin. I was very proud of my wife for her contributions and loved reading about it. She was planning an extended leave of absence to come to my graduation and travel to my next assignment with me. We'd have six days to get there, no matter where it was, so we were hoping it wouldn't be too far. That way we could have some fun instead of just rushing. In the meantime, I had plenty to keep me busy at Luke. The training was intensive, and we got a lot of information thrown at us in a short amount of time. We began to wonder why we were being rushed so much. We were too busy to get news, so we didn't really know what was going on in the war to that point. We began to wonder if they were rushing us because we were needed overseas. At any rate, in about three weeks they were going to take about half of us and put us through some twin engine training. They wouldn't say what they meant by that, but we all hoped it meant P-38's. I couldn't wait and I volunteered quite overtly every chance I got. Being a Lightning driver was all I could think about when I was flying.

Chapter 22
Sacramento

How's my sweetheart tonight? Fine, I hope, 'cause I sure am. Guess why? I received a swell letter from my darling tonight in which he told me he thinks he might be assigned to an instructor's school. That makes me very, very happy, dearest, and I know you're doing it just especially for me. That's swell, and sweet of you, and I love you so very much. Thanks, sweetheart, for always thinking of me. I hope that you will like being an instructor if they put you in that class.

Gee you're cute! I have your picture right in front of me, in that little frame in my writing folder. It's the picture of you in front of the house, taken while you were home the last time, and only time of course, since August 3rd, 1942! You sure look swell! Oh me, oh my! I'm so excited about your swell letter that I am neglecting to tell you all about my experience at Sutter Maternity tonight. It was a lot of fun and I loved every bit of it. I had a mask to wear and everything. I worked in the nursery and helped take care of the mothers. I showed a brand new baby to its father. I took several around for their feedings. I fed a few their bottles, changed and cleaned them, and did just all kinds of things. It was certainly swell, and the nurses were so helpful. They surely appreciated me too, they said. I sort of hope that they will let me put in all of my time out there now. It will certainly be swell to have had all of this training when we start raising our family, won't it dear? Gee, that will be fun!

We are having a swell Red Cross meeting on Monday night. Mrs. J.H. Polkinhorn, a laboratory technician, who works now at Afleck's Pharmacy, is going to talk about blood plasma, how it was prepared during the Pearl Harbor emergency (she has just returned from Honolulu, after having been there for 2 ½ years) and the important part played by civilian volunteer workers in time of disaster. She is a swell person and I know she will have lots of interesting things to tell us. The Lucky Strike Hit Parade is on the radio now, maybe you're listening to it now too. Do you like 'I've heard that song before?' It's a pretty song, I like it. There are a lot of good ones out now, or maybe I've been listening more lately.

Gee whiz! You're doing 'Rat Races' already! I can't believe it! I suppose the next phase I hear of will be 'Dog Fights!' Oh my, take it easy darling is all I can say. I'll try not to worry about you too much. I bet its lots of fun, huh? The planes from Mather fly over the house all the time and it sounds like they are doing 'Rat Races' too.

I love you darling, with all my heart! I was so lonesome for you over the weekend that I could hardly stand it. No fooling, I felt like going out and shooting Hitler and all of the rest of his gang just so that you could come home and be with me again! Of course I guess we've got to kill off a few others besides that bunch of scalawags before we can have peace again, but we'll do it, and soon!

Gee honey, I'm so excited tonight, as usual, over plans for our visit! I hope it is a permanent one! I made my reservations on the Santa Fe – one way trip ticket (do you mind?) to Phoenix, Arizona. I leave here on Friday, April 2, 1943, and arrive in Phoenix at about 11:30 A.M. I still love you with all my heart and always will. I think you're the swellest guy in the world too, no fooling, and I can't get to Phoenix fast enough! Good night for this time, honey, and God bless you always! Love and kisses-from your Mrs. Margaret.

Cecil was going to be graduating the first week of April, so I was beginning to get very anxious about the whole thing. I wanted so badly to be able to see him. He had mentioned that he may be a candidate for instructor pilot school, which meant he would be able to stay stateside and we could be a normal family again. You never knew what would happen because of this war, though, so I was planning on taking a leave of absence from my job so I could spend some time with him after graduation. Regardless of where he was assigned there would be yet another school somewhere, so I wanted to be together before he had to report there, and with any luck I'd be able to go live there too since he would have received his commission. Even if he had to stay on post I could get a place in town and we could do things in his off duty time and on his days off. My temporary paid position at the Red Cross had ended and I found myself back in my old position in the engineering section in the War Department. Getting the leave of absence wasn't as easy as I thought it would be, however, because my boss, grumpy britches Bob, just had this thing about him that made him want to be as ornery as he could for some reason. It just seemed like he didn't much like me, or any of the girls for that matter. I think his boozing and jealousy of the boys in the service made him a bitter man. One of my friends was able to take a leave for the same reason about a month ago, but now Bob wouldn't allow it. I did some research and found out that since I was in a government position within the War Department that I could resign without prejudice and maintain my good standing, meaning I could find another position within the government somewhere else and maintain my time and salary that I had achieved in Sacramento. Bob was not happy when I turned in my resignation on March 12th, effective April 1st (at the conclusion of accrued annual leave), but at that point he had no options. He should have given me what I wanted in the first place. When I handed it to him the other girls stood up and clapped they were so happy for me and that was such a thrill! Bob asked me to come into the addressograph room for a conference. When I got in there he told me he wanted to know my real reason for resigning (my official letter stated only that I was going to travel to be with my husband in the service in Phoenix). I guess he had a guilty conscience. I stuck to my guns and told him that this was my only reason and things were just now working out so that I could be with Cecil. He rattled on and on how good my work was and blah, blah, blah. About how much more he thought I could get done. I thought to myself, what am I, a machine? I gave him a good argument and in the end he was convinced that he doesn't realize how much detail there is to my job. That's what happens when someone is in charge of people doing things that the boss doesn't completely understand, doesn't know how to do, and was never qualified to do.

If I was moving to Arizona, I would have to find something to do with our stuff and our house. We had a nice two bedroom house with a basement, a nice yard, and a garden that I just put in after having an area plowed under. My friend Betty was living in the second bedroom and kept me company as much as possible. After a while, though, Betty began going out more and more and was hardly ever there on weekends. I was frustrated, but at the same time I understood. Betty was single and a little bit of a wild thing and she didn't want to just sit around with a fuddy-duddy married woman who was faithful to her husband. She loved me, but she had to get out and be happy too. That's one of the reasons, also, that I joined the Red Cross and went to nurse's aide school. It gave me something to do to keep me busy. Sometimes, even if I wasn't scheduled, my loneliness would begin to get the better of me so I would go down to Mercy or Sutter hospital and just show up and they would put me to work. We decided to sublet our home and all its furnishings, but Betty would never be able to afford it. Plus, even though I loved her dearly, I didn't think she would take very good care of my furniture. I found a nice couple named Ken and Kay Dunn. They had been married about the same amount of time as Cecil and I and they seemed like a very nice responsible couple. They came over and looked at the house and fell in love with it. We came to an agreement on rent and they also agreed that if Cecil gets stationed anywhere near Sacramento that we would, of course, be moving back into the house. They agreed to take very good care of my furniture as well. I would be storing everything that I didn't take with me in the basement. I cleared everything with the landlord and as a final precaution I took out an insurance policy for fire on the furniture. Betty wanted me to ask the Dunn's if she could stay with them, but I didn't go for that so she agreed to move in with another friend.

Everything was set for my visit to Phoenix that I was hoping would turn into a permanent move. I knew the location would never be permanent as long as Cecil was in the Air Corps, but I was hoping that the permanence would be with him with no more separation. I got real nervous when Betty went out on a date with some boys who were graduating from Mather Field. They were supposed to go to a show but then they got sent out immediately to other assignments. It made me wonder what was in store for Cecil after his graduation. I was hoping at that point that he would at least get a few days off before having to report to his new assignment. If that happened, I hoped that I could at least ride on the train with him to his new post. Perhaps it was premature and naïve of me to have made so many plans. This old war certainly held a lot of surprises and we never knew what was going to happen. The only way to be halfway normal, though, was to make the plans and then just accept what comes, otherwise you just lose faith. I would continue on with my plan to travel to Phoenix and accept whatever happens when he graduates. My mother was living in Long Beach, so if I had to I could travel over there and stay with her until something works out.

My brother Ray decided to go in the service. He wanted to join the Navy, but when he went to San Francisco he was a day too late. They had already met their quota of men for that time. He was awaiting induction into the Army and would be going into the signal Corps. Ken was already in the Army, so here it was 1943 and all the men in my life were off serving our country in some capacity or another. Yes, I would keep my plan of traveling to Phoenix. Film was getting hard to find but I had been stocking up on it so I could take some pictures of Cecil in his officer's uniform and I even managed to get ahold of some color film to take with me. Cecil hadn't been able to get any pictures at Luke Field as they had confiscated everyone's cameras when they arrived on post. I guess they were worried about security and such. I thought it was a little overboard since it was just a training base, but I guess the Army has its reasons for doing things. Cecil was a bit concerned that I was getting there a day before his planned day off but he got me a room at a hotel and we would find other arrangements after that. He was supposed to get off Sunday afternoon, the day after my arrival, but you never know what may transpire. I had money with me and was able to take care of myself but that didn't stop him from worrying about me. I tried to tell him to keep his mind on what he was doing because I was afraid I would be a distraction and I surely didn't want him to get hurt, or worse, because he was thinking about me instead of what he was supposed to be concentrating on. I didn't have as much money as I should have because Bob arranged for my last check to be delayed until after my departure, even though I had asked him if I could have it early and he had agreed to do so. What an ass!

Chapter 23
Commission

Hello, again, darling! It is a very lovely Sunday today. I got it off to a good start with a nice talk with my honey. I'm sorry to get you up so early in the morning, but it just seems like that is about the only time that I can get ahold of you. Besides, I like to talk to you early in the morning. It always seems more cheerful and I can always seem to hear you better. I guess 'cause there aren't so many people on the wires. I had one hour of flying again today with my instructor. I was scheduled to have an hour of combat also, but I didn't get out there early enough because I had to go back to the infirmary for my ear. Gosh honey, the time is growing short now until you will be here and in my arms. I can hardly wait. Maybe that's the reason that you sounded closer this morning, 'cause it won't be very long until you're right here. Then, I will really be able to feel those kisses that you were giving me over the telephone. They sure sounded real and made me all atwitter for you. I haven't been to a show for a while, so I guess I will go to one tonight. 'Hello Frisco Hello' is on tonight staring Alice Faye and John Payne. There was a good one on last night that I wanted to see, it was 'The Keeper of the Flame' staring Katharine Hepburn and Spencer Tracy. We were kinda late though, and it was crowded, so I didn't try to go.

I'm glad that the Dunn's will be renting our place. It will be nice to have someone there who we won't have to worry about, and as long as you know them it will be better. I guess everything will all workout for the best, as it always does. Anyway, it will be good to have a place to leave all our stuff. I'm glad to hear that Bill got himself a furlough so he can go home to see his new son. Some of the fellows here in the cadets have had kids for about a year now without ever getting to see them. They don't believe in giving time off for such things when there is a war on. It sounds as though you are really going to town with all your hospital work these days. I imagine that it was quite an experience to work out at the Sutter Maternity and help take care of all those newborn youngsters. I am not worried about you quitting your regular job. We will get along alright once I get my lieutenant's pay. I didn't like you working for that grumpy old Bob anyway.

We showed up on the flight line prepared for a cross country trip the other day and they had a surprise for us. They changed the trip and only gave us ten minutes with our maps to figure out the course. That made it more interesting alright. We went to Blythe, then to Wickenburg, and back to Luke. I got to California for a minute at least, about ten miles across the border. Boy, you should have seen the B-17 bomber that was buzzing Luke Field yesterday! I was just starting up an AT-6 and getting ready to taxi it out to take off when he came zooming over at about ten feet above my head! He came over a couple of times and then went on. They couldn't get his number, or I would feel sorry for him if they did. Those things sure look big so close by. I would like to fly one sometime. It probably had some former Luke Field graduate in it.

Red Skelton was here today so I went down to the hangar to see him, he was pretty good. He was there with just his wife. He put on about an hour show though. Just crazy stuff like he usually does. Showing how different people would do different things. We received all our officers flying equipment. We sure do get a lot of it. Boy, those winter flying suits are sure swell. Real heavy sheep lined coat and pants and boots. I don't see how anyone could ever get cold in them. Then we get a regular flying suit, dark glasses, combat goggles, a heavy sheepskin lined helmet, and a light one; an oxygen mask, a life preserver vest, gloves, a traveling bag, our own private parachute and a bag to keep it all in. I also got my regular leather flying jacket and my officer's hat with the big gold eagle on it. We are supposed to take the flexible band out of it so head phones will fit over it. You can always tell the experienced

pilots by how much their hats sag on the sides. It's the sign
of a real veteran flyer!

I sure hope that we don't fly next Sunday afternoon so
that I can get an early start from here to get into town and
give you a big squeeze and a big kiss, maybe even a couple
or so if you will permit me to take the liberty. I'd better say
so-long now darling, until tomorrow. I love you an awful
lot. May God bless you and bring you safely to me. Love
and kisses-for my Mrs. Cecil.

Well, I finally was seeing the end of the tunnel. I was getting closer and
closer to graduation and getting my commission. Margaret's loneliness
seemed to be getting worse and I was beginning to worry more about her.
Her roommate was taking off constantly to go to the cadets club at Mather
and her boss was being a big blow hard at her office. I was glad that she quit
that job. Of course, it was a gamble having her in Phoenix because I never
knew from day to day what I was going to be doing and where I was going
to be doing it from. But I was pretty confident that we would have some
time together as we had been planning. Graduation was getting closer and I
was all caught up on everything. Even if they whisked me away after
graduation she could visit her mother in Long Beach. At the very least we
would have a couple weeks together, and maybe longer if it all worked out
well. We finally had our gunnery training and boy was it fun. We all piled
into Army trucks and they convoyed us out to Gila Bend. We left Luke a
little after 1930 hours and had a nice hard sitting trip in the trucks for about
four hours. We stopped after about an hour and had soft drinks and stuff.
One of the trucks hit a cow right after we started. It didn't hurt anything
except to kill the cow. We got into Gila Bend at about 2345. We hit the sack
at 0100 and they got us up at 0630. Needless to say we were all a bit tired
our first day out there. I finally figured out why we were shooting skeet with
the shotgun. It was to teach us to lead the target. It was at Gila Bend that that
training became valuable. The gunnery training was sure fun. We had
ground gunnery and aerial gunnery. In the air we used camera guns at first
until we got the hang of it. I guess they wanted to make sure that we were
skilled enough not to shoot down the plane that was towing the target. My
regular instructor didn't go out to Gila Bend with us; he was flying P-40's. I
had a new instructor out there and he was plenty fun. After practice one day
we played follow the leader in the planes. We flew down low over one of
the gunnery ranges at about ten feet off the ground and at 225 miles per

hour! Finally they let us use real ammunition in the airplane guns. It was a thrilling sight watching the tracer rounds glowing as they flew toward the target. We had 100 round belts and I got 22 hits on my very first aerial try. It didn't sound good to me, but my instructor said it was pretty good, especially for a first try. I figured ground gunnery would be a lot easier because you could see where the rounds were hitting, and I was right, but just barely. I was hoping to get a good score so I could get an expert rating. When we did our runs for the record we had 200 round belts for the ground targets and 400 rounds for the aerial targets. We had to get 15 percent to qualify as marksman, 23 percent as sharpshooter, and 30 percent as expert. We flew for four hours when we qualified on multiple runs. Landing, rearming, taking off again, tight turning to get on target and firing. It was all very tiring. To make it even worse the wind was blowing extremely hard that day, which made it very difficult to line up on target. With every gust of wind the rounds would fly off target. I was exhausted by the end of that day but I managed to put up a marksman score and got a badge to wear on my uniform. One of the fellows in the squadron brought his clarinet with him and he played it in the barracks at night. He was real good with it and knew all the popular numbers. It helped pass the time at night and really relaxed us, taking the edge off after our stressful day. I wished he was in my barracks back at Luke. He was real-real good with his clarinet.

When I got back to Luke I found out that I almost lost another instructor. He was doing some training in P-40's while we were out at Gila Bend. When he came in for a landing one day he found his brakes locked up right from the get go. One of the landing gear collapsed and he skidded to a stop on one wing, barely managing to keep the plane upright. It was a very close call. He had to go before a board but they found the accident to be mechanical failure and cleared him of any errors on his part. I guess that flying is more dangerous than I thought it was, at least in high performance airplanes anyway. One day we had a demonstration by a famous flyer. His name was Al Williams. He was a famous pilot that helped pioneer military aviation with Billy Mitchel. He gave us a nice long talk on flying and furthering military aviation and how it can win the war. Then he gave us a flight demonstration in his Grumman Gulfhawk. He flew inverted at maximum speed just a few feet off the ground and picked up a handkerchief when he went by. It was an amazing exhibition that showed us just how little we knew and how far we had to go, but very interesting just the same. He flew better upside down than I did right side up!

After gunnery qualifications the rest of my time at Luke was spent doing cross country flights and night flying, as well as, of course, the Link trainer. We affectionately called it the "Blue Box" because that's what color it was painted. I wasn't sure by this time what I wanted to do after advanced training, other than to keep flying of course. I wanted to be an instructor so I could settle down and be with Margaret, but I also wanted to contribute to the war effort too. I was beginning to hear that I was too old already to be accepted into fighter school. I talked to my instructor about it and he said that that was a possibility. I was already 26 years old and would just get in under the maximum age if they accepted me. This was all very disconcerting for me to hear at this point. I really wanted fighters, especially the P-38 that I had seen, but now I may have to come up with an alternate plan for the future. I took some time to think about it and when the time came for me to tell my instructor I had my answer. We all got interviewed by our instructors and we had to give him a wish list for what we had hoped would be our next assignment in aviation. My thoughts kept going back to that B-17 bomber that did the low fly-by. It was such an awesome display of power and a beautiful four engine plane to boot, with guns sticking out of every window. So that's what I picked, the Boeing B-17. But I also told him that I would also prefer to be an instructor if they would allow it. He said he would pass it on in my file. Margaret came down as planned and she was sure a sight for sore eyes. She got a room at the hotel for the Saturday that she arrived and I met her there after flying on Sunday and we spent as much time together as we could up until graduation. She was stunning in her peach colored gown at our graduation ceremony and she was grinning from ear to ear, as was I, as the silver wings of an Air Corps pilot were pinned to my chest and the gold bars of a 2nd lieutenant were pinned to my shoulders. I made it dad, was the thought that went through my mind. We danced every dance together. It was a grand time and it was sorely needed by both of us. I got the news just before graduation that I wouldn't be going to instructor school. I would be in B-17's after all, kind of. Things were heating up in Europe and there was an emergency need for co-pilots to fill spots so we could get more bombers in the fight. They took almost our whole class and told us we were off to fill co-pilot spots in the B-17's. I would be going to Walla Walla, Washington, for assignment to a bomber crew.

Chapter 24
The Crew

My leave vanished as if it was never there, and I guess it never really was. I was hoping that I would get some time after graduation before going on to my next post. Some fellows did, and some fellows didn't. I did have a few days to get there but traveling by train would take up all of those few days and I was supposed to leave the very next day after graduation. The good news was that Margaret could travel with me. We secured a sleeper room on a civilian Santa Fe train heading north out of Phoenix to Seattle. The very nice accommodations of the Santa Fe were just as good as a vacation. We had nothing but time to spend together, and that's really all we ever wanted. We spent the days talking and playing cards, looking out the window at the scenery, and in general I spent a lot of time just staring at her and memorizing her smile all over again. That fellow that had the clarinet out at Gila Bend was on the train and he played it for everyone. There was another fellow there who had his trumpet with him and I guess he used to belong to a professional band too. They played together as we transited our way north. It was a magical ride along the rails. My next post was to be some 170 miles east of Seattle at an airfield called Ephrata. It was at a town of the same name with a population of about 1000 people. It took us three days and three nights on the Santa Fe to get to Seattle. We had to pull onto side tracks all the time and let other trains pass. Once we finally reached Seattle we had a four hour layover, so some friends of ours that met us at the train station took us out for a nice steak dinner. When we got back to the station we were surprised to find that our new ride would be a passenger car attached to a milk train. It was only 170 miles so I figured, how bad could it be? Well, that last 170 miles took all day because we had to stop at every farm along the way and fill a tanker car with milk. Fine way to run an army I thought. Oh well, it would make for a humorous story someday.

Once we finally rolled into Ephrata I got a ride on an army truck out to the airfield with several other fellows. Margaret went around town with three other wives to find lodging. At this point in our training our wives could billet off post and we could go into town whenever we weren't assigned duties. Margaret soon found that Ephrata was a very small town and there wasn't anywhere to stay. The girls walked from one end of town to the other but couldn't find anything. Finally, someone suggested they try a two story house down at the edge of town. They thought the woman who lived there was considering renting a couple of rooms. When they arrived at the house they talked with the lady who lived there and she confirmed that she had been considering it but had not done so yet. When she discovered that the girls were all Army wives and their husbands were out at the airfield flying she let them have the rooms. It was a huge relief for Margaret. She had waited patiently for all these months to spend time with me, and I felt the same way when I found out how close we were to not being able to be together again. Of course, we knew that we would be separated again because of the war, but we wanted to have as much time as we could while we could. Once settled into a room at the airfield I sacked out for the night to get some rest. Bright and early I went to the commander's office and checked in. On my way I could see B-17's parked all over the place but I didn't see much activity. The biggest surprise came when I reported for duty. I discovered that I was to be assigned to a crew right away and I would be traveling on to Walla Walla, about 140 miles south east. I wasn't the only fellow in that boat. Most of us new arrivals got the same news. Up to that point I had still been holding out hope that I would be assigned to P-38 training. I had heard that there was a field up here somewhere where they were stationed, but to no avail, B-17's was all I could see from one end of the field to the other. It wouldn't be bad, I tried to convince myself, they're big airplanes and very fast and powerful for their size. Plus, they had machine guns sticking out all over them. That night I went into town and told Margaret what was going on. She talked to the lady that rented her the room and she was very understanding about the whole situation. We would be in Ephrata for a week, so Margaret would stay there as planned and then she would hop another train to Walla Walla while I flew down there with my new crew.

In the morning I reported for duty again and was introduced to a fellow named Flight Officer Jack Pry. He was the pilot in charge of the B-17 that I was assigned to. I thought it was a bit odd that I outranked the fellow who would be my boss but I didn't mind at all since I had no time and no training in B-17's. I just thought, shouldn't the pilot outrank everyone else on the plane? I guess I had some things to get used to. What I learned about Jack was that he began his career as an enlisted man in maintenance and worked his way up to a flying sergeant, then received his warrant as a flight officer. Jack knew B-17's inside and out, from top to bottom. He also had a reputation as one of the best pilots around who figured he needed to constantly prove how good he and his crew were to the other higher ranking pilots. Jack was not at all happy that I was assigned to him and he made that loud and clear. He didn't like that he was getting a brand new wet behind the ears 2nd lieutenant that only had single engine training. He told me to just sit there and do what he told me and I figured that was probably good advice, especially after I saw the B-17 cockpit for the first time with what I thought was a mass of intimidating gauges and switches compared to what I was used to. Unfortunately, we never got any orders to fly anywhere so I could train. We just sat around for a week until they told us to load up our aircraft and head down to Walla Walla. In the meantime we went to town every night and Margaret and I got to know Jack and his wife Polly. By day we just sat around on the flight line waiting for something to happen, but it never did. I got to know the rest of the crew while we waited. Ted Snyder was our bombardier and was a real Hollywood type. He was authentic Hollywood though. His father was a composer for the movies and wrote "The Sheik of Araby" and "Who's Sorry Now," and he owned a night club in Hollywood. Art Wilson was our navigator, but he pretty much kept to himself. Jack Pry was from Houston, Texas, and seemed like he was a full foot taller than me. The enlisted guys kept to themselves at first, maybe they thought I would bring them bad luck or something. Eddie LaPointe was our flight engineer and top turret gunner, Russell Frautschi was our radio man, Al Johnson and Carl Baird were our waist gunners, Irving "Smitty" Smith the ball turret gunner, and Martin "Tex" Brandt our tail gunner. The Army was darn sure going to make sure that we were properly trained in the concept of hurry up and wait. In my down time I read some letters that came from my family in Modesto, California. Most of the family had gathered there at my sister Esther's home for a celebration. They took advantage of the gathering to pass around pencil and paper.

> We're sure missing you today. Hail! Hail! The gangs all here (but you and Lester, Min & family, & John & Thelma). It is a beautiful day. You're nephew celebrated his 16th birthday yesterday and he also received his Eagle Scout Badge in a Court of Honor. Mother Quinley came home with us and was quite thrilled to see this honor bestowed on Winson. He has worked hard for this occasion. Now he can be on the council at Scout Camp. I'm so glad you can be with Cecil, Margaret. You can have your second honeymoon, huh? We are all sitting around visiting on the screen porch, there is a nice cool breeze blowing across the river. Everyone has been riding in the boats. Whoops!

Corabelle was feeding Tommy and dropped a glass and broke it. We all laughed because all she said was 'oh, God bless it!' Milly, Jimmy, and Robby are here too. Well, Esther says to pass the paper on and let someone else write. Here's thinking of you and God bless you Cecil. Helen.

How's everything? How do you like Army life Margaret? Cecil, I want to congratulate you on getting your wings and commission. Best of luck to you and hope to see you safe and well some of these fine days when your job is done. We are all gathered here on Esther's porch about to have some pot luck supper. Wish you folks were here to help eat it up. This end of the family is all fine and dandy. Bye-Bye. Love, Lulu & Girls.

Here we are on the big screen porch at Esther and Earle's, wishing you could be with us, and hoping you are having a good time. I went to Clarence's last night to celebrate Winson's 16th birthday and attend Scout Court of Honor, at which he received his Eagle Scout Badge. Lester and Johnny didn't get down today but they sent something special delivery for Winson. Esther took us out to the cemetery and we put flowers on Daddy's grave. Well, I will write more soon, so I will say bye-bye for this time. Mother is thinking of you always. Love you both, Mother.

Greetings and so forth. How's Washington? We're having fun out here at Esther and Earle's. The water is fine! Orma.

Just a line or two to stick my two cents worth in with everyone else. How's everything in Washington? Gee, I bet you're enjoying being together. Charles was just home from Florida on a 15 day furlough. We certainly enjoyed the short visit, it took him 4 days coming, and 4 days going back. We spent 2 day in the hills together and stayed at the same place we spent our wedding night. I rode as far as Los Angeles with him on his return trip and saw him off at the train station and then came home. We're all proud of what our 'Uncle Cecil' has accomplished so far! Congratulations! We're behind you all the way!!! We hope to see you real soon. God be with you both, till we all meet soon again, Barbara.

Sure wish you could be with us today. Most of the family is here at Earle's. I received my Eagle Badge last night at a Court of Honor. Congratulations for getting your silver wings. Good luck, Winson.

Here we are again; sure do wish you were here with us. Our thoughts are with you. We arrived here rather late. All have enjoyed boat riding. The kids are having a swell time. I was surprised to know you're being moved again so soon. I'm so sorry you can't be living in an apartment together, but when this is all over you'll have years and years to enjoy everything. Take care of yourself, both of you, Viola.

Just a line to let you know that we are having a nice time. I brought my swimming suit to go surf board riding but the boat hit a submerged log in the river and it damaged something on the front, so it could no longer go fast enough to pull the surf board. Thanks so much for the pair of wings you sent me. I wear them everywhere. Take care of yourselves, both of you. Love, Carolyn.

Everybody is gone, dishes done, and it's bed time. I'm sitting here barefoot resting my tired feet. I have read all the other letters, so I won't repeat. If I could only write every time I think about doing so you would be showered with letters. But I write in my mind while my hands are busy and never seem to get a second to really put it to paper. It's terrible to be so busy and rushed all the time. Mother told you we took flowers to dad. It was such a quiet peaceful evening out there. Earle hit a submerged log the last thing yesterday afternoon, so it sort of put a crimp on the boat riding. Took a few slow trips, but no surf board riding. Earle says to tell Cec he will give him a surf board ride next time he comes here. I haven't tried it yet! Earle says come to bed, so good night. Love you both, Esther.

Chapter 25
Walla Walla

Hello again darling. I would have liked to have called you up today, but we have no telephones as yet. But I believe we will have one tomorrow, so I will call you as soon as possible. I still don't know anything about what day we are leaving here or anything. I imagine it will be about the middle of next week. As far as I know we are still going to Grand Island, but I can't guarantee it. I will let you know as soon as possible. We had a kind of a tough time today. We had to be down at the flight line at 11:30 P.M. last night. We didn't get off the ground until 3:00 A.M. this morning, that's 0300 hours Army time. We were gone for almost eight hours out over Seattle and out over the ocean a ways and back again. We couldn't see Seattle or anything because it was overcast. We could see the ocean a little after we got out a ways. We got back in a little before 11:00 A.M. Then, we had to go back and fly again at 4:30 P.M. and fly until 9:00 P.M. I think I could use a good night sleep tonight! I'm already in bed, so I won't have much further to go.

I didn't get my stuff sent for home from Walla Walla 'cause I couldn't get into town to send it, so I will have to send it whenever I get a chance to do so. I guess they will give us a chance to do such things in Nebraska. Gosh sakes honey, I sure do miss you down here in this desolate place! Of course, I would miss you anyplace if you weren't there. I guess that I will be seeing you soon though, and I hope it will be for at least several days or weeks, but I wouldn't know about that. I understand that we won't be in Nebraska very long, but maybe so, we never do what is planned ahead of time anyway. I think I had better be saying good night for now 'cause my eyes are getting heavy. I'll be a writing some more and also calling you some in one manner or another. In the meantime, be good, and I'll be thinking of you and praying for us to be together soon. Bye now

darling. May God bless you. Love and kisses for my Mrs.
Cecil.

Finally the time had come for us to head down to Walla Walla.
Margaret and Polly came out to the airfield to see us off. After that, they
would make their way down there as well. We were now in the 88th
Bombardment Group, 317th Bomb Squadron. The flight was uneventful. All
Jack let me do was raise and lower the landing gear. It wasn't anything we
could talk about on the intercom while we were flying. We had already
discussed it a little during our sitting around time back at Ephrata. Jack was
already having some problems with Art, our navigator, before I joined the
crew. He wanted to take care of that before he put too much effort into me. I
guess, according to Jack, Art wasn't very good at figuring out where we
were flying and that's not a very good quality in a navigator. Fortunately,
though, Jack was extremely good at pilot navigation and he never got lost.
There would be times, however, that he (we) would be using all our
concentration on flying and would need to be able to rely on our navigator
to get us where we needed to be, or get us out of trouble faster than we got
into it. Jack said that we would be doing a lot of flying while in Walla Walla
and he would sort out our little problem there. He was all business alright, I
could see that this ship was going to be run in a no nonsense manner.

We landed at Walla Walla Army Airfield, taxied to our assigned
parking area and completed a post flight check of the aircraft. After that we
checked in with the squadron commander and then received our billeting
information. Jack and I received a briefing on what we would be doing here,
which consisted of training flights, some formation training, aerial gunnery,
and some specific B-17 maintenance training. At the end of the day we
checked into our quarters and waited for the girls to arrive. After they got to
Walla Walla we went into town to meet them and have dinner. We found a
nice cafe and the four of us had a nice relaxing evening together. Margaret
and Polly got a room at a hotel for the night and the following day they
located a nice boarding house that had a couple rooms to let. There were
already a couple pilot wives staying there, so they would have some good
company while we were out flying. We trained pretty heavily while we were
there. Jack was determined to have the best crew in the outfit. We flew
almost every day for nearly two months. The gunners got a lot of practice on
air to air firing and some air to ground firing as well, just to keep the feel for
the gun when we weren't doing air to air practice. We flew out into the
desert to a gunnery range at some little mountain with targets all around it.

Jack and I took turns flying around a low altitude orbit of the mountain and range while everyone took turns shooting at the targets. Even I got trained on all the different guns and their positions while we flew in orbit. I trained the most on the tail gun and the top turret because in some formations, depending on our ships location, an officer has to man one of those two guns to help keep track of the trailing formation. When Jack's turn came to fire all the guns I got to fly that big ole ship in circles. It was quite a thrill for me and I felt good that Jack trusted me enough to leave me to do it.

With all the training we were doing at Walla Walla, we never really had enough time, or long enough flights to be able to evaluate the navigator very well. It was obvious that he was pretty unsure of himself, but we needed more information and a better evaluation if we were going to take it to the commander. In the meantime, we flew our training missions and got into town as much as we could. Ted was working the dance hall and hooking up with the girls there. Art pretty much kept to himself. Jack and I would either hang out with the girls together, or sometimes we would just get some much needed alone time with our wives. One night while we were having dinner together in late May we heard over the radio that an 8th Air Force crew had completed their 25th mission and were coming home for a tour. They said the name of their ship was the "Memphis Belle." Jack said that he was going to name our ship after his wife. Polly was a bit embarrassed and giggled some with her hand over her mouth. Margaret said that his gesture was very cute. He said he was going to name our ship the "Polly Jo." Jack said that I would be getting my own ship someday and suggested I name her the "Maggie Marie" or "Maggie's Irish Rose" or some such name. Now he had Margaret blushing and giggling too. I figured I'd have to think about that one. I have to admit, up until that point I hadn't given much thought to having my own crew and ship. On Sundays I would attend mass with Margaret. She continued to try and convert me, and she especially wanted it done before I deployed somewhere. I figured that the day would come, but not right now. My belief in God was in my heart already, so I concentrated all my time and energy on my flying.

Around the first of June we got orders to fly down to an airfield at Redmond, Oregon, for a couple weeks. They didn't tell us much about what we would be doing, but we didn't have much time to take care of business. Margaret took the train back to Sacramento and stayed with the Dunn's at our house, waiting to hear from me. We loaded up our crew and flew on down to Redmond, about a 250 mile flight to the mid-state area. After arriving Jack and I reported to the commander there and he advised us that we would be flying anti-submarine patrols twice daily. He said to take advantage of the flight time and get used to flying out over the water, that it would be good practice for us before heading overseas. It was a grueling two weeks, as our flight times were sometimes back to back with not much rest in between. I guess that was good preparation too. We would fly north to Seattle and then head west until we got out over the ocean by a couple miles, or at least clear the fog if there was any. We would head south from there until we reached California, then we would reverse our course and come home. Our flights were usually about 2000 feet AGL (above ground level) altitude, sometimes lower depending on weather. We could see right down into the water but we never did see any submarines. What this mission did do for us was give Jack a real good chance to evaluate Art. Jack would ask him from time to time where we were and he always had trouble figuring it out. Once, Jack flew off course on purpose and asked Art where we were and how to get back to the post. I piped up that even I knew where we were and all we had to do was follow that river down there. Jack told me to pipe down, that we needed to see if he could do it; he couldn't. When we got back Jack had all the ammunition he needed and he went to see the squadron commander to talk about the problem. He recommended that Art be retrained into another position or return to navigation school for some remedial training. In any event, Jack flat out refused to allow him to navigate for our crew, fearing that he would get us all killed. It certainly wasn't an issue with his personality or attitude, he was a swell guy. This was a dangerous business, though, and a navigator can get every one of us killed if we try to let down through a cloud layer right into a mountain. The next day we were introduced to our new navigator, Lieutenant Roger Burwell. He was a big guy, as big as Jack, but a little more solid. Jack had already interviewed him before we were introduced and he questioned him quite extensively. During the introductions to Ted and me we were told that Roger had been on another crew at Walla Walla, but the pilot had encountered some sort of medical issue before they were able to deploy, so the crew had been split up. Roger had graduated in the top of his navigation class and was offered an instructors position, but he turned it down to fly combat. Jack propped us up too during the introductions, pointing out that I had graduated the top of my class as well, albeit single engine school, and Ted was the tops in his bombardier class as well. We had a little meeting where Jack stressed to us that he wanted us to be the best aircrew in whatever squadron we ended up in. At the end of our meeting he surprised us with the news that in two days' time we would be leaving for Grand Island, Nebraska, by train to pick up our very own brand new ship right off the factory floor. From there we would fly more training missions and then be deployed to England. Wow, I thought to myself! My stomach turned over and over. England! The war! Here we come!

Chapter 26
Grand Island

Hello again honey dear. Just received your most welcome phone call and want you to know how happy I am again after having a chat with you. Gee, I was surely lonesome, but I knew you would phone if possible. The only bad part about not hearing from you for so long was that I had visions of your having left the country without getting a chance to even tell me good-bye by phone or telegraph. I know I shouldn't have such illusions, darling, and I promise not to be a worrywart from now on. It was wonderful to hear your voice again, and those kisses were super. I almost felt them they sounded so real! Gee, I really wish things could be worked out so you could just stay here, unless you prefer the excitement of 'active duty.' I'm really just like all of the other wives who hate to let their husbands go into the thick of the fight! It's much nicer to have you right here in the good old USA, even though I know it is selfish of me to want that privilege. If you do have to 'cross the pond,' my dearest, you will always know that I'll be waiting for you and praying real hard that God will take care of you and bring you back to me real soon. I promise to try to be a good soldier too, honey, so please don't worry about me – just do your usual good work and hurry back home! Today, Sunday, I went to 11 O'clock mass. Kay and Ken were here so I asked them to take your messages if you should phone because I didn't know if you'd have another chance to call back. The kids went on a picnic to William Land Park with Louise and Bill. They all tried to persuade me to join them, but I declined 'cause I wanted to be here in case you should phone – and you did too!

I really haven't much news, honey-dear, except how much I love you and miss you, which is old stuff, but still goes! I'm looking forward to hearing from you real soon now and receiving that signal to 'take off' to join you in Grand Island. Well, I guess I'd better 'sign off' for this time my darling. Be a good boy, as I know you always are, and fly 'em high. In the meantime, and always, May God bless you and keep you safe and happy, 'cause I love you so very, very much and I want the best of everything for you. Goodnight, now, I'll be a-writing and seeing you soon. Love and kisses – from your Mrs. Margaret.

It was a long and uneventful train ride to Grand Island, almost 1,500 miles! This time there was no Margaret, and no one playing a clarinet or trumpet. We did play some card games to keep us busy. I learned real fast how dangerous it was to play poker with Roger, our new navigator. He was quite good at the game! When the game switched to black jack I won my money back from him, though, because I'm real good at that. We were like two gunfighters sizing each other up. Margaret was headed to Grand Island also and her ride was just about the same distance. She got a ticket on the "Challenger Train" out of Sacramento. The day after we reached Grand Island we were introduced to the newest member of our crew. A brand spanking new B-17. True to his word, Jack already had her name, "Polly Jo," painted across her nose. She was a site to behold and carried with her that specialness because she was all ours. After our orientation and inspection of our new ship we were allowed to head to town and get our affairs squared away. Those of us who were married would be allowed to stay in town with our wives while we were here. The reason for that is because in a few weeks we would be heading to England and the war. I got us a room at the Hotel Yancey on N. Locust Street. Boy was Margaret ever surprised when she arrived. Everything was all set when she got to town later in the afternoon. We had a nice Fillet Mignon steak dinner for only a dollar in the hotel restaurant, and then spent a much needed long overdue night alone in our room. The next day our work began. We were to report every morning at 0600 hours and we spent the next few weeks training and flying every day. Jack received his promotion to 2nd lieutenant so then all the officers on the ship carried the same rank. Our first flight in the "Polly Jo" was to Salina, Kansas, to pick up some equipment and parts for the ship. Jack would use that flight to test Roger and he came through with flying colors. The majority of our flight was in the clouds, but we arrived right on target and right on schedule following Roger's directions. Jack also trained in and received his instrument rating in the B-17 while we were in Grand Island. The "Polly Jo" was well equipped and tested by us in the short time that we were in Nebraska. Jack's wife, Polly, got a real kick out of seeing the ship for the first time with her name on it. Another real surprise for us was finding out that Polly was pregnant. The crew was beginning to form a bond, so getting news like that was great for everyone's morale. Each long day ended at 1800 hours and Jack and I would head into town to spend the evening with our wives. It was almost like having a real job, but we knew that would end soon. Like my mother used to tell me, all good things come to an end. I've never eaten so much steak in my life, but how could we resist at only one dollar a meal for a Nebraska steak? I think we ate steak every night for dinner.

One afternoon when I was beginning to sign myself out for the evening I heard a voice from behind me shout, hey lieutenant. It was the Operations Major. He asked me what I was doing and I said, nothing at the moment, sir. He told me that there was a B-17 warming up out on the ramp and the crew needed to test flight a new navigator. He said it was a last minute thing and they couldn't find their co-pilot. He told me to run on out there and go with them and that it would only take an hour. Of course I complied, grudgingly running out to the ship I climbed in, introduced myself to the pilot, and we took off for places unknown. It was an uneventful flight until we were just about back to Grand Island. We were second in line and turning for final when the B-17 in front of us was struck by a massive bolt of lightning. He banked hard left and looked like he was going to roll over but the crew managed to right the ship. At that altitude they surely would have crashed had they gone any farther over. It was a testament to their reactions and training that they were able to right the ship at all. When they came back to level flight they looked pretty wobbly and their bomb bay doors flew open. It's a good thing their wheels were already down or they may not have been able to lower them. They were able to land her alright and I understand no one was even hurt. The tower closed the runway immediately and ordered us to divert to Lincoln, Nebraska. After seeing that mishap right in front of us we gladly complied by sliding the throttles full forward and getting the hell out of there! Our flight to, and landing in Lincoln, went without a hitch and without any more lightning, but we just barely beat the storm front there. There was no room for any of us on the post so we had to drive into town to find accommodations. In town we discovered every room was booked and there were majors, colonels and generals running around everywhere. That wasn't good, because none of us was in a proper uniform. We had jump suits over undershirts, no hats, you name it. We were sitting ducks if anyone wanted to push it, but it was only supposed to be a one hour flight!

We found out that the brass was in town because there had been a WAC, Women's Army Corps, graduation somewhere and the women would be stopping in town where the brass had a big graduation party and dance planned for them. Well, needless to say, this interested the crew greatly and everyone went scurrying around town trying to round up a uniform to buy so they could attend the party. Surprisingly enough, everyone, including me, found uniforms to wear. I didn't attend the party, but I did want to be able to find a place to eat without looking like a hobo and getting a shellacking by a colonel or general. At one point I climbed out of a car and walked past a general, still looking like a garage mechanic. I just saluted him and said; good evening general. He just saluted back and said good evening to me in response. That was a close one. After getting a uniform we managed to find a small room for us all to pile in and I got cleaned up and called Margaret to let her know what happened. She had been worried about me and had asked Jack, Ted, and Roger where I was, but no one knew because they had just left the post ahead of me when I got snagged for this little detail. Now that she knew I was safe she got quite a laugh out of my little predicament. I assured her I had no interest in going to the party and was just going to eat and hit the sack. I ended up buying dinner for all the enlisted men on the crew because no one had any money with them on this short training flight. The next morning we went back to the base, got in our ship, and flew back to Grand Island. I'll never forget my little trip to Lincoln, Nebraska.

Back at Grand Island we continued to train and get ready for the big leagues. They hadn't given us a departure date yet, but we knew it would be soon. I tried to fit a lifetime of moments in with Margaret in the few days that we suspected we had left. We dined together every night, walked side by side through town together, and loved each other every night. Finally, we were all called into a briefing. The word came to prepare for deployment. The colonel added that a complaint had been lodged by officials in Chicago about a flight of three B-17's that had performed a much too low fly-by of the city by completing a circle around the downtown area. He said they failed to get any tail numbers so he didn't want to know anything and to take the information with us to England. Ted piped up and said,

"Should we say anything?"

"Shut up!" Jack and I said simultaneously.

And that's the last time we said anything about that. It's a good thing we were leaving. Things were beginning to get a little wild. After we were issued our 1911 pistols, guys were getting in trouble going out into the fields and shooting things. One 2nd lieutenant got drunk and shot up the mirror behind the bar in the officers club. We thought he'd get in a world of trouble for that, but we saw him later in England. In the Army's infinite wisdom he got a promotion instead. I guess they didn't know what to do with him.

We had to plan for the upcoming long distance haul. We would be flying to Presque Isle, Maine, then up to Gander, Newfoundland. From there we were to head "across the pond" to Scotland to a refuel point and then make the final leg to England. We had one last night together and we fell asleep in each other's arms wishing that this day hadn't come. But it did come, and in the morning Margaret, Polly, Jack, and I all drove out to base operations and made preparations for the flight. The operations officer said he would take the girls out to the ramp and let them watch us leave. He said it was the least he could do after stranding me in Lincoln. That was very nice of him, I thought, and we thanked him repeatedly for his kindness. There would be about a dozen ships leaving for the trip to Maine that day. I hugged and kissed Margaret repeatedly as Jack looked at her and said,

"Cecil and I will take good care of each other. Will you help take care of my little Polly and baby? I'm counting on you."

Margaret told him she would. With that, we both pulled ourselves up through the hatch and began our preflight check and engine start up as the operations officer drove away with the girls crying and waving to us.

Chapter 27
Crossing the Pond

Just a short note before I check out and head for the depot. Wanted to tell you how swell all of you looked when you left. It was beautiful! And, of course, you saw us waving. Pat, Edith, Polly and I watched all of you and we waved to everyone, as you noticed if you saw us. Grand Island will never forget us for all of our cheering. We're proud of our darlings, as if you didn't know! Honey, this is a rush note but it's wonderful to be able to send you a little letter and know you'll receive it soon. Lt. Manning and some of the other fellows who are leaving tomorrow are going to take them (our letters) to you boys. Edith, Polly and I have been keeping each other and Pat from being too blue this morning. Of course we miss you heaps and heaps, words can't describe that, but we're going to try to be good soldiers too and keep up the 'home front,' so don't you worry about us – just remember that we love you very, very much and will be patiently but anxiously awaiting your happy landing near home!

I have a feeling that it isn't going to be very long before you'll all be home with us and we can once more be happy together for always. In the meantime, as always, I love you my dearest, and I'll be thinking of you always, wishing you the best of everything, and praying for your speedy and safe return to my open arms! We are at the depot now. Pat and Lillian came to see Polly and me off. The train is late, but is coming at 12:30. I will arrive in Caliente tomorrow night at 8:35 P.M. I have wired Ken and Dee accordingly. It's afternoon already, so guess we'd better go and see about our baggage. I'll be seeing you 'in all the old familiar places' darling, real soon, I'm sure, and we'll have the best Christmas ever, even if it has to be late! G'bye now, sweetheart, and God bless you always. XXXOOOXXX. Margaret.

"Wow, I'm sure glad we got that six day leave before shipping out," I said to Jack.

"Ya," he said, "I wish it was longer. I hate that my baby is going to be born while I'm gone, but I guess we knew what we were signing up for."

"Ya, you're right. But that doesn't make it any easier, it's still real hard."

"Yep!"

We pushed the throttles full and started our roll down the runway. We were a bit busy watching what we were doing, but we could see the girls over between the taxiway and the runway on the jeep with the major. We were now headed on the first leg of our journey to jolly old England. Our first stop would be at Presque Isle Army Airbase in Maine. It was about an 1800 mile flight. We flew most of the way in heavy clouds. Jack snickered a bit as he said,

"This will test Burwell alright."

Roger fed us a heading from time to time and we broke out of the clouds right on schedule and right on target. I asked Jack,

"Well? How did he do? We ended up right where he said we would and right when he said we would."

All Jack did was grunt and chuckle a little. That alone made me laugh out loud, and right when Eddie stuck his head up into the cockpit. He said,

"What's so funny lieutenant?"

"Oh, nothing."

We taxied to a hard stand and checked in at base operations for the night. We ended up having to stay in Maine for a few days because of foul weather, but the food was good and the beer was even better. We got in a few card games while we were waiting for the weather to clear. I got my fill after losing a couple hands in a row to Roger and I sat down on my bunk and wrote a letter to Margaret.

> Hello, once again, my darling. Gee whiz, it's been a long time since I have had to write letters to you, and of course I wish that I still didn't have to do so. But maybe I will be able to say hello in person again soon – I hope. Jack is feeling sad also, I guess, like I am, that you are no longer with me – 'cause I guess he misses his Polly like I miss my Margaret. Of course, I don't know anything about what is

going to happen yet, as we are still grounded. I forgot to tell you, I got another letter from the draft board. It was addressed to Lt. C.W. Quinley this time. What a bunch of idiots! They want a note from my commanding officer stating that I am in the Army, yet they mail their notice to an Army post and address it with my rank. I guess they won't believe you and me. I ought to just let them keep wondering, but maybe I will send them the verification just to shut them up. I still love you very very much my darling. Keep your chin up and take care of yourself. May God bless you. Love and kisses. Cecil.

After a few days we received our orders to fly up to Gander, Newfoundland, as a last stop before heading across the pond. Gander was a 643 mile flight. Just a little hop, what could go wrong? It was clear beautiful weather when we took off but we soon had a solid cloud layer below us for the rest of the trip. It was time for Roger to be tested again. I think he was going to have to earn his money working with us, and we were going to get our money's worth out of him it appeared. At the appropriate time Roger came on the intercom and told us we could start to let down. Jack asked him if he was sure, after all it's quite stressful intentionally losing altitude through the clouds, trusting your instruments, but being totally unfamiliar with the area where you're flying. There has to be a lot of trust to do that. Roger said he was sure. He was confident in his abilities and never hesitated to let Jack know that. We circled down in a slow descent and broke through a low cloud layer into a driving rain storm, but right on target. I laughed a little and Jack half glared and half smiled at me. I was wondering if every flight was going to be like this. We had a few days to wait in Gander again because of foul weather. Accidents were increasing on the North Atlantic route to England, so they were trying to be cautious. But planes had to get to the war, so sometimes chances had to be taken.

Gander was an interesting place. Even though it was June there was still about ten feet of snow on the ground everywhere. I ran into my friend George Riegal, who had gone all through flight school with me. He was on his way to England too. He joined the four of us, Jack, Roger, Ted and I, and we walked about the base looking around. We came upon the officers club and we went inside to get out of the weather. The only person in there was the bartender. We were sitting and talking about the flight when a number of Royal Canadian officers came in and got very upset that we were in their club. Roger took exception to their highbrow attitude and we could see that this was going downhill fast. Jack ushered us all out before it got out of hand. We were walking along again and came upon some Royal Canadian Sergeants who overheard us talking about our experience with their unfriendly officers. They said they just got a new shipment of beer in and they would love to have us as their guests at their sergeants club. Well, how could we turn down an invitation like that? They saved us from the opinion we were forming about the Canadian Air Force. They were the nicest bunch of fellows you would ever want to meet. They entertained us most of the night and let us drink their beer with them. I don't know what was up with those other fellows, but this bunch was swell. There was a piano in the club and Ted played it while we all sang songs. Eventually, we had to call it a night because we never knew from day to day when the weather would clear and we'd get the okay to takeoff. After a few days Jack and the other stranded pilots were called to operations to meet with the meteorologist. He took Roger with him, a clear sign that he had accepted our new navigator. When they came back they said that in the morning the weather was going to be as good as it was going to get for a long time. They said that we'd still be flying in a storm, but it looked doable.

In the morning we did our preflight and everyone took their positions. We knew it was going to be a rough flight because we were taking off in a rain storm and not long after takeoff we flew right into the storm front. It was a bumpy ride and our longest flight to date, about 2100 miles! Every once in a while we could see Roger trying to shoot a position in the bubble in front of us. Finally, Roger came on the intercom and said we were a hundred miles south of our planned course and we had to make a correction of 30 degrees left to get to our check point at Ballymore, Ireland. Jack and I looked at each other and we talked off com about it. I said,

"He's really confident, and so far competent in everything he's told us."

"I know," Jack said. Then he asked Roger, "Are you sure?"

Roger said he obtained a three star fix and then added a bit gruffly that if we didn't want to end up a prisoner in France we needed to turn 30 degrees left. Jack simply said okay and we changed our heading, again on Roger's say so. As had been our luck so far, though, we had a solid cloud layer below us as we were reaching our check point. Then, suddenly, as daylight broke, there was also a break in the clouds and we could see Ireland. All of a sudden everyone got on the com and piped in how glad they were to finally see land again. I guess we weren't the only ones who were getting stressed out over the flight. I think the only one who wasn't stressed out was Ted. Roger stuck his head up in the cockpit and told me that Ted had been sleeping for the last few hours and he had no idea what we'd been through, and if I was going to get him, I needed to do it now. It was a little plan I came up with while we were having ales at the sergeants club back on Gander. Ted's family knew some people in London and he already had a date lined up with their daughter. I yelled on the intercom,

"Hey Ted, wake up!"

He came up on the com and asked where we were. I told him that we got blown off course in the storm and that we were crossing the coast of North Africa and we'd have to stay there for a while. Man oh man was he upset; swearing and yelling. He finally got clued in when he noticed that Roger was laughing his head off behind him and he swore vengeance.

As we passed over Ballymore I remember thinking that I couldn't wait to tell the family that I had flown over the green green grass of Ireland, and green it was. Roger gave us a heading for Prestwick and off we went. So much for Ireland I thought. Maybe someday I'll get to set foot there. We started down below the cloud layer for the remainder of the flight and we found ourselves breaking into the clear at 1000 feet above the water of the Irish Sea with a Navy destroyer steaming right at us. He was sending us blinking signals with his lights so Jack hollered down to Roger to get on our lantern and send the proper code back to him, which he did. The cloud layer was getting lower and lower, and our fuel was getting lower and lower too. Jack was getting a bit nervous, and when he got nervous, I got nervous. We weren't sure if we could make it to Prestwick on the fuel we had, and we darn sure knew that if we got lost in the cloud cover or fog we'd run out of fuel for sure. We saw a short runway ahead of us and we made a bee line for it. It was an RAF fighter base and they called us on the radio and tried to divert us, but Jack told them we were low on fuel and coming in, like it or not. As we touched down we could see that the end of the runway was coming up on us fast. Jack yelled at me to help him with the brakes and we were both practically standing on them. We could hear and feel the tires skidding as we finally came to a stop just short of the end of the runway. As it turned out, we wore flat spots on the bottom of the tires and our brakes were smoking hot. Several RAF pilots were standing at the hardstand as we shut down; mouths hanging open. They said they'd never seen a bomber land successfully at their field before, and they pointed to the broken down fence past the end of the runway as evidence of several prior attempts. Ted said,

"You should have seen it from my seat!"

"Welcome to Scotland Yanks. Hot coffee or tea anyone?" One of them said amidst their laughing at Ted's statement.

Roger and Ted said thanks, but they would prefer something more stiff after being in the nose and watching that fence at the end of the runway coming at them. Jack reminded them that we wouldn't be here long and we could all get drinks in Prestwick. Roger said-fine! We left Tex at the ship to take care of things and the rest of us caught a ride to base operations for our drinks.

Chapter 28
Wheels Up Damn It

July 13, 1943.

Another day gone by with everything going well and I hope you can say the same, as always. Didn't have to take any drill tonight. Everyone's interest here, at present, is centered on the invasion of Sicily, just as I imagine it is in the U.S. It really looks swell to see some sort of invasion into Europe – even if it is a long way from Germany. Every little bit helps and makes that much less to worry about. I imagine that you get just as late if not later information on it over there than we do here. We have a very good daily paper called 'The Stars and Stripes,' which is distributed to all the U.S. camps over here, and it is a very good one, for only about two cents per copy. One penny British money is equivalent to two cents our coin.

Gosh honey, if you think that there are quite a few bicycles in the U.S. you should see them over here. Everybody from about four to ninety rides them. They are all about like the Victory models at home. I guess they have to have them to get around. There are an awful lot of busses and taxi cabs over here too. In London you can see about fifty cabs going down the street right behind each other, and the busses are just as thick. All the busses and street cars are double decker. A bicycle over here is called a wheel and a train a tram. There aren't many cars on the road though, all that are-are about the size of an Austin with anywhere from six to twelve horsepower engines in them. One thing that I've never seen over here yet is a road that crossed a railroad track. They all either go over or under. Ted said to tell you hello for him. He is about as bad over here as he was in the states. When it comes to women, he is always looking for one, and then he keeps talking about how swell his gal at home is that he is going to marry. Some people are sure hard to figure out. I guess they're just made that way. George Riegal is still around here with us. Bob Pelton left

here today for someplace, he got here several days before
we did. We have an officers club here on the base, which
isn't too awfully bad and the meals really aren't so very
bad. Most of the guys do a lot of griping about it but it
really isn't bad, I don't think. We get a package of gum a
week and a couple of candy bars, a package of cigarettes a
day, and a package of mints a week, it's all enough to
satisfy me. I'm still looking forward to a letter from you,
my darling. I run over and look every day but no luck so far.
But there will come a day, of course, as it really hasn't been
so awfully long since we've been in England, and I guess
they didn't send our addresses until after we arrived here,
which has only been about nine or ten days.

My darling, I guess I'd better be saying so-long for
now and signing off for tonight, as long as I don't have
much of anything of interest to relay to you. I just threw a
kiss to your picture so you can consider yourself kissed. Of
course, I'd prefer it in person by far. Bye now darling, I
love you and think of you always. May God bless you. Love
and kisses. Cecil.

While the rest of us were drinking some awfully bad coffee Jack was
told we didn't have to hop over to the main airfield. We could just refuel
here and fly down to RAF Bovington. He stayed at operations and arranged
the fueling and flight plan while the rest of us went back to the ship. When
we got there Tex was nowhere to be found. I asked Roger to see if he could
find him while I started a pre-flight check. About fifteen minutes later Roger
climbed in through the hatch and I asked him if he found Tex. He said he
had and he'd be here in a few minutes. I asked where he was and Roger
said,

"Don't ask."

"What do you mean? Did you find him or not?" I said.

"I think Tex just broke the all-time record for finding someone to have
sex with in Scotland! I found him just off the taxiway in the bushes with a
red head."

"You have got to be kidding me!"

"No, I'm not!"

"As long as he gets here in time, maybe we shouldn't tell Jack until some other day, after he's had a few drinks."

"Good plan."

When Jack got back to the ship the fueling was already done and Tex, luckily, was back on-board. We finished the preflight check and engine start-up and taxied out for takeoff. As we sat at the end of the runway staring down a strip that looked like the length of a football field we both kind of just swallowed hard and looked at each other. Ted came on the intercom and said,

"You sure about this?"

He didn't get a response. We locked the tail wheel, set the brakes, set full flaps, and throttled forward to full while standing on the brakes. On Jacks order we let loose the brakes and started our roll. As the end of the runway came up on us we began to pull back on the yoke and Jack ordered,

"Wheels up."

"I can't," I said.

"Wheels up!"

"I can't!"

We were almost to the end of the runway and Jack yelled this time,

"Quinn, God dammit, wheels up! Wheels up!"

"I can't Jack, we're still on the damn ground!"

Right then we lifted off and I raised the gear just as we cleared the end of the runway and scraped through the top of some bushes with the gear as it came up. Ted came back on the intercom and said,

"I'd like that drink right about now!"

"I'll second that," Roger said.

"I'll buy the first round," Jack said.

The guys in the back of the plane had no idea how close that was. It was only about a 350 mile trip to RAF Bovington and it was clear sailing once we climbed up through the low cloud layer. The rest of the flight was smooth and uneventful and we landed right on time. We taxied to a hard stand where a couple trucks were waiting for us. They took us to base operations where we received a billet until we received our assignments.

We were at RAF Bovington for a few days until they figured out where we would be stationed. We just meandered about the base and had some fun at the officers club most of the time. Finally, Jack came back to our barracks one morning and told us to pack up, that we were being sent to Ridgewell Station 167 in East Anglia. We were being assigned as a replacement crew to the 381st Bomb Group (Heavy), 532nd Bomb Squadron. It was close to a town called Cambridge and about fifty miles from London. To our surprise, though, we wouldn't be taking the "Polly Jo" with us. None of us were very happy about that. We felt like she was ours. We named her and brought her all the way to England with us. We formed an attachment. But I guess the aircraft was needed elsewhere, not where we were going. They put us on trucks and drove us the last 140 miles or so to our station. I thought; imagine that, a bunch of flyers driving to our base. When we got to Ridgewell the enlisted men received a billet in an open barracks, which was a large Nissen hut, and us four officers were assigned to a smaller Nissen hut. Some of the officer's huts accommodated the officers from four crews, or sixteen men. Our Nissen hut held just two crews, or eight men. Our roommates were Lieutenant's Bill Baltrusaitis (the pilot), Art Sample (co-pilot), Martin Honke (navigator), and Carl Potter (bombardier). Baltrusaitis went by "Baldy." He and Art were swell people and we got along great. Baldy had a reputation as a fantastic pilot who didn't let anyone mess with his crew. Art was from Mississippi and spoke with a good old southern drawl. He was a swell fellow and would become a good friend. They arrived March 26th but didn't start flying missions until late June. They already had a few under their belts by the time we got there. We would be one of the first replacement crews in the squadron and we had a long-long way to go to get up to speed, get our time in trying to beat the odds, and get home. We were told that there was about a 25% casualty rate so far. That was pretty unsettling news to hear.

It was going to be a while before we were cleared to fly combat, so we spent our time getting used to the lay of the base. It was huge and was about a two mile walk to the officers mess and back. We learned real quick to buy a bicycle to get around on. The first order of business, after getting a bicycle in Cambridge of course, was to get to London and look around while we weren't assigned to flying yet. Our whole crew caught a train (or tram) into London on our first weekend. Roger and Ted headed off to see what trouble they could get into. I'm not sure what Jack did but he told me to keep an eye on the enlisted fellows and keep them out of trouble. He told me that because I wasn't much for hitting the bars like Ted and Roger, and I had already mentioned that I was planning on taking the rest of the guys out for a nice dinner. So, that's what we did our first weekend in London. I guess we looked like a bunch of tourists. We rode the double decker buses around town and saw the sights. It was all very nice, except for the bombed out areas. It was a sober reminder of why we were there. As planned, I took the rest of the boys to dinner at a nice restaurant. After our meal the waiter made a big fuss about us not paying our bill. I argued with him that I had paid it and didn't understand what his issue was. The more he yelled at me the more I just stopped listening to him. I just told the boys, C'mon, let's go. We got about a block and a half away and then we heard a whistle blowing and then someone yelled,

"You Yanks there, stop!"

It was two London Bobbies. The darn restaurant called the police on us. I was thinking, oh great, and Jack told *me* to keep them out of trouble and I get us all locked up in London! The Bobbie told me that the waiter said we hadn't paid our bill and I said that yes we did. He explained to me that, in England, the gratuity was written into the bill. He was very nice and explained it in a way that I understood it. I told him that we left the gratuity on the table, that we didn't know the custom. He just told us to get out of there and he'd clear things up with the waiter. Soon, we were assigned our first ship. We'd be getting some training flights to learn the countryside, the routes, form up areas and so forth. The war was about to get real for us. Our ship was a B-17F, tail number 229854 short for serial number (42-29854). Our squadron letters were VE and ship letter B. There was a big white triangle on the tail with a black L in it, signifying the 381st BG. It was already named in big block letters on the side, "OLE FLAK SACK."

Chapter 29
Kassel

Another Sunday is here and another week has gone by, which makes just two weeks since we first arrived in dear old England, which of course is two weeks too long. If you were here it wouldn't really be so bad, of course. It's kind of a quiet day around here. I'm about the only one around the barracks here. I didn't even get up until about 11 A.M. Aint I awful? Then, I went and had dinner and have been playing pool over in the club for a couple of hours. It's good not to have anything to do for a whole day once again.

Went into town last night and went to a show. I saw 'High Explosive' and some other picture, which I don't recall the name of. They are putting on a USO show here tonight, which I guess I might just as well go to see. From the sounds of it I guess it should be a pretty good one. I have your picture sitting here in front of me on my table, you sure do look beautiful, which of course you really are. But even so, your picture gets more beautiful every time I look at it. I sure do wish that there was some way for you to get yourself over here, but of course that isn't possible, as we know.

Our old commanding officer, Colonel Hoyt, is over here now. He is in command of a fighter group. He was at Luke Field the first month I was there - he is a general now though. I don't know just where he is, but I saw it in our paper. He is a pretty good fellow, I guess, from what they say about him. I only saw him a couple of times while at Luke.

I guess the war down in Sicily is going along very good now, which really sounds encouraging. I wish that Italy would give up and shoot Mussolini, 'cause he will get it anyway, very soon, and it would mean that things would come to an end that much sooner, and it can't be any too soon to suit me. Every day it goes on is one day too many! Anyway, I believe in being optimistic and believe that it

195

will be over here very shortly. About the war in the Pacific, I'm afraid I can't say though, but that shouldn't be so long either, if this was finished over here.

I sure do wish this week would hurry by, 'cause by that time I should be getting some mail from you, and I will be about one hundred percent happier when I finally do get one of your precious letters. Maybe writing to you then will be easier, 'cause it will be more like a conversation. As it is now I do all of the talking, and I run out of things to talk about, except to say that I love you, and am thinking that constantly every day. Bye now my darling. Say hello to everyone for me and May God bless you and take good care of you, just for me. Love and Kisses. Cecil.

Roger, Jack and I were at base operations one day. We'd been flying training missions and practicing close in combat formation flying. The group was coming back from a mission and the three of us went out to the hard stands to welcome them home. A ship by the name of "Old Coffins" pulled up and an ambulance was waiting for them. The ship commander climbed down through the hatch and looked at the ambulance fellows and just shook his head. Our Chaplain, James Good Brown, went up to assist them in pulling out the body of their navigator. As his body was tilted to get him through the hatch a massive amount of blood poured out from his flight suit, all over the chaplain, but he didn't miss a beat and they lowered the body to the stretcher. That was the first time I had seen anything like that, and I could tell by the look on Jack and Roger's face it was a first for them as well. It must have been a first for the dozen or so men who were standing their watching too. We all just stood there in silent disbelief at what we had just witnessed. We had been hearing about the twenty-five percent casualty rate, but thus far had not seen combat ourselves, and didn't know anyone who had been lost. Seeing this was like we got an immediate slap in the face. This is it, I thought, this is where the war is. Roger was especially disturbed by what he saw because it was the ships navigator who was killed and no one else on the ship was injured. The three of us just stood there and watched the ambulance drive away with the body. After that we got back on our bikes and peddled over to the club and downed a few beers while talking about what we were getting ourselves into. It wouldn't be long now. We'd been cleared to join the squadron on active missions.

Thus far we had been operating as a spare crew and we weren't officially assigned until the 21st of July. I was left behind on the first three missions so Jack could be checked out on his tactics and formation flying in actual combat. A veteran pilot flew right seat with our crew so he could train them under combat conditions, and it would be Jack's job to catch me up when I rejoined the crew. The thought was that the offset in the number of missions wouldn't make any difference because, if we were still alive by the end of our tour, I would have my own crew by then anyway. They took part on a mission to Hanover, before our having been assigned, and to Hamburg as a spare, and Altenbuna, Germany, after assignment. Roger was also tasked with accompanying a 534th squadron crew, 1st Lt. Tucker (pilot) aboard "Battlin' Bombsprayer," on a flight to Kiel, Germany, for an unscheduled mission to try and catch the German battleship Tirpitz, which was seen steaming in the area. The navigator for that crew was in the hospital. Back at Ridgewell I felt like an expectant father in a waiting room. I paced around the barracks until I couldn't stand it anymore, then I would pedal back to the barracks and pace more. Finally I heard the drone of the first returning bombers approaching the field and I raced out to the ramp to greet them. The planes with injured on board had priority for landing and they would fire a red flare on final approach. From where I stood I couldn't tell which ships were which, so every time I saw a red flare I expected the worst. Fortunately, no flares came from our ship! The boys were happy to get back and, although quite weary from flying high altitude, talked with excitement about the missions. They saw very few fighters so far but they said the flack over Hamburg was pretty heavy and some of the experienced crews said it was the heaviest they had seen so far.

"Gentleman, your target for today is Kassel, Germany."

30 July 1943, this would be my first combat mission, and the 16th for the 381st group. I sat in the briefing room along with the officers of numerous other aircraft. At the head of the room was a large map that was covered. Colonel Nazzaro, our group commander, entered the room and we were all called to attention. He walked quickly to the front of the room and told us all to be seated. At that time the cover was pulled from the map and he made his statement about our destination. After the words Kassel, Germany, there was a loud moan from everyone. Then, he called the group communications and radio officer, Lieutenant Robert Thayer to the front of the room. The lieutenant briefed us on the rest of the mission. Specifically, identifying the Fieseler Flagseugbau Aircraft Component Works at Kassel

as our target, our munitions load of ten 500 pound bombs, our form up point, route in, initial point of the bomb run, expected fighter and flak opposition and so forth. Then, Colonel Nazzaro dismissed us. My job was to head out to the aircraft and prepare it for the mission and assure that the rest of the men were getting their guns and ammunition in place. Jack and Roger attended a secondary briefing for first pilots and navigators. When Jack arrived at "Ole Flak Sack" he and I did another walk around and spoke to the ground crew briefly. Then, he threw his flight gear through the hatch and we did a final walk around. At the appointed time we ran through our check list and engine start procedures and taxied out to the runway. When the flare was fired from base operations each bomber began their take-off roll thirty seconds apart down runway 28. After takeoff we joined up with the rest of the group and then joined with the rest of the first air division heading into the thick of it.

We slowly climbed up to 26,000 feet as we headed toward Germany. Our "little friends," P-47 fighters, joined up with us across the channel, but they had to turn back when we needed them the most. They just didn't have the range to escort us into Germany. After they left us the German fighters appeared and came in for their attack. The chatter on the intercom was incredible.

"Jerry fighters 12 O'clock level. Ted, fire your guns! Ted, fire!"

We could hear Roger yelling at Ted. Roger would later tell us that Ted was sitting there, just staring out the nose of the aircraft, saying prayers while holding his Rosary Beads. I guess he just got in a trance like state and Roger literally had to hit him in the back to bring him out of it and fire on the fighters that were coming at us head on. This would become Ted's routine on missions, except that he learned to snap out of it on his own. A matter of mental self-preservation, I suppose. It continued on like that.

> Smitty he's coming around to your side. Tex, how's it
> looking back there? He's shooting at us! Well, shoot back!
> Pilot to turrets, fighters coming in head on, watch for them
> as they slide over or under. 3 O'clock high, slicing down
> our way, watch for him. Let him have it! Pilot to crew, flak
> up ahead! Fighters are peeling off skipper.

As we turned on our initial point (IP) and headed in for the bomb run we entered the flak field and "Ole Flak Sack" shook violently up and down from the concussion of the exploding shells. It was difficult to keep good formation because of the turbulence, but Jack was a great formation flyer and he only needed a little help. It took all his concentration to fight the yoke and keep our proper distances, which left me to monitor the gauges and engines. There wasn't much time to think when flying through a barrage of enemy planes and shells that are all there to kill you, but there are a million other places you'd rather be. The 381st was leading the division today so we would be near the front in dropping our bombs. Ted had the ship now as the auto pilot was engaged through his Norden bomb sight, although it was the lead ship bombardier that would zero in on the target and announce the drop. After what seemed like an eternity, but was probably only a few minutes, we heard Ted say over the intercom-bombs away. The ship lurched upward a little from the sudden loss of 5,000 pounds of bombs. Jack took back the controls and we made a turn to the north east for a few minutes, then turned back North West for a few minutes, all intended to confuse the enemy as to our route and try to avoid flak positions. As we made our third turn to the west I could see a ship dropping out of formation with at least two engines out and smoking. From what little I could see it appeared to be under control heading for some low clouds with several German fighters chasing after it and shooting. I saw a couple of parachutes, but my attention was soon drawn back to our own predicament. The enemy fighters seemed to come back at us from everywhere and the chatter of calling out their locations filled the intercom again. As we came within reach of our own fighters, close to the coast of Holland, the enemy fighters turned back. Not having the fuel, ammo, or will to mix it up with the P-47's and British Spitfires. Either way, we didn't care which it was, as long as they were gone. Somehow we endured the mission without a hole in the ship anywhere, although we could hear some shrapnel clanging off the fuselage from time to time, it never penetrated the skin. Upon landing back at Ridgewell, we were all exhausted from flying at 26,000 feet for so long at a brisk 30 degree below zero temperature and having our adrenalin rushing through us for what seemed like the whole day. It was good to be home, but I thought to myself; I have 24 more of these to do? How is that going to be possible? The odds are against me ever seeing Margaret again. My hopes were further dashed when I learned that the ship I saw going down over the Netherlands was our squadron commander, Major Post. I had only known him for a few weeks, but my impression was that he was a very nice fellow who deserved the position he was in. A commander that led by example. The kind of man who didn't say-go do it, he'd say-follow me. He was already the squadron commander, but he'd just been promoted to major three day ago, and this was his 12th mission. He'll be sorely missed. Our day wasn't over yet. We had to attend a debriefing, interrogation they called it, and we were interviewed by group personnel. Red Cross girls handed out coffee. As I raised my cup to take a drink I couldn't stop my hand from shaking. I couldn't figure it out. I didn't feel scared anymore, just worn out, but the shaking was still there as I just sat there and watched my hand in curiosity. I wasn't a drinking man, but tonight we four officers of "Ole Flak Sack" downed a few after interrogation. It was the only thing that made my hand quit shaking. We wouldn't fly again for almost two weeks.

Chapter 30
Thank God for Mail

Dearest Brother Cecil.

I know that Margaret has written to you all about our little Phillip Cecil, so there isn't much left for me to say about him. Naturally, I think he's a very handsome baby, but that's just the matters of opinion you know. Jim had to work on Sunday, so he came down Monday morning after work and had a few hours to spend with Robbie and had a chance to see his new son and visit with me before going back. It's been swell seeing Margaret these last few days and we hated to see her leave. She left last night around 9 P.M. It was supposed to leave at 6, but was three hours late. She and Corabelle were right here when the baby was born, in fact, they practically delivered it. Your cablegram arrived in Ceres a few hours after Margaret did, so talk about excitement! After rushing back and telling mother the news we started calling everyone on the phone we could think of. Guess the train couldn't move fast enough for Margaret last night, for she had phoned Sacramento and found out there was a V-Mail letter waiting for her there.

It was swell of you to write to mother from New York. I know she was very happy to know she was in your last thoughts before you made your long flight. Of course, we're all very anxious to hear more news from you if possible. Just where you are stationed, but really, that may be a military secret. Wherever you are right now and whatever you may be doing, our thoughts and prayers are with you. We're all so proud of our little brother and know he will be coming home again soon. I'll be staying here in the hospital until next Sunday and then won't be able to go back to Oakland until the last part of this month. Robbie named the baby 'Two Bits' before he arrived and Jim's afraid that name will stick with him for a while. Robbie went last night to stay at Carolyn's for ten days. He's probably having a grand time, and Carolyn too. I'll write again soon. God bless and take care of you. Milly.

Dearest Cec.

Hiya Honey! Gee, I'm happy tonight! I received two swell letters from my darling today! Thank you sweetheart. My spirits are up once more. Forgive me dear, for writing sort of blue letters the past few days. I know you understand how disappointed I am when I don't get letters from sweet you, you said so in your swell letters that came today. Don't ever think that I'll be mad at you, though, 'cause I don't get angry, I just feel awful blue. I know that you write at every possible opportunity and I surely do love you for that, among a million other things. I try real hard to keep the old chin high but have to admit that it quivers once in a while. You just keep on writing as often as time permits and I'll ask no more, except for you to hurry on home quick and fast!

This is Saturday once more and we have a two and a half day week-end, which is of course appreciated. I guess I'm still not quite used to working, 'cause I surely looked forward to the extra day off. Almost can't believe it, though, that I am working on a job that leaves a little time for leisure. It's swell, and I don't feel unpatriotic about it either, 'cause when we work, we really work, and we keep plenty busy, which is how I like it. Speaking of my job, dear, I really like it, and don't feel so terribly green at it, after this week on my own. Haven't had to call but once, but Helen has been swell to help me over the rough spots. I've sort of neglected my shorthand since I started to work, but hope to pick up a few of the loose ends over the holiday.

I hope to be able to go to Modesto and Ceres tomorrow for a long planned visit with the folks. Corky called tonight to see if I was coming for sure. I had told your mom that I would try to make it down this week-end. There will probably be lots of people traveling by bus, though, so it may not be as easy as I hope for. We shall see. I'm kind of counting on seeing everyone 'cause it's been a long time since my last visit and Milly and Jim are going to be there too. Naturally, I'm anxious to see our precious little Phillip Cecil and Robbie, and all of the kids! Corabelle said that Roberta is to have her tonsils out this coming Wednesday. I'm glad, because they have been very bad, and you know how many terrible colds she has always had. Corky should do the same for herself. I didn't do very much again today, darling. Jeanie met me for lunch and it was too hot to go shopping, we didn't feel too flush either, so I was home soon after 3 O'clock, just after our new mailman brought your two wonderful letters. Gee, it was swell to hear from you, as always. Tonight I read the papers and caught up on the latest war news and funnies. I am glad to hear that you fellows are able to have some sort of paper there. I guess sending ours really wouldn't be so good because you would probably get a whole bunch at one time and have too little time to read them all. Anyway, I shall continue to save them all for you, dearest, and some cool evening soon, I hope, we'll sit by our fireplace and you can catch up on everything as we have heard and read it – all of the things you're doing these days to make history.

In Polly's last letter she sounded pretty perturbed that Jack never writes her any news of what you boys are doing and she begged me to call her if I ever hear of anything from you regarding same. It seems that Bill Tuscott wrote Anne all about things and stuff, in general, and also sent her some clippings from the 'Stars and Stripes.' His crew was all split up after their arrival and Bill had been in one crack-up and had a seven day leave afterward, but wasn't hurt I guess. Anyway, Polly was sort of upset when Anne called long distance and told her all about it. When I wrote to her, darling, I tried to explain how you fellows are duty bound not to write details of your business and how very much you spare us by not telling us everything, you sort of keep up civilian morale that way, darling, even though it is hard for us to stifle our curiosity. Speaking of Jack, is he still having a good time for himself, entertaining the 'native' gals over there? I must say, I don't think much him for it, if he is!

Darling, were you on that last mission of Doug's when his crew was lost? I know I shouldn't ask such a question, but I can't help but wonder. If you were, and if you know for sure that none of the boys had a chance, please tell me – it would help to know how to write to Pat. Her notification from the War Department merely listed him as 'missing,' which to me means there is yet hope. However, I'd just as soon not try to build that idea up too much if it isn't possible. Please try to answer me somehow, darling, 'cause Pat is really in a bad way – poor gal! She hasn't phoned me yet this evening, so she may be with Doug's relatives up in Seattle. I just can't believe that his number came up so fast! He was really a nice fellow, as were all of his crew members, including Jimmy Luce. He rode back to the base with you and Doug that morning you left Grand Island, you probably remember him, he was Doug's bombardier. I guess that's just how it is to be, though, as much as we hate to have it that way, and we just have to take it, huh? Life and death are two things that only God controls and he wills them as he sees fit, the latter always to the unhappiness of loved ones who are left behind.

Well dear, to get out of my 'morbid rut,' so to speak, what's cookin'? Have you received any of the three packages that I have sent to you? When you do get them let me know what the contents are 'cause I'd like to know what all the P.O. takes out! Those fellows probably have some pretty nice feasts, I'll bet, at times. How would you like to have some candied figs? I'm going to make some for you next week. Sound good honey? Evie is going to save me a big sack of figs from their tree. Celia was telling us how to candy them last night.

Well, dearest darling, this seems to be about all I can cook up in the way of a letter for tonight, I seem to have covered just about everything. I surely do love you honey (I saved the best subject for the last) and I miss you more and more every day! But I keep hoping and praying every day that you'll be home real soon and then we'll be happy again together for always. I make a little visit to the Cathedral (up the middle isle, remember it dear?) every morning on my way to work, and surely hope that God will take care of you always and keep you ever safe and please bring you home in a very little while, 'cause I need you. Until I see you again, on paper tomorrow, and always, I love you, dearest. May God bless you and watch over you forever! Good-night, honey-bun, pleasant dreams. I love you very much, with all my heart. All my love and kisses.

Hiya, honey! Boy, I'm happy tonight. The mailman brought me five swell letters from my darling today. That is the most I have ever received at one time from my honey. Thank-you, sweetheart! Someday I'll give you five big kisses for today's treat! I wonder if our letters may not even pass each other en route sometimes, as yours seem to travel faster than mine. I really think that most of yours come by air, darling, because they could hardly reach me in five days to eight days by boat, unless the boats travel much faster now than I've heard. Anyway, I'm surely happy to hear from you so often, my darling, and I still think you are the swellest guy in the whole world for being so sweet to write often, and for lots and lots of other things, naturally! You're really tops with me, honey, and I love you just an awful lot! Hm, Hm! Consider that a big hug, darling.

You mentioned something in one of your letters about Doug being officially declared missing. From the sound of that letter he was not stationed at your present base. It's surely tough to lose a swell fellow like he, and his crew too, but I know we're losing lots of others every day too and the world isn't going to stop turning because of such individual tragedies! I can readily understand why you other boys can't let it get you down, but please God, to end this awful war real soon, before you and lots of other fine boys become brutally hard-hearted as a result of such events!

Received a wire from Pat, who is now in Burbank. She is with Doug's sister and family. She called me tonight and she sounded pretty low. I did my best to build up her spirits. I also asked her to come for at least a few days visit here, as I think it would be very good for her. At least she could see new places and faces, if that would help. She really wants us to have her piano and said she had written several times to me about it, but has had no answer. I never received her letters, though, so can't figure it out. Anyway, I told her that I'd still like to have it if she wanted me to, as long as you don't mind, darling. I'll really and truly learn to play for you dearest.

Today, honey, I bought an anniversary greeting card for Ken and Dee and it brought back the memories of our first date. Remember our meeting, honey, that night we went to the fair and had such a wonderful time? Gee, we've been having lots of fun ever since that big night, haven't we dear? You've really been the swellest date any gal could ever dream of finding! No fooling, I'd do it all over again a thousand times! No matter what comes to us from this awful war (and I pray daily and nightly) that nothing will happen to mar our happiness. I know I shall have a huge store of beautiful memories that no one or nothing can ever take from me, and I wouldn't trade places with any other person I know! I guess I sort of, kind of, love you, darling! A little bit, anyway.

I'm sorry if I asked a lot of foolish questions that I should know you can't answer, but anyway, you know I'm interested, huh? I like the sound of the name of your new ship, dear, and I'm glad that Jack is going to leave it that! I think the 'Feather Merchant' sounds swell, and a name that my darling might have chosen for his ship! It's really cute! I'm sure glad you aren't flying that other old ship with the awful name. 'Old Coffins' gave me the wooleys! You can kid me if you like, darling, or try to do so, but I know very well you're doing lots of exciting things in the air these days. More power to all of you great fellows, only take good care of yourself and hurry home.

I think I forgot to tell you the latest news of Jack Opdyke. He has been at Kearney, Nebraska, (where I thought he was) and had been to a field in Kansas where some officer took him up for a ride in the new B-29. He was really crazy about the ship and even got to handle it in the air. Celia says that he says that he won't be contented now until they give him one of those to fly across the pond! I guess it is a pretty swell ship.

Gotta go to bed now, honey-bun. I've enjoyed talking to you, as always. You are a son and brother any family should be mighty proud of, and I know you rate plenty high with all of the folks. Thanks for not going dancing, etc. without me, darling, we'll make up for it when you come home. I don't even miss such fun 'cause it wouldn't be fun without you, sweetheart! Good night, my dearest, May God bless you always and please keep you ever safe 'cause I love you truly and need you always. G'bye for now! I'll be seeing you soon 'in all the old familiar places.' All my love and kisses. Margaret.

Chapter 31
Schweinfurt-Regensburg

The lights in our Nissen hut clicked on at around 0300 hours and Bob Nelson, our squadron operations officer, was standing at the door.

"Good morning gentlemen. Get up! Combat mission today. Briefing at 0400."

Baldy wasn't one to wake up easily and he mumbled something in Lithuanian.

"Breakfast is at combat mess," Nelson added.

We knew something was going on because we were told to expect a mission today and we could see a lot of activity out at the hard stands at night. We didn't know the particulars, but from the looks of things it was going to be a maximum effort, meaning everything and everyone that could fly, would fly. It was just enough to clue you in that maybe you should try to get some sleep instead of drinking all night down at the club.

"Good lord, what day is this?" Ted mumbled.

"It's Tuesday," Art said.

"No, I mean what's the date?"

Ted rubbed his eyes. No one answered, no one really knew. Baldy stumbled over to the calendar on the wall; it was Tuesday-the 17th of August. We hurriedly got cleaned up and shaved and then we mounted our bikes for the awkward half asleep ride to the combat mess. I was surprised to find a meal fit for a king. Fresh bacon, fresh eggs (not powdered), coffee, milk, fresh fruit. I was happy indeed to see this. I hadn't caught on yet, I guess I was slow on the uptake because, after all, this was only my third mission. Art and Baldy had been here a while, this would be their 17th mission. They clued me in that when they fed you like this it was kind of considered a possible last meal. It meant that the mission was going to be a tough one. After breakfast we lingered outside for a while and grabbed a smoke, then headed over to the briefing room and took a seat. At 0400 the room was called to attention and Colonel Nazzaro walked briskly to the stage at the front of the room. He told everyone to be seated and then spoke those words again. As he pulled the tarp from the map on the wall he said,

"Gentlemen, your target for today is Schweinfurt, Germany."

As we all sat there staring at the map a loud moan was repeated throughout the crowd of fliers. We saw the ribbons on the map indicating our flight plan and it seemed like it went all the way through Germany. I was still green, so I didn't quite fathom the meaning or consequences of what I was looking at. It looked like a complicated mission, for sure, with a lot of ships taking part. Colonel Nazzaro called Lieutenant Thayer to the front for the particulars. This was to be a three stage attack. There would be diversionary raids on numerous German airfields by B-26 and B-25 medium bombers designed to confuse the German fighter response. Meanwhile, the 4th Bombardment Wing, made up of seven groups and 146 bombers, would strike the Messerschmitt fighter factory at Regensburg. Additionally confusing the Germans, this wing would then continue on to North Africa instead of turning to return to England. Our wing, the 1st Bombardment Wing, would follow closely behind the Regensburg force making it appear that we were headed to Regensburg as well. Short of Regensburg, however, we would turn toward Schweinfurt, presumably before the German fighters could refuel and rearm and counter our attack. This indeed would be a maximum effort with all flyable ships utilized. The 1st Wing would field 12 groups, 230 bombers, including three composite groups made up of various ships from all the regular groups. The 381st would be contributing 26 bombers today. What could go wrong?

Even though we had been assigned "Ole Flak Sack," she was still undergoing some serious maintenance after a non-mission belly landing in early August by our friend Leo Jarvis. Leo got in some trouble for that one, because I don't think it was on purpose. At the next mission briefing after the belly landing the colonel made Leo sit on a stool at the front of the briefing room. He had to wear a dunce hat and when the colonel walked by someone kicked the stool out from under him. Leo wasn't too happy about it, but he took the ribbing in good form. All he had to do was wait a week and somebody else would do something and the focus would be off of him. That's the way things were. To Roger's shock and dismay we had been flying "Old Coffins" since our ship got damaged. He was none too happy about that after having seen that poor navigator being hauled through the hatch and spilling his blood all over Chaplain Brown. Margaret, I'm sure, wouldn't be too happy about that ship's ominous name either. Fortunately, we wouldn't be flying "Old Coffins" to Schweinfurt. We were assigned a ship called "The Hellion," tail number 23177. Engine start-up time was scheduled for 0600 with take-off at 0630. I ran through my usual routine of hopping a ride out to the hard stand, grabbing my flight gear on the way, and preparing the ship while Jack and Roger got more detailed information for the mission. Ted picked up his and Roger's guns. The enlisted men were already in the ship and preparing their stations when I arrived at 0530. As I sat in the right hand seat I could hear the steady low drum of the ground generator and the clicking of metal as the boys nervously went over their fifty caliber guns again and again. Jack and Roger came on scene at about 0545 and we began our final pre-flight checks. At 0600 sharp we began engine start-up and warm-up only to be called by the tower and told that we would be delayed for an hour due to very low and heavy cloud cover. At 0700 we started the engines again and sat at idle for several minutes awaiting the order to taxi, but instead we were again advised of another delay due to weather. At 0900 we again went through engine start-up and sat on the hard stand warming up. A red flare was fired from the control tower signaling another delay and we again shut down the engines. This time, as we sat there discussing the many aspects of this mission that have to go perfect in order for us not to die, someone brought around some spam sandwiches that we all ate while we were waiting. Finally, at 1100 hours, we were given the signal for engine start-up and taxi. Our lead ship started his take-off roll at 1130. As we made our way to the head of the runway Jack and I were talking about the delay. It occurred to us that, unless the Regensburg force delayed also, we would be sitting ducks when we got within reach of Galland's Luftwaffe boys and the Regensburg force couldn't have delayed this long and still hope to reach North Africa in daylight. Oh shit, we both said almost simultaneously, we're going to get hell from those fighters today for a long-long flight deep into Germany. As we pushed the throttles to full and started down the runway I said it again over the intercom-what could go wrong?

After form up over England we continued our climb out over the North Sea to 26,000 feet with a heading toward Germany as we picked up our P-47 fighter escort. We were flying in the low squadron and Leo Jarvis was off of our starboard side in "Ole Swayback." The flight seemed colder than usual with more humidity. When we got close to the Dutch border our leader, Colonel Gross, ordered the formations down to 17,000 feet to get under a solid cloud layer. He was afraid that there may not be a break in the layer by the time we reached Schweinfurt. I'm sure it was a tough choice to make, but it would be to our heavy disadvantage. The German fighters could perform better at that altitude, and the flak gunners would have an easier time ranging in on us. What a wonderful day this was turning out to be. The P-47's left us near Eupen, Belgium, and it was only a few minutes later that all hell broke loose. Almost every gunner on the ship began reporting enemy fighters at the same time. As they swooped by I could clearly see the 20mm cannon firing through the yellow noses of their FW-190's. It was a good thing that the boys loaded extra ammunition for the flight. We were going to need it. There wasn't much for me to do except watch for fighters so I slumped down in my seat and pulled my helmet down low, somehow thinking that would protect me. Five ME-109's came at us from 12 O'clock level flying line abreast with their guns firing and tracer rounds flying by each side of our ship. I don't know how they missed us! All our guns were firing and the squawk box was filled with the chatter of calling out fighters and other expletives. Jack yelled at the boys to can the chatter and only call out useful information for other gunners. It wasn't long before we saw our first ship go down. He wasn't the first in the wing, but he was the first we saw. It was our deputy group lead, Lieutenant Painter and Captain Nelson in "King Malfunction II." He dropped out with an engine on fire. Thankfully, at least, (some) parachutes were seen. The Jerries came at us relentlessly and from all directions. The bam-bam-bam of Eddie's top turret guns right over my head was deafening. I could see enemy fighters going down in flames all over the sky. At least we were making them pay. Smitty yelled that he got one, so did Tex.

> 3 O'clock high, five of em, coming down through the formation! Eddie, Al, get those guys! Here they come again! Going around to your side Carl, light those bastards up! Watch your ammo, we have a long way to go! Short bursts guys, short bursts! God damn it, wait till they're in range! Now! Now! Ted! 12 O'clock shoot those bastards! Frenchy, you've got Eddie's back, don't let any sneak up on us from 6 high! Roger that! Here they come again! Fire. Fire! Skipper, Darrow in 'Our Mom' has an engine hit, but it looks like he's keeping up! Roger that! Keep an eye on him!

The path to our initial point, or IP, took forever. The terror was real, but we became numb to it because there was just too much to do, too much to see, smell, hear. The pop-pop-pop of the guns, the smell of gunpowder, the clinking of the empty shells hitting the deck and being kicked around by Eddie, the sight of 20mm guns flashing, and each flash, you know, carries an exploding shell with someone's name on it. We were on overload but the boys fought on because it was all we could do. We took a couple hits that passed right through us, but it didn't hit anything vital. "The Hellion" was flying magnificently and she responded promptly to every small evasive input or engine adjustment. All the gauges remained within normal limits and we weren't losing any oil or smoking. The fight just went on and on. Finally, we reached a point between Mannheim and Frankfurt and we turned left toward the IP. Most of the fighters departed at that time, no doubt running low on ammo and fuel after chopping us to pieces. A few hung around to give us hell and we soon lost two more ships. We didn't know for sure how many ships the wing lost, but we could hear the constant call out of another one going down and the helpless pleas of-c'mon guys, bail out! Bail out! We also knew that our group had lost several so far too. How many we didn't know. We had six ships flying as part of a composite group within the wing, and twenty ships in our normal group formation. Obviously, we hadn't fooled anyone on this multi-faceted brainstorm of a mission. I'm sure every last one of us wanted to get our hands on the guys who planned this and wring their lousy necks. There was no question that the targets were important, but for a mission like this to succeed the timing has to be perfect. When the weather delayed us like it did, it should have been scrubbed.

The flak was getting thick now, but at least the fighters backed off of us while we were in the flak field. The guns were quiet, but the sounds of the exploding flak had taken their place. Loud bangs and little black clouds of death floating around in the sky. Shards of metal bouncing off of the skin of our "Old Hellion" and sliding down the side of her fuselage like nails on a chalkboard.

"C'mon baby, you can get us home, I know you can," I said.

"I hope she can Quinn, I surely hope she can," Jack said. "Take the controls for a few minutes, my arms are killing me."

I took the controls as we continued on through the flak. All of a sudden, up ahead, there was an ugly black flak explosion directly under Baldy and Art in "The Joker." They were thrown straight up into the prop wash of another flight of ships and they nearly lost control but somehow managed to get back in position.

"Holy shit," Jack said, "did you see that? That was close! I hope they're all okay!"

As we approached the IP Jack took back the controls and we turned on the IP toward the bomb run. Control of the ship was turned over to Ted. We continued to be knocked about by the turbulence and concussions of the exploding flak. Finally, Ted announced bombs away and we lurched upwards and the bomb bay doors were closed as we took back the controls. Right at that instant there was a loud explosion over at Leo Jarvis' ship and he nearly rolled over to his starboard. When he did we could see his number 4 engine was on fire and part of his fuel tank had been blown away. He regained control briefly, but took another hit on his number 3 engine. Leo waved goodbye to us in his window, signifying that he was dropping out. He slid to his right and dropped rather quickly, probably intending to dive to put out the flames. Man-oh-man. Painter, Nelson, Jarvis. I wondered who else wouldn't be back at Ridgewell tonight. God be with you Leo, God be with you, I said over the com as we watched "Ole Swayback" fall from sight. What could go wrong?

Hello Darling! How's my honey today? I received four V-Mail letters from you today, so things are improving right along. I also received a missing you card from yourself, a very cute one indeed. I loved the smell of perfume on it! One of your letters had a running account of the newly acquired Perry, namely Phillip Cecil. I also received a birthday card from mom with a letter, and Milly had written a letter on the card. I haven't been doing an awful lot more today than yesterday, except that I did do a few hours of work, and also playing cards for about an hour. As soon as I finish writing to you I am going to have to go and fix a tire on my bike, though, 'cause I'm getting tired of pumping it up all the time.

That was too bad about Lola May's younger brother getting killed in action. But that is just something to be expected, but always hurts someone, nevertheless. You are doing pretty good to be putting up peaches and pears. I'll bet they are really good, and maybe they will be coming in handy some fine day this winter. As for the fellows whom I have met from Sacramento, the only one whom I remember is George Darrow. You might know him, but I didn't before. You aren't supposed to mention who all you see over here anyway. But a few won't matter if I don't mention what they're doing. As far as Judge Timmons' son goes, I haven't seen him, but I guess we're all doing about that same thing, and quite frequently besides. I forgot to thank you yesterday for all the airmail stamps that I received from sweet you. I will try to do them all justice. I guess I should be writing V-Mail letters to save space and such, but I don't imagine the boats are going back from here as crowded for space as they are on the road over here.

I guess it's about time for me to be canning all the chatter as I haven't much of anything in the way of news to impart to you at this time. So-long for tonight darling. I love ya an awful lot and miss you something terrible! But it can't all last forever, so I'll be seeing ya. May God bless you darling. Cecil.

Chapter 32
All The Brave Young Men

There wasn't time to dwell on Leo and his crew going down. Our business at hand was to not join him. With all the scattered yelling on the radio about bombers going down, parachutes, Jerry fighters and flak, I couldn't believe that we hadn't been hit hard yet ourselves. I wondered how long our luck would hold out. After bomb release we made a sweeping left turn and began re-assembly procedures. Ships were scattered all over the place and it seemed like we were a little bunched up. After clearing the clouds on the way in we climbed back up in altitude again and this may have altered our timing and formations a bit. But now there was no need to maintain radio silence, they knew we were here and where we were. Unfortunately, they knew where we had to go to get home too, and they'd be waiting for us. A fellow Sacramentan, George Darrow, had fallen behind the formation earlier with a feathered engine. He managed to keep up for a few minutes, but soon started falling back. We thought he would be a sitting duck. I could hear him talking about sliding back into the formation somewhere in a more rearward group. I'm glad he was still there. It didn't take long for the fighters to come after us again. There were five ME-109's lining up for a head on. Eddie and Ted blasted away at them until they swooped down low. I don't know if they hit anything, but they didn't hit us, thank God. The com was alive again with the chatter of the guys calling out Jerry fighters,

> 190's at 3 O'clock, holy shit there's some twin engine
> bastards out there, looks like ME-110's! I don't know what
> they're shooting but it looks like a flying fence post! Smitty,
> 9 O'clock low! Short busts guys; we have a long way to go.
> Wait till they're close enough to hit!

It went on and on and the pounding of Eddie's guns over my head gave me a splitting headache. I swore I'd be joining the boys tonight for a drink-if we make it back-and I'd buy. It would take us a little over an hour to make it to Eupen, where our own fighters were scheduled to rendezvous with us.

Flying fence posts, huh! I couldn't understand what Eddie was talking about, but then I saw one. They were white cylindrical things with smoke coming out the back. We had heard about rockets, but we hadn't seen any yet, and there they were being shot by the ME-110's. None of them came close to us, but we could see them off in the distance. They weren't very fast, and it would just be a curious thing to see if it weren't for the fact that you knew it would blow your plane apart if it hit you. Our group was doing pretty good on the return flight and we hadn't had any ships go down for a while. The fighters were still hitting us, but not as heavy as before. All along the return trip we could see billowing smoke columns rising up from the ground. Those smoke columns were the final resting place of B-17's and some crew members who never got out of their ship. Oh my God, I thought out loud, there's so many! I couldn't bring myself to count them. Jack called them death pyres. We droned on and on until we reached the Rhine and then all hell broke loose again. The fighters jumped us from every direction and the fight was on once more. It would be our final push to get out of enemy territory. Another 381st ship went down and our hearts began to sink. Bam-bam-bam, our guns blasted away. Finally, Jack told them to let those bastards have it with everything we've got. We're getting close enough that we don't have to worry about conserving our ammunition. The boys really let loose when a Jerry plane came around. The whole group must have had the same idea. Suddenly there was the sound of bullets hitting us. Frautchi, our radio operator, said there were some holes in the bomb bay area and that he was going to check it out. A couple minutes later he came back on and said it didn't look like it hit anything important. Thank God, it must have been a regular machine gun round and not an exploding 20mm shell! On and on it went until, all of a sudden, there they were, like angels from heaven, P-47's! We were still about fifteen miles from Eupen and we saw a huge formation of fighters a few thousand feet above us. At first Eddie called out enemy fighters at 12 O'clock high but the more we looked at them the more it became apparent that they were our guys. It must be farther than they had ever been before. My thought was that they could hear the panic and terror on the radios and they were putting themselves out there to help us. We have got to buy those guys some drinks when this is over! They flew about midway past our lead ships and then they peeled over in great waves, splitting into smaller attack formations as they sped downward, lining up on the Jerry fighters. I don't think the Krauts ever saw it coming. With a great swoosh the P-47's sliced down through the Jerries and took out many of them in the process. There were great dog fights all over the sky, and then, as suddenly as it began, it was all over. We were home free! I began to scan our formation to see what I could see and finally realized how chewed to pieces we were as a group. I said to Jack,

"My God, there's a lot of ships missing Jack. A lot!"

We flew the rest of the way across the Netherlands and Holland and out over the North Sea. Once we had water underneath us we really began to breathe a sigh of relief. British Spitfires began to form up around us to escort us home. Not too close, though, they didn't want any trigger happy gunners still in shock to let loose on them thinking they were bad guys. The P-47's had to cut and run for home, they must have been running real low on fuel. I couldn't believe how far they came to rescue us. They certainly earned a drink in our book. Then, there it was, the most beautiful sight in the world at that moment, the white cliffs of Dover. Seeing those cliffs really meant we had made it, especially since our ship was still flying beautifully. Our fuel load was still pretty good, and we had no injured crew members, so we would have to wait our turn to land. When it finally came our turn we lined "The Hellion" up with runway 28 and slowly descended toward our let down as Jack ordered gear down.

"Gear down and locked," I said.

A few minutes later our tires chirped that we had made it. We rolled out like normal and caught a taxiway to our hard stand where the ground crew and several others had been sweating us out. That's what we called waiting for the return of the ships and crews-sweating it out. As the brakes were set, and the ground crew chalked the wheels, we shut down the engines and breathed a huge sigh of relief. We both just sat there, unable to move, staring out the windshield, totally exhausted and spent. Even though it's ice cold in flight, I think we both lost ten or fifteen pounds in sweat. At long last we lowered our gear bags and ourselves down through the hatch and saw the rest of the boys down on their hands and knees kissing the ground. Jack and I looked at each other and simultaneously dropped down and kissed the earth with them. I walked over to "The Hellion" and inspected the holes in her side while running my hand over her. She got us home. Somehow we made it. Through the grace of God, we made it. So many other fine young men did not. Soon, the rest of the ships that survived were all in their assigned spots. George Darrow was not among them. After a mission like that there was no way that any one of us wanted to go to a debriefing, but it was mandatory. We all hopped in a truck that was there to give us a ride and we bounced our way over to the interrogation building. It was there that we would learn just how bad the 381st had been hit.

The man who woke us up just this morning, Captain Bob Nelson, was gone. Painter was gone, Darrow was gone, and Leo Jarvis was gone. Jarvis was the one I knew the best. He was on his 14th mission. Is there no hope for us to finish 25? It looked hopeless. I didn't really know most of the others who were lost. It was a common practice to keep your circle of friends small for just this very reason. A man can only bear so much loss and grief. It is better to know who they are, if you have to, rather than to know them. It was a self-preservation technique that we all practiced. I recalled being told that by the veteran crews as we got to Ridgewell. It made some sense, although curiously so, but now it has really sunk in. Now I understood what they meant, and how right they were. We completed interrogation and a couple of the boys got credit for several fighters confirmed down. Man, they earned their money today! We were questioned about Leo going down but there wasn't much we could tell them. We hadn't seen any chutes by the time we lost sight of him. We caught a ride back to our hut and got cleaned up, then we headed down to the officers club and began drinking. It was a somber and quiet place that night. The Mighty Eighth, the Mighty 381st had lost a lot of great men. The shock of what happened was sinking in as we looked around the room and saw all the empty chairs. We didn't know each and every man who fell today, but we had a list of ships. We raised our glasses almost silently to each ship lost, the men if we knew them, and simply the memory of their crews if we didn't, and the hope that they all got out and would get home after the war. Baldy posted the list on the wall and God Speed was sent to the crews of "King Malfunction II," "Ole Swayback," "Our Mom," "Lucky Lady," "Chug Alug LuLu," "Sweet Le Lani," "Uncle Sammy," "Strato Sam," "Hell's Angels," "Damfino," and an un-named ship from the 534th squadron. Chaplain Brown came in and sat with us and shared our grief. The chaplain would sweat out all the boys on all the missions. Roger and he had become close friends. I, as well as most the men on the base, had sought counsel and solace from Chaplain Brown from time to time. He was truly upset, as were we all that night. He was a good man who understood us and genuinely felt our pain. He wrote a fine letter to the family of all those who were lost. Colonel Nazzaro wrote letters as well, but he also had the responsibility of planning for the continuation of operations. Chaplain Brown was deeply affected by the losses and keenly aware of what we were feeling. I didn't often see the chaplain drink, but on this occasion he sat down with us and Baldy's crew and we took turns drinking English Ale and Irish whiskey.

"Here's to Leo, and all the fine young men who fell today," the Chaplain said.

As we raised our glasses someone came charging in the club door and announced that George Darrow had successfully ditched in the channel and was picked up by a British rescue boat. All ten of his crew were safe and should be back at Ridgewell tomorrow! The chaplain blessed the room and the sudden announcement and with swelling in our eyes from the good news, we called it a night. It had been a long day, too long!

I am writing to you as the Chaplain of the 381st Bomb Group and also to reflect the minds of all the officers and enlisted men of the command. It is by no means easy to write on a matter which has been a severe blow to us and which came to you as a shock. To say that we feel the loss as keenly as you is hardly true, but permit me to say that, if you were here with us, you would see the effect which a loss of a buddy has upon us.

Living away from our homes as we do is not the most pleasant circumstance; hence we cherish the friendships we have in the 381st. When these friendships are broken, it makes our life on the base even more unpleasant. To see our buddies taken from us is something which we cannot even describe in words.

May we of the 381st Bomb Group express as best we can our deepest sympathy to you in the loss of our comrade. He died with a number of his companions while in the performance of duty, on a dangerous and hazardous detail, necessary for the accomplishment of our mission. An impressive memorial service was held in our chapel, attended by the members of the group.

I would like to quote here from a prayer offered at the memorial service; 'We are grateful in life for the privilege of friendship, and our minds now go back to the days of association we had with these men. We who are here have laughed with them, played with them, and worked with them. Together we fought for the best interests of humanity, willing to give our utmost that goodwill might be established on earth as it is in heaven. These men have given not their utmost: they have given their all. May we not forget the purpose for which they sacrificed their lives.

Ever mindful of this purpose, may we so live that these dead shall not have died in vain.'

Sincerely,

Chaplain James Good Brown.[3]

---

[3] James Good Brown, <u>The Mighty Men of the 381st: Heroes All</u> (Salt Lake City: Publishers Press, 1984) 82.

Chapter 33
Reflection and Resolve

Greetings again to my sweetheart. I didn't get a letter again today, but I'm not whining, just hoping hard that I'll get one tomorrow. That will make the long weekend easier to take. Had a postcard today from Bonnie Pelton. She says Bob has been missing since the 17th of August. Bob McCowen (remember, he and Marcia were in our Pullman from Phoenix to Washington, they had the typewriter, he sang and she was such a good sport). He is missing as of that date also. Guess all of you boys participated in that raid! Sure hate to hear of the possible losses of these fine boys, but guess we have to take it. Bonnie also wrote that Bill Nelson, who was with you at Gardner Field, was killed in Lancaster, California. Bonnie seems to be taking her news much better than Pat did, but then she is younger. I admire her, though, for keeping her little chin up and hoping and trusting in God that Bob is alright somewhere. That is really the best way to take such a report. I wrote her a letter tonight 'cause I've been thinking of her lately, and I plan to write her at least a card this weekend.

I got a letter from Polly and she told me of you boys being the lead ship in your flight. Gee, that's swell, darling. Sure wish you could write me a few details now and then, but I know you hesitate to do so 'cause you wouldn't want to get anyone into trouble. Polly also spoke of Jack's 'mentioning' that you are making lots of flights here and there and that you'll all be home real soon, so here's hoping that will be any day now. It sounds as though you boys have really been making some long and tedious hops, with the lack of sleep you mention! Polly also wrote of one mission you boys went on, at which time Jack lost about eight pounds. Sounds like maybe it was that big jaunt we read about recently over Germany and on to North Africa bases. Nice going darling, wherever it was, but do take care of yourself always, and catch up on your sleep as much as

Daniel J. Quinley

possible. You looked so swell the last time that I saw you that I want you to come home looking as much that way as possible. She also said that the doctor had told her that she couldn't possibly carry 'junior' the full length of time and he expects him any day now. She has been in bed almost ever since she got home from Grand Island, so I guess she really paid for that trip. I would have done the same, though, I imagine, so she shouldn't be blamed too much. Poor kid, I hope she doesn't have too much trouble before it's all over. That would be pretty hard on her, especially without Jack there to hold her hand!

Gee honey, I sure do wish that you could get some snapshots taken and send them over. Other fellows send them over; won't they let your bunch do the same? I saw a snapshot of Clark Gable and a bomb the ship he was in dropped on the 4th of July. It said on it 'To Hitler from Kay,' she is the cashier in DeVon's Jewelry Store, and the pilot of the ship was Carl Stackhouse. It was a good picture. I guess it was taken when Clark Gable was taking those aerial photographs. Anyway, I'd sure like to have some snapshots of my darling 'cause I haven't seen him for so long, not that the pictures around here aren't swell, but I'd just like to keep up to date. Do you still have your camera and the film that you had at Grand Island? It really should be used before too many months because it gets old. C'mon, honey, take some and send them to me! I'm more excited now than ever to hear all about your activities over there. Sure wish that you could put me wise a little, but suppose you really shouldn't mention anything about everything, but I'd sure like to hear some of the news. It must be plenty thrilling to be the lead ship of your flight, that's a really fine accomplishment. But then, I knew you and your gang couldn't help but be right in there in the very front row for your part in the big show!

I went to a show with Jeanie Heitman. Her hubby had to work till midnight. We went to the Alhambra where we saw 'Heaven Can Wait,' in Technicolor, and 'Henry Aldrich Swings It.' Both were swell pictures and we

224

thoroughly enjoyed them, but now I'm sleepy, it's only a quarter of 1:00, so no wonder! This is the latest I've been up for a long long time! I love you with all my heart, as always, and surely miss you more than you'll ever know, but I'm sure it can't be much longer before you boys will be on your way home, then I'll truly be happy once more! Until next time, sweetheart, and always, May God bless you and watch over you, 'cause I love you very much and want nothing more than to have you come home to me real, real soon. Good night, honey-bun! I'll be seeing you soon! All my love and kisses. Margaret.

The officers mess was half empty. What a sight to tear your heart out, all those empty chairs that were filled just yesterday were now a ghostly reminder of how fragile our time here is. We slept in till about 9 O'clock, no one really wanted to get up and moving. Schweinfurt was on everyone's mind, and would be for the rest of our lives, if we lived through this. After breakfast we meandered about the base for a while wondering what was coming next. The maintenance crews were already busy trying to patch up the damaged ships from yesterday. I imagine some would even need new engines after a day like that. We didn't spare the engines while trying to get out of Germany and back home. The maintenance crews had their work cut out for them, that was for sure. Around noon a truck arrived with George Darrow and his men. They were all dressed in British flight crew attire, packing their wet and salty clothes in bags. They were whisked off to interrogation so they could debrief the mission. After they were done it was our turn to talk with George. We all told him how great it was to see him, and that we had feared the worst when he didn't return. He said it was rough and the Jerry fighters kept raking his ship over and over and that it was a pure miracle that no one was seriously hurt or killed. He said by the time he reached the North Sea he lost his third engine and had to ramp up the power on the only remaining engine so far that there was no way to tell how long it would last. He had the throttle full and his supercharger running at full boost and could tell his cylinder heads were overheating and were going to blow at any time. He said they threw everything overboard that wasn't bolted down so they could stay airborne as long as possible. Eventually, they ditched without much difficulty and climbed into their life rafts. He said they were only out there a little over an hour before they were picked up. He excused himself and went to get checked out by the flight surgeon. He spoke in a monotone voice and we could tell he wasn't himself, but who could blame him after what he'd just been through.

Not much went on for the rest of August. There was a mission on the 19th, but we only contributed one ship from our squadron. The rest of the group had some aborts due to weather and what not. Our crew didn't fly again until the 27th, when we took part on a mission to Watten, France, about 120 nautical miles north of Paris. It was a milk run, and all our ships returned. That was a nice feeling for once. There was very little flak and only a few enemy fighters that acted like they weren't too interested in mixing it up with us. It was actually the most beautiful flight I think I had ever been on. The air was brisk and clean with a clear bright blue sky. The thing that caught my attention and almost made me forget we were at war was when we were close to Watten we could see both Paris and London at the same time. It was an amazing thing to see. Everyone in the ship was silent for a few minutes as we stared at the view. Tex brought us back to reality as he called out an enemy fighter that was circling our formation. But it never came in for the attack. I guess since it was France, and not his fatherland, it just wasn't worth his risk. I suppose he felt it was better to live and fight another day over Germany when he had greater numbers.

Back on the 20th Colonel Nazzaro had a pep talk with us because he could see how our morale was falling apart. My crew got a break after Schweinfurt for some reason, but many others continued to fly, even though the missions were milk runs. I guess they tried to give us a break while they rebuilt the group. Many of the surviving ships needed major repairs before heading back into combat. The evening of the 18th the colonel was in the officers club having a few drinks with us. Art Sample was sitting next to him and talk turned to Schweinfurt, what had become known around the base as Black Tuesday. The colonel made a remark that made Art nearly insane with rage and he began yelling and looked like he was going to attack the colonel. Baldy and Roger managed to hold him back. The remark the colonel made-made it sound like he was more broken up about his job of having to replace personnel and ships than he was about our lost friends. I didn't take it that way, but that's the way it sounded. Many of the officers didn't like Colonel Nazzaro because he seemed cold to our losses and frustrations, but he's the boss and he had a lot on his plate. He *has* to think about those things. He *has* to think beyond the losses because that's what he has to do to be able to manage an air group that's in a war. He was also criticized for only flying on milk runs, but I didn't think that was so unusual

226

either. How would we manage if our group commander kept getting shot down? If one stops and analyzes it, the colonel was doing a fine job. That didn't help us, however, with our frustrations and feelings of doom. I didn't know how many crews had completed their tour of duty yet, but I think it was only a couple, and none from here. It was beginning to look like it was nearly impossible, especially if they planned to be sending us deeper and deeper into Germany without fighter escort. We all thought it was just a matter of time before our number came up and that's all she wrote. Everyone began to have a pretty fatalistic view of our time at Ridgewell. The worst part came when the Colonel left the club and everyone went back to drinking. Baldy had a few more drinks and then a ground officer sitting at a table with a few of his friends began talking loud about how we combat officers think we're hot shit and we get spoiled with whatever we want. Words were exchanged but it seemed like it was blowing over until that officer went into the latrine. Baltrusaitis followed him in and the next thing we knew there was a terrible commotion coming from in there and yelling and screaming. His friends tried to go help him, but Art and Roger blocked the door. After Baldy came out, alone, we scooped him up and got him out of there. He had beaten the living shit out of that ground officer without getting a scratch on himself, except a few bloodied knuckles. Baldy was one tough Lithuanian! He fell off a bridge that provided a walkway over a small ditch near our hut while stumbling back from the club one night. He came in all muddy and hit the sack that way. At 0400 the operations officer tried to wake him for a flight but he just cussed him out in Lithuanian. The officer got mad and tipped Baldy's bunk over and he came up swinging and cussing but never hit anything. Needless to say he didn't have to fly that day. I don't know how, but he never got in trouble for anything. Perhaps because he was such a courageous pilot and great leader. The men would follow him through anything, and the colonel knew it.

The colonel's pep talk did do some good within the group. He talked about the war and how tough other groups had it and especially the ground forces and how it was our job to pave the way forward. To eliminate Germany's ability to make war by blasting their factories and infrastructure. He spoke of our fallen comrades and the men who were in prisoner of war camps; how they would not appreciate our giving up after their sacrifices. It was a powerful speech and I think many took it to heart. If you already didn't like the Colonel, it probably didn't change your mind, although I think it instilled some given responsibility in us as officers to move forward and fight this war to the end. He said missions would be smaller for a while as we built our forces back up, but to make no mistake about it, when we are back up to full strength we would be seeing deep penetration raids again. We were happy to have a break, so to speak, but we knew it was only a matter of time before we suffered another maximum effort; another Schweinfurt.

The 24th was a sad and stressful day. Poor George never quite got over the Schweinfurt raid and his ditching. I guess he had been telling the doctor that he couldn't fly anymore. He had gotten really depressed and was sure he was going to die. He couldn't hardly drink a cup of coffee or light his cigarettes his hands shook so badly. The doctor talked to Colonel Nazzaro and recommended that he not fly, but the colonel didn't agree. He thought there wasn't anything wrong with George that wasn't wrong with everybody and he ordered him to fly. We could all see that he was cracking up. All he needed was some R&R, but the colonel would have none of it. A mission was scheduled for the 24th and as George was taxiing out, his ship suffered a blown tire. The loud bang scared the life out of him so bad that he slammed on the brakes, dropped out through the hatch and took off running across the field. It sounds like a sad state of affairs, but it's how everyone felt. He just needed a break. The doctor this time put his foot down and he arranged to have George sent to a big hospital for treatment. We hoped we would see him again soon. He's a valuable member of our group and a great pilot. Roger spoke to the Chaplain about it and we were assured that George would be back, but only when he was ready.[4] The crew spent a lot of time either at the officers club, or at the King's Head Pub in town. Eventually, September would arrive and our mission schedules would increase. Whether or not everyone was filled with a renewed resolve didn't matter. Being good men who wanted this war to be over, we would mount our ships and fly wherever they told us to fly. I don't think the feeling of dread or doom ever goes away, you just become numb to it and you get on with what you're paid to do. We would soon find out. What choice did we have? We could all run off through the field or break up a pub in town and get thrown in the brig, or we could get on with it. No one wanted to climb back in the ship and be shot at again, we knew we were all living on borrowed time, but this thing was bigger than us. We would all do our duty. I suppose we would all drink just a little bit more to numb the images burned into our minds.

---

[4] . George Darrow did indeed come back. He went on to have a distinguished combat career.

Chapter 34
Stuttgart

Greetings again and how is my honey this cool evening? Fine, I hope, 'cause this is the kind of weather you like the best. I just finished watering the yard, lawn, and flowers, and swept the sidewalks before dinner, and also started the water running, then finished everything after I had done the dishes. Boy, that was surely swell news that came through today! Italy surrendered last Friday! That is really a good thing for them as much as for us. They were taking a plenty rough beating from you boys these past few weeks, so it's about time they got wise to themselves. That should mean that it won't be so many more days until the European mess will be cleaned up and my darling will be home again. Gee, that's going to be a wonderful day, honey, when you come home to me. I'll sure be a happy gal, no fooling. Please God to make it come real soon. Darling, your wife is the new Nurse's Aide Corps chauffeur starting next week, the 15th. The Red Cross has decided we're worthy of transportation provisions (finally), so since it was my idea in the first place, and I gladly offered my services, I shall see that all of the aides get safely home from the hospitals. I shall drive five nights each week (Monday through Friday) to get the thing going and the Motor Corps will take care of Saturday and Sunday. Before the bad weather starts we want to work out some plan whereby the girls can be taken to the hospitals as well as delivered to their homes after their evening work is through.

How are you and the 'Feather Merchant' getting along these days? The name of your other ship really sounded bad, 'Old Coffins.' I wouldn't have blamed Jack for wanting to change it to the 'Polly Jo II.' Whoever thought up such a moniker? They must have been like that other crew back in Grand Island. Remember Ken Alexander and that bunch? I'm glad you didn't change it to the 'Mad Maggie' though. At least you're out of that ship and in the

'Feather Merchant' now. It's very nice of Jack to leave the name alone to honor the man who named her in the first place. I'm sorry Leo was lost, honey. I pray that he was picked up and is safe. Gee, some articles in the paper tell about fellows writing home about missions they've been on and even mentioned things that happened. I thought (and do think) that that was illegal. Maybe they just get away with it, huh? I'm still counting on hearing some good tales when you come home, dear. You save me everything, unless you'd rather forget it all, as you like it. Just heard the 10 O'clock news and things are really looking up, but I know there's a lot farther to go. Germany and Japan are still plenty powerful and will be tough to lick, but we'll do it!

I got a nice letter from Bonnie. She hasn't heard anything further from the War Department concerning Bob, but still has her hopes up, which is the best way to be. She is working, and that helps a lot. She had a letter from Vince and Hildred in which Vince wrote that he would be in New Mexico about four more months and then he would be looking for Bob. Guess he'll be joining you fellows over there too, only I hope my sweetheart will be headed for home long before that length of time! You try real hard, honey, to get home soon, huh, 'cause gee whiz but it's lonesome without you. Just read in tonight's Bee that Jack Noce is missing in action. I received a card from Jean today also and she said a letter would be following. The article in the paper said something about his mother having received a letter from one of the gunner's mother in which she advised that her son had been reported killed in action. It is certainly hard to realize that so many of the boys, the very ones who were with us on that trip to Washington, are actually missing and perhaps even gone forever! War is really terrible, as we all know, but we realize it so much so when it strikes so close to our own loved ones. Let us hope and pray that all of these boys, and millions of others too, will be found safe before many more days are gone. Guess we can't stop to worry and wonder about them, there is so much more to be done, but it does cause a sort of anxious feeling in the hearts of those left behind. Jeanne seemed to be taking her news okay.

> I still love you my darling, with all my heart, and miss you just an awful, awful lot - more than you'll ever know – but I'm sure you'll be flying home any day now, so I'll try and be a good sport and take the lonesomeness on the chin, as lots of other gals are doing. Be good, as I know you are always, take care of your sweet self, darling, write to me as often as possible, and I'll be seeing you soon 'in all the old familiar places.' May God bless you always and watch over you for me and everyone else who loves you. Good night, honey. Margaret.

It was the 6th of September 1943 and we were on our way to Stuttgart, Germany, for another maximum effort mission. Something caught my eye not long after our fighter escort turned back. I noticed far off to our left there was a lone B-17 keeping pace with our formation. I thought it was odd and we all kept watching it, but we couldn't quite figure it out. Here we were cruising along at 23,000 feet in 25 degree below zero temperatures getting closer and closer to engaging enemy fighters and here was this lone bomber outside our protective box formation. What was he doing out there? Soon, all hell broke loose as Jerry fighters jumped us from every direction. Our lone wolf bomber became an after-thought as our minds switched into survival mode. The intercom in the "Feather Merchant" was filled with the usual chatter. Roger was yelling at Ted to shoot. By this time he didn't have to remind Ted anymore, but it had kind of become a tradition with Roger.

> Tex, coming front to back, get his ass when he goes by, 190's at 3 O'clock high, coming in fast. Short bursts fellas. Don't waste ammo if they're out of range. Two more 9 O'clock high, they're diving in. 12 O'clock level Ted, get those bastards!

I hated having to just sit there and watch a 190 coming head on with us and seeing the flash of his 20 mm gun. At least the rest of the guys had something to shoot back with. Jack and I just had to sit there, stare at it, and take it. Nowhere to run-nowhere to hide. No evasive action, sitting ducks! Back at Ridgewell it was this that I dreamed the most about. I hunkered down as much as I could, as if the thin metal skin would stop the 20 mm shells. My nights were becoming sleepless, as were everyone's. I would lay there after lights out and stare into the darkness. I could hear the sounds of the battle, feel the cold on my face, smell the guns and hear the chatter. It's a wide awake nightmare that we all shared. Today, however, it wasn't a dream, it was the real thing, the real thing that the dreams were made of. At this point I couldn't see how anyone could make it to 25 missions. I snapped out of it as Jack made a slight erratic move to throw off a fighter coming right at us, then it dawned on me. I knew why that bomber was out there all by itself. I watched it some more to confirm my suspicions. None of the fighters were going after it, even though it was a sitting duck out there all by itself. It was a captured B-17 being flown by the Jerries, it had to be. Those bastards were out there following us and calling in our exact location to the fighters along our route. My suspicion was confirmed when we hit the flak field and all of a sudden that lone bomber was nowhere to be seen.

On through the flak field we went. We were old hands at this by now. We had flown a few missions in our new "Feather Merchant" and she was holding up quite nicely. Jack had planned to rename whatever ship they finally gave us, but when we received the "Feather Merchant" we both agreed to leave it the same. This was the ship our friend Leo Jarvis named and brought over from the states. It was an original 381st ship, Leo's ship. No, she would stay the "Feather Merchant." The flak bursts knocked us around quite a bit. I was nervous and wanting to get rid of our load of incendiary magnesium bombs that we were carrying. One hit in the bomb bay and we would be blown to pieces. Ted called up on the intercom and told us the target was obscured. That was okay, I thought, we'd just go on to a secondary target, drop our load, and skedaddle back home. That's when we realized the group lead was going around on target again. Jack and I were furious. What was this idiot officer thinking! Going around on a target is not only near suicide, but we didn't have the fuel reserves to be doing that kind of thing. As the whole group pivoted, the ships on the outside of the pivot had to increase power to keep in formation. That meant using more fuel to keep up, and the older ships without Tokyo tanks carried less fuel load. If the ships were unlucky enough to have been early on in the take-off scheme, well, they'd never have enough fuel to make it back to England. There was plenty of cussing going out over our intercom and we told everyone to can the chatter, but that didn't mean Jack and I weren't cussing up a storm off com in the cockpit at the new development. I nervously watched our fuel gauges. The insanity of it all was that we didn't just go around once, we went around three times! Four bomb runs on the same target! We were burning up gas like there was no tomorrow! We were constantly on the intercom with Roger to plot a course home and calculate fuel. It was becoming more and more obvious that we wouldn't make it home. Finally, we dropped our bombs with the group lead. We have no idea where they fell; the city remained covered by clouds. Now we faced a dreadful decision. Cut and run for Switzerland or try to make it home with the rest of the group. Our ship was relatively undamaged and all the engines were running smoothly, so we decided to try for England. We knew we'd never make it to Ridgewell but perhaps we could make it to a base along the coast, or at least ditch in friendly waters. I watched while the gauges dipped well below half as the Luftwaffe fighters again came after us.

"Shoot, shoot, shoot! God damn it Ted, shoot!" I yelled.

I saw an FW-190 roll onto his back and fire at us from 12 O'clock level. I saw his tracer rounds walking toward us, then the Plexiglas panel above my head exploded out from a direct hit and a rush of iced air came in and filled the cockpit. Eddie was in the top turret and yelled over the intercom that I'd been hit, but I yelled back that I was okay. I think Ted hit the 190 but they had armor plating on their bellies, that's why they inverted as they fired and slipped below us as they passed. It had to have been his machine gun rounds that raked us, since I saw tracers, and if it had been an exploding 20 mm round I would have been a goner. The fight went on and on as our gauges dipped lower and lower. Finally, some specks appeared in the sky at our 12 O'clock high that we knew had to be friendlies. P-47 Thunderbolts diving in to mix it up with the Jerries. The P-47's were undoubtedly lower than usual on their fuel too since we were running so far behind schedule. They must have been waiting around for us for at least 30 minutes to an hour. They made a good show of it by making one devastating pass through the Jerry fighters. Low fuel was probably the story of the day for the Jerries too. They cut away from their attack and headed home.

Our fuel was reaching critical as we crossed the coast and headed out across the channel. Jack leaned out the engines and put the ship in a long power glide to get every last drop out of her. Back over France when the German fighters cut off their attack we had ordered the crew to throw out everything that wasn't bolted down; machine guns, ammunition crates, whatever. If it wasn't loose, we pried it loose and threw it out to lighten the ship and extend our range. We finally approached the white cliffs of Dover and, fortunately, we still had enough altitude to clear them. Roger had given us a course that took us to a small RAF fighter base right on the coast. It wasn't much, but there was a short landing strip there and we had already proved we could do a short field landing back on our trip across the pond.

Looking behind us we could see a long line of bombers that had the same idea we did. As we approached the field they were shining a red lantern at us and firing red flares. They frantically called out on the radio to abort our landing, but we told them we had no choice, we'd be coming in on the first pass, like it or not. With flaps at full and two of our engines already sputtering, Jack set her down just feet past the beginning of the runway and the end of the strip came up fast. As we rolled out as far as we dared we turned off the strip, got about 25 yards, and all four engines sputtered and quit, bone dry! That scene was repeated over and over by several more ships. Many more would end up ditching in the channel, not from battle damage, but out of fuel because of an idiotic and short sighted decision made by an officer that had no business leading a group. As we surveyed the damage to our "Feather Merchant" all we could find was the blown out window panel and a few holes here and there. Our luck was holding out, and our new baby proved she was a fine old gal. I guess this is what they meant by coming home on a wing and a prayer.

Chapter 35
Tinker Toy

Just reread that swell letter of yours that came yesterday. I didn't get a newer edition today, but maybe tomorrow I hope. That British stationary is alright, darling. How do you like my new American style? Maybe you are wondering what has happened to the typewriter in connection with my letters. Well honey, I decided that after typing off and on most all day at the office that it would be much more relaxing and more fun to write to my sweetheart in longhand. It's the personal touch, I guess. Of course, it's always a pleasure, and fun too, to converse with you on paper, dear, and longhand letters probably make you feel more at home anyway.

Boy, honey, you guys are still going to town over there! Last night you bombed Paris again! Sure do hope and pray that wherever you may be you won't be having any kind of trouble on any of your trips. Keep good old St. Chris around your neck, darling, he's really a big help I think. Do a good job, as I know you will, and hurry home my dearest. I was glad to hear that you were able to have some time off in August and get to London. It no doubt helps a lot to relieve the tension of your long hours of work. Have a swell time whenever you get a chance 'cause you really deserve some fun and relaxation now and then for all you are doing. I am glad to hear that the colored snapshots arrived okay and also that you like them, dear. There is an improvement over the ones we took a year ago, huh? It's swell that Vi sends you nice letters often and also continues to tuck in those little clippings. I must write to her soon and thank her for being so faithful. On the whole, though, I think that the whole family is doing pretty well on the writing end. I just hope they will all keep it up.

You boys must be keeping plenty busy, honey, from the sound of your letters. You sounded plenty tired too! After I finished your letter last night, dear, I wrote one to

Polly, and also one to Jean Noce in Palo Alto, so I'm getting caught up again. Tonight I should write to mom and Emil, also your mom, although I phoned her yesterday, and about sixty other people too, but I just like to write to you. I have your picture here in front of me (in Technicolor) also the one of your crew, so I see you very clearly. But I sure do wish you could be right here beside me, 'cause I'd love to reach over and just hold your hand. Sentimental, aren't I honey-bun? If you happen to have a copy of the picture of the crew how's about naming off the fellows for me and giving me their respective titles and positions, or I shall try to get it from Polly. I'd like to have it for your scrapbook, darling.

I surely do love you and miss you just an awful lot, but I'm still hoping and praying (real hard) every day that you'll be home very, very soon. Then, I'll be truly happy again. I'll say goodnight for this time, dearest, but I'll be back again tomorrow and every day until you're home with me to stay. Until that day, and always, May God bless you and take care of you for me, 'cause I love you very much and will need you always. Goodnight honey-bun. Margaret

It was a miracle that we made it to the RAF fighter base, out of gas, with one window shot out, and no injuries. Our guardian angels were with us on our trip to Stuttgart! I'm not sure how many bombers landed there, but there were a lot. The Brits were gracious hosts and gave us a ride to their operations center where Jack made arrangements for fuel. Problem was they only had fuel in five gallon cans. It took a little while for the ground crew to dump enough in to get us to Ridgewell. In the meantime our hosts took us over to their officers club and treated us all to a nice ale, except Jack and I, we abstained because we still had to fly. Eddie sent a driver for us when the ship was ready. It took a little bit to get the engines primed again since we ran them dry, but we eventually managed it okay. Being as light as we were, because of dumping everything overboard, we didn't have any problems taking off on the short strip. We did a very thorough walk around to inspect for damage before takeoff and the ship looked practically untouched. While we were doing the walk around "Frenchy" (Sgt. Russ Frautschi), our radio man, told us about throwing his helmet out over France. Jack and I looked curiously at each other and I couldn't help myself.

"Sgt. Frautschi. Why did you throw your helmet out?" I asked.

I surely didn't expect the response I got. "Frenchy" said he had to take a crap so bad he couldn't hold it anymore, so he took his helmet liner out and went in it while there were enemy fighters all around us. Right in the middle of combat at twenty-some thousand feet in sub-zero weather "Frenchy" took a huge crap in is helmet. When we were flying over France and throwing out everything we could, he tossed the (loaded) helmet down through the camera hatch in the radio room and yelled-take that! I hope it hits one of my relatives in the head down there! The laughter that erupted between us and the Brits was enough to make us forget the hell we just went through, at least for a while.

The runway reminded us of that short strip we landed at on our way across the pond in the "Polly Jo." Drawing on that experience now, we revved the engines up full while standing on the brakes, let loose and began our roll. "Feather Merchant" responded beautifully and we went airborne easily. It was a short hop over to Ridgewell, about twenty minutes or so. Upon landing there we taxied to our hard stand and hitched a ride to interrogation. It was a miracle, everyone in our group made it home except two ships that crash landed, out of fuel, in southern England, but there were no casualties at all. The total losses, however, for the raid was 45 ships. Undoubtedly because of the bone headed decisions that was made over the target. Someone's head would roll, I hope! The rest of September was very busy. I'm glad we were able to get a leave to London back in late August. Roger and Ted were busy finding girls and parties to attend. Jack and I found a British representative who was giving out tickets to a USO show. She asked me for my serial number because she had to keep track of who she gave the tickets to. I kept telling her over and over again,

"Zero-743 Oh 87."

She couldn't understand what I was telling her and she kept asking me to repeat it. This went on for several minutes until an RAF fellow happened by and he heard us. He said us Yanks like to say zero and Oh, but they call it nought. We all got a good belly laugh out of what must have looked like a scene from Abbott and Costello. We saw the show and some of the sights around the city, popped into a few pubs, played some darts. It was a great trip to unwind and try to forget what happened on August 17th. Of course, that day would never be forgotten, but at least we were able to get some of it out of our minds for a little while.

As if Stuttgart wasn't enough, we would go to Brussels the very next day, the 7th. Then, Lile Nord in France the day after that, on the 8th. They weren't missions that were deep within Germany, but the fighters and flack were still there waiting for us every time just the same. We had another long flight scheduled for some submarine pens in Bergun, Norway, on the 9th, but it was scrubbed. I wouldn't fly again until the 15th, when, to my surprise, I was tasked as first pilot on a mission to bomb an airdrome at Rommily sur-Seine, France. Jack would be training someone in the "Feather Merchant," so I would fly with Baltrsaitis' crew. He was going to let me fly the whole mission because we were going to be the deputy group lead, and he'd be in the right seat to watch the formation. I did the same thing with Jack, but Jack wouldn't relinquish control of the ship. Baldy didn't mind giving up the controls to mentor another first pilot. It would be an unusual mission because for the first time we would be carrying two 1,000 pound external bombs in wing racks, as well as our normal bomb load. It would be the heaviest load yet that we have carried. The ship would be heavier than hell with no room for engine problems on take-off. At the morning briefing things went as usual. This is the target, this is the route, expected enemy fighter concentrations, expected flack areas etc. I received my ship number, 846. It was a 535th squadron ship. Baldy and I headed out to the ship to get ready. As we rolled up to the hard stand my mouth just dropped open. Holy shit, I heard myself saying, it's "Tinker Toy," the jinx ship of the 381st. If you didn't believe in good luck, bad luck, or jinxes, you've never been in combat. You cling to whatever gives you confidence, and "Tinker Toy" didn't give confidence, she scared the hell out of everyone. She seemed like she always came home, but with crew members with horrific injuries, or she was a mechanical nightmare. On the Stuttgart mission she tried to kill off her entire crew by losing all her oxygen. She was so infamous that even Lord Ha Ha, the German propaganda guy, talked about her on the radio. Baltrasaitis' ship "The Joker" wasn't mission ready, so we got "Tinker Toy."

Me, Baldy, and the flight engineer did an extensive walk around, as much as we had time for anyway. We checked and double checked the oxygen system and all seemed good to go. I even talked nice to her out loud, calling her Baby. Man, the things a man won't do when he's scared for his life. I was already nervous enough being in command for the first time, but I'd be flying with a crew that I was completely unfamiliar with, in a ship with a reputation, with an impossibly heavy load, being graded, I'm sure, by our squadrons newest captain. What could go wrong? We joined the rest of the ships waddling down the taxiway and when it was our turn we positioned ourselves at the head of runway 28. At the thirty second interval I revved her up and let loose the breaks and we began our roll. As I rotated us up off the pavement everything was going smoothly, that is, for only a few seconds! The number two engine ran away on us and was revving out of control. I muttered to myself,-ya, what could go wrong? I shut the engine down and feathered it as fast as I could and adjusted the other three engines the best I could to keep us straight and climbing out. It was slow going as our overloaded and lumbering "Tink" struggled to gain altitude and keep from stalling and falling to earth in a huge fireball, but she did it. We flew around at 10,000 feet until the rest of the group was airborne. We discussed flying out over the channel and dropping our bomb load, but we decided to keep her close in case we had further engine problems. I figured that 10,000 feet was good in case we needed to bail out. After we got the all clear we landed without incident and parked our ship on the hard stand where we were met by the ground crew and maintenance chief, who just stood there shaking his head. I have to hand it to Captain Baltrusaitis. He never did panic or try to take control of the ship. He let me do it all. Although I'm sure he was ready to grab it if I made just one wrong move or hesitation. Chaplain Brown was waiting there too.

"Nice flying Quinn," He said.

"Thanks. I never left England, but I think I still sweat out ten pounds worth." I said.

"C'mon, I'll buy you guys a cup of coffee, then we can sweat out the rest of the group until they get back."

We followed the Chaplain to the officers club, had our coffee, changed out of our gear, and went over to operations to sweat out everyone's return. Chaplain Brown was already there. True to his word, he had told Roger one day that after missing a returning flight, he would never again not be there waiting for the group, and he never did miss another return. He was our rock.

For the rest of September we had pretty bad weather over France and six missions were scrubbed. We managed to get all the way to Nantes, France, on the 17th, where the target was a port area, but the target was obscured and no bombs were dropped. We didn't jettison bomb loads over France willy-nilly for fear of hitting the civilian population. We needed a clear military target to drop in France. We returned to Nantes on the 23rd and were able to drop with good results, pulverizing the port area. Jack received his promotion to 1ˢᵗ lieutenant and they made us the "A" flight lead plane. Art Sample received his promotion to first pilot and moved out of our hut around the first of the month. He was assigned our old ship "Ole Flack Sack." October started out just like September ended. There were two missions planned for the same day, the 2ⁿᵈ of October, and we were to fly on the second mission. The first flight went off without a hitch, but we were scrubbed due to weather over the target. On the 4ᵗʰ we had a raid to Frankfurt and we were assigned as group lead. Lt. Colonel Hall flew in my place as per protocol. Normally, I would be assigned as tail gunner in this case but the rest of the crew protested and wanted Tex to remain at his post because he was a better shot, and they were right, so I stayed home. I'm glad I did. Just short of the IP "Feather Merchant" lost her number 2 engine. The colonel ordered Jack to abort and head for home. Jack told him that it would be suicide to abort at that point and they should stay in the formation for protection, that they could manage that just fine on the three remaining engines. The colonel, apparently, was in a near panic and ordered Jack under penalty of court martial to drop out of formation. Jack slipped out of formation and put the ship in a dive with fighters right on his tail, scaring the living daylights out of everyone, including the idiot colonel. Jack gained as much speed as he could and slipped her into as much cloud cover as possible, cloud hopping all the way back to the channel to avoid flack locations and fighters. By the grace of God they managed to make it home alright.

We got a two day pass, but most of us hung around the base, only going into the nearby town to the local pub, or to the officers club. We came up with a great way to entertain ourselves in the Nissen hut after a few drinks. We would listen for when we heard someone walking up to the hut and someone would throw a 50 caliber shell into the coal stove. Our visitor would come in and after a few moments the shell would explode and scare the crap out of him and we would all get a big belly laugh at the visitor's expense. We did a 20 millimeter shell once, but it blew the pipes away from the stove and we didn't do that again. One day, however, the joke was on us as we heard someone coming and threw a shell into the stove. To our surprise, in walked our squadron commander and then (POW) went the shell. He was so mad he threatened to ban us from the pub, but after a while he laughed also and told us not to do that anymore. Another popular sport someone came up with was to have a few ales and then participate in some bicycle jousting out behind the huts. Leo Jarvis used to be good at it. Art Sample and Baltrusaitis played, as did Roger, me, Jack and Dexter Lishon and several other guys. We weren't supposed to do it anymore, though, as Colonel Nazarro put out an order to cease and desist. It seems that too many men were ending up in the infirmary from jousting injuries instead of actual battle injuries. But when no one was looking and our judgment was clouded by the local ale and scotch we would sneak in a bout or two. We called the jousting games early on the 7th and headed back to the club for some supper and drinks. There was a rumor circulating of something big happening on the 8th, another maximum effort. We'd turn in and try to get some sleep, but it usually meant you just stared into the darkness, envisioning a fighter firing right at you and wondering if your time was up.

Chapter 36
Willkommen nach Deutschland

Thanks for those swell letters that arrived today. They were a real treat, believe me. This is going to be just a few lines tonight as I have to leave a little early for my trip with the Red Cross station wagon. This is the first night of our transportation system and I have to go by Mrs. Wilson's for a chart, otherwise I wouldn't have to leave until almost 10:00. It is after 8:30 now and I have to change to my other slacks so I'll have to leave in a few minutes. I just wanted you to know that I'm thinking of you, darling, as always, and surely do love you, for lots and lots of things, especially because you are so sweet to write as often as you can. You'll never know how much your daily letters mean to me, honey, with an ocean and a whole continent between us! It's wonderful to hear from you as regularly as I do. If my letters mean even half as much to you I'll be happy! Don't worry, dear, about getting the money to me in a hurry. I'm getting along okay now, really. I want to save as much as possible of what you send, so there really is no big hurry for it to get here. At the rate we're going at the office I should get a pretty nice check this month, here's hoping. It will help a lot.

Hello again, my darling. It's just 11:00 P.M. and I'm back home again already. Practically all of my gals got other rides home, but I had one gal to take way out near the fair grounds. She lives at 50th street and 11th avenue and worked at Sutter General Hospital! I took her right to her door and saw that she got in okay. It's sort of fun driving that nice station wagon. It even has a nice radio in it. Don't know what kind it is, a Mercury I think. I meant to look, but I forgot. It really drives easily and smoothly. You'd like it, honey, unless it's too tame after a B-17! I kind of enjoyed being out in the nice cool air, only I wish you were with me. We used to enjoy such nice rides together, remember? We'll do it again sometime, though, and soon too. Here's hoping!

Gee, to get back to answering your wonderful letters. I'm glad to hear that you were able to find some nice clothes. I imagine that you were about out of everything by this time. Did you ever get one of those blouses you mentioned some time ago, honey? Be sure to do so soon if you still care to have one of them. I had to laugh when you wrote of your flannel pajamas! You used to tease me about mine, remember? They feel sort of good on cold foggy nights, don't they darling? I'll probably have mine out again soon if you don't come home soon to keep me warm. I surely wish you could tell me something of what you're doing dear, 'cause you sound so full of news that can't be written! Be sure to save up a lot of the highlights for when you come home 'cause I'll be anxiously waiting to hear them. We'll go back over your letters and that will help you to remember what happened at each respective time, but which you couldn't tell me about. That will be fun! Interesting too!

I love you with all my heart and am just about to start counting the days now until you'll be home with me once more. Until that great day, and always, May God bless you, watch over you, and bring you safely home to me real soon. Good night, darling, I'll be seeing you real soon again, on paper at least. I love you, honey-bun. G'bye for now. Margaret.

Two men stood over me, looking at my face that was reddened from the below zero temperatures, my useless leg and beaten up body with blood streaming down my face, and they just shook their heads. One of the men was clearly a farmer and he did all the talking,

"Willkommen nach Deutschland, Fur Sie ist der Krieg uber!"

He had a very old rifle that was slung over his arm but he never did point it at me. The other man carried a pitchfork and spoke what sounded like Russian. I didn't have a gun. They made us stop carrying them. I guess instead of helping they just got guys killed or because the Jerries just ended up with a lot of American pistols anyway. They motioned for me to get up and walk toward the road where they had an old truck with a flatbed full of hay and vegetables. I tried to walk, but I just couldn't. The farmer urged me a bit, but then motioned for the Russian to help me when he realized how much pain I was in. The Russian pulled my arm around his neck and half carried me while I hobbled across the field. The pain was horrible and almost made me pass out, or maybe it was the loss of blood or the concussion, it didn't much matter. The Russian helped me up onto the flatbed. Pretty soon four soldiers came along on bicycles and the farmer motioned for me to lie down and he held his hands together in a manner that looked like he wanted me to pretend to be asleep. I did what he wanted just before the soldiers got there. I kept my eyes shut but listened to what sounded like a pretty heated argument. Back and forth the argument went, with the farmer yelling at the soldiers and the soldiers yelling back. Pretty soon all the soldiers went on their way, so I guess the farmer won. I think he was afraid he'd lose his reward for capturing me if he let the soldiers take me. They shoved me a little more onto the flatbed and climbed into the cab of the truck and started it up. We drove for a few miles to a Russian prisoner of war camp where the farmer turned me in to a German officer there. I guess he did business with them and that was where he got his helper. He was a trustee from the camp and was loaned out to the farmer. They lifted me off the truck and a German sergeant, to my surprise, allowed me to lie on his cot. After a while a truck arrived with another American prisoner lying in the back. He was a sergeant from some other outfit that was also shot down on the Bremen raid. He had a badly fractured leg and was in a lot of pain. The sergeant and the men with the truck hoisted me into the back and they took off down the bumpy country road. The other prisoner with me moaned loudly every time the truck lurched from the bumps in the road. They took us to a building in Diepholz that was some sort of small prisoner intake or something. It was full of other Americans that had been captured from this raid, although I didn't see anyone I knew. I was beginning to get worried about our crew and couldn't figure out why none of them were here. I hoped they hadn't been killed in the ship before being able to get out, or having been trapped and unable to get out, that would be horrible. There was a doctor at this building that had gotten his license in Minnesota several years ago and spoke good English. He wanted to give me a Tetanus shot. I told him that I had just gotten one a couple weeks ago, but he said, I don't care what you got before, we believe in giving good ones here! He x-rayed my leg and said that the shrapnel would have to stay in there and that the pain would subside after a while, but for now I'd just have to grin and bear it. After intake they shipped those of us that were injured over to an infirmary at a nearby military base.

At the infirmary the tetanus shot did just what I thought it would do. I started sweating and feeling like I was swelling up all over. I was out of my head all night, but it finally went away in the morning. I was in a cell with a wooden bench to lie on and by now it was soaked with sweat from my rough night. I was more than happy to just lay there staring at the ceiling all day. There was a peep hole in the door and every now and then it would open and someone would look in at me. After a few hours someone brought me some food. The guy who brought it told me in broken English that it was rabbit stew and it wasn't too bad. Eventually, the door opened and a German soldier, a corporal I think, motioned for me to come with him. He looked all of 17 years old, but he was pretty big. I tried to walk but couldn't manage it, so I hopped across the room to him. He could see I was having a hard time and he motioned for me to hang around his neck and he helped me to the entrance of the building we were in. Using hand motions he indicated to me that we were going to cross the street and go to another building. This enemy soldier had me climb up on his back and he carried me across the street, but when we got to the door he made me get down so no one would see what he was doing. This new building turned out to be another doctor's office. When I went inside I found one of our waste gunners, Carl Baird, laying on a gurney. Carl had gotten some pretty serious flack in his groin and the doctor was going to operate on him. The next day they brought an ambulance by and they put me and the other sergeant with the broken leg in it and took us to Bremen. I didn't see Carl again so I never knew how well he did after surgery.

When we got to Bremen they took us to St. Joseph's hospital. We were taken to the third floor, where there were already three other Americans. The floor was loaded with x-ray machines. The hospital was run by Catholic Nuns and the one working with us took a real liking to me and went through me when dealing with any of the other Americans. I suppose it was because I was an officer and the rest of the men were sergeants. Either that or it was because I had a St. Christopher medal hanging around my neck and she thought I was Catholic because of the medal, but I wasn't. Margaret had given it to me before I went to England. Either way, I had it pretty good there for a while. I had more x-rays taken of my leg and stayed at the hospital for a little over a week. She had an orderly that was a French prisoner of war. I guess there were three of them working there at the time. This one guy kept coming in wanting to talk to me and he'd lean way in close to me and kind of whisper his conversations. I didn't like him that close to me, but it was nice having someone who was trying to communicate what was going on. I never knew too much of what he was saying though. One day the sister came in and motioned me to come to the door. She motioned me to stop at the door and she scurried down the hallway clear to the end where another hall intersected it. When she got to the end of the hall she looked both ways like she was up to something and then she motioned for me to come down the hall too. She took me in a room and there was that Frenchman, along with two other Frenchmen. One was in a bed recovering from a bullet wound to his back. He stole a jacket out of the laundry at the hospital and tried to escape by simply walking away from the hospital, but he was discovered and shot. He looked like he was recovering well, though. When I went in their room they had some bottles of wine that they wanted to share with me. They said don't tell anybody, but this is French wine, not that stuff the Germans drink. It was smuggled in special for them by other French underground people. That was impressive. I didn't know they were active inside Germany. One day the sister brought in a young German soldier to talk with me. He must have been about 18 years old is all. He was recovering from having his face badly burned by a flame thrower at the Russian front. He was from Hamburg but they couldn't send him there because the city was so badly destroyed by bombing. Perhaps that's why the sister wanted us to meet, so he could tell me all about what our bombing was doing to the German cities, even though it was the British at the time that were bombing Hamburg. I didn't tell him much, but I asked him a lot of questions. He told me that the Brits bombed his home town five nights in a row, coming over in waves. The first wave would drop heavy bombs and everyone would head for the air raid shelters. The next wave would drop barrels of gasoline or kerosene and saturate the whole town with the flammable fuel. Then the next bunch dropped incendiary bombs and the result was a fire storm that must have resembled hell on earth. He said there were 100,000 civilians killed there. That kind of information really makes a man reflect on things, but it's over for me now, I guess, and there won't be any more raids to go on. In reflection, war is a terrible thing, but how else do you stop a country that supports a man's ambition to take over the world by doing the same thing to his enemies? He was a good natured young fellow and it seemed he held no ill feelings toward the U.S. or the Brits. One day the nun had him participate in a prisoner exchange. He took two British merchant sailors down to the docs where he met someone and exchanged them for two German merchant sailors. He came back with boxes of British cigarettes, tooth paste and other things that the nuns couldn't get for the injured people in their charge. It was all very surprising to me and it was a very interesting week and a relief to see that the Germans took care of their prisoners. I don't know what I expected, but it wasn't this. I wasn't looking forward, however, to finding out what my final destination was going to be, but I figured why would they fix me up and take such good care of me if they were just going to do something bad to me? At least that's what I prayed every night. Margaret is going to be in shock when she hears what happened. I felt bad for her. All I could think about was how this was going to devastate her. Had I not been shot down I probably would have been home by Christmas. The hard part for her will be not knowing what happened to me. It will take a while for the news to get to her that I'm alive. Even back at Ridgewell it took a long time for us to hear whether or not our friends were alive or dead. Yes, for me the war is over, but for Margaret it's just beginning.

Chapter 37
We Regret To Inform You

It's only I again, back to tell you I love you and miss you very, very much! Surely have felt low today. I know I shouldn't, dear, but with no letters since Monday, and the news of your latest activities, I just can't seem to help it. Even though the news is almost a month old and I've had letters from you dated after that. You boys certainly did a wonderful job on that ball bearing plant near Munich a couple of days ago. Nice going! General Arnold commended all of you in a news release today. Sixty flying fortresses lost on one mission is plenty tough, though, and especially hard for us wives to take. As I promised you, darling, I'll keep trying hard not to worry too much, but it's awfully hard not to do so. I know we must all have and hold our faith and trust in God, so I'll keep trying dear, for your sake. No news is good news, I suppose!

Here it is already after midnight, which makes it the 16th day of October, and our monthly anniversary again. We've been married 4 ½ years, darling, and I still love you with all my heart. Happy 54th anniversary, darling, may we celebrate in years that many! Sure wish we could be together for this one, and all of our anniversaries, but guess we can't have all of the good things in life. I'll be hoping and praying that we'll be celebrating together again real soon, honey. Until that is possible we'll just have to be content with pleasant memories of all of the good times we have had together. I remember the night that you came home to surprise me. Gee, I was glad to see you! Do it again, soon, huh? Bet I'll yell even louder next time!

Another Sunday is here, and almost gone, but I'm back again with my daily chatter. Esther, Earle, and Peter just left a little while ago and I had no sooner addressed the envelope to your letter when Eve and Car came by. They were all dressed up on their way to see the McClellan Field All-Soldier Show at the Sacramento High School auditorium. The show is called 'At Your Service' and is sort of like 'This is the Army.' It is playing here for a week and then will tour California cities and camps. Jane saw it last night and said it was very good. Faye Travis and I, also June Brill, have tickets for next Thursday night, the last night it will be showing here. I think it will be fun to see it. Wish you could come along. Esther, Peter, and I had a swell day together. We went house hunting, without much luck, but enjoyed the ride. We took Peter to the zoo, which we all enjoyed. Then, we drove out to Municipal Airport where we saw lots of planes, including a couple of P-38's, several P-39's, and lots of B-25's. Naturally, Peter was in his glory! Esther brought us a big piece of salmon, which will be good some night next week.

We are having the sorority social on Tuesday night and Faye Travis and Elgeane Lauppe are staying in town and overnight so we are having them for dinner too. We'll have a pajama party after the social! The reason we're having the party at our house is because nobody else wanted to bother or wasn't sure she could have it. You know me, I always offer them our house, and I really don't mind. I'm not on the committee, though, so that helps. I'll just have the house to clean up afterward, but I don't care.

Gee, you should get a kick out of this, honey. Mrs. Middlestadt (you remember the colonel. He is now a general and is over in Hawaii) directed Esther to our house. She remembered me from the other day. She was out in front washing her car when I was house hunting on my bike. I stopped to ask her if she knew of any houses for rent, I ask anyone that I happen to see outside. Anyway, I chatted with her for a little while and she seemed very sweet and interested in helping me out. I had told her my name, and our address, and that we lived by the fire hydrant. Also, of course, that my husband is over in England bombing the Nazis! So, I found out the next day from the man next door, whom I've talked with before, who the very nice lady was. I've got a lot of nerve, huh, talking to strange people. It just goes to show you, you never know who is a general's wife, or something. But to get back to the funny side, Esther told her my name and she remembered right away; the house number, fire plug, and all. She said, 'why, she is a little blonde girl who rides a bicycle and stopped by just a few days ago to ask about houses for rent.' Esther had forgotten our number and stopped to ask her because she was raking leaves into the street and was handy. Isn't that something? I'll have to stop by and thank her next time I ride by their house.

Gee, honey, I sure do hope I get a letter tomorrow. It's been so long, 19 days since the date of your last one that I have received anyway. You probably know how much I worry when I hear news like that of Thursday's activities! I spent an hour in church yesterday afternoon trying hard to snap myself out of an awful worrying mood! I succeeded, to some degree, thank God. I got to thinking of the other ships, perhaps several hundred that did return from that raid, and just must trust in God that you were in one of that number! It's still tough though honey and is certainly breaking me in to the life of a war-birds wife! But ruggedly, and how! I've made up my mind that it isn't fair to you for me to worry so hard about you. I can't help it, though, honey. You know how much I love you and if anything should happen to you I think that I would die too, or want to awfully bad! I can't even think of life without you by my side!

Gosh sakes, I've really dashed off a note to you, honey. Hope I haven't worn you out. Guess I'd better be signing off for this time, though. I love you with all my heart, darling, and surely do miss you like the dickens! I'm hoping and praying hard, though, that you'll be coming home real soon, now just any day would make me very happy, as long as it's soon. Until that wonderful day, and always, God bless you, my darling, and keep you ever safe. Goodnight for tonight and pleasant dreams to you. I love you, honey-bun! Margaret.

I stood out on the 10th floor balcony of the medical dental building where I now worked in Sacramento. I was working at my desk when I heard a plane coming and went out to watch. We often heard planes flying over from the nearby McClellan Field, but this time it caught my attention. As I stood there, staring into the sky, I saw a lone B-17 bomber come into view and pass over my head. I felt a chill go down my spine and goose bumps and a cold sweat overcame me. I said under my breath, I hope to God Cecil isn't having to bail out today. I turned and walked back to my desk and looked square at the calendar. It was October 8th, 1943. I shook off the chills and went back to work. I went about my normal routine of writing letters to Cec every day, working at the medical office, volunteering for the Red Cross and driving nurse's aides home at night after their shifts at the various hospitals around town. Sometimes I would go a few days without a letter from Cecil, but they always eventually arrived, sometimes bunches at a time. I kept in close contact with Polly. She was due to have her baby in a couple weeks. No matter what was going on, though, I would always stop in at Sacred Heart Church and pray for my husband's safe return. I always tried to keep a stiff upper lip, as the Brits would say, but for some reason it was getting harder and harder for me to do so. I don't know what it was. It isn't something you can easily describe, but as the month wore on I became more and more uneasy and less composed. The afternoon of the 19th I was feeling much better because I received three letters all at once from Cec. I had a party planned for that night, but I still took the time to sit there and read every last word of them. I didn't just read them once, either, I laid on my bed and read them over and over again and dreamed that he'd soon be done with the war and could fly on home to me and we could run off on a second honeymoon to a beach somewhere.

I was hosting a going away bridal shower party combined with a sorority social in my house for Peggy Tyler. She was going back to Ohio to get married. All our sorority sisters were there and we were having a swell time gabbing as she was opening gifts. I heard a knock on the door, but I was across the room, so one of the other girls opened it. I could see the head and cap of a messenger man over top of the crowd, so I made my way over to him. I was expecting news any time about Polly having her baby and I didn't want to miss that. I thanked the man and turned to take the letter back to my bedroom to open it. Whatever it was, I didn't want to ruin Peggy's party. I kept telling myself that it was about Polly, but I think that was just wishful reasoning. I knew in my heart that it couldn't be good news, not delivered at night by messenger. I began to shake, feeling light headed and weak in the knees as I went into the room and I stood there for a few moments trying to work up the courage and steady myself before opening the envelope. Finally, I took a deep breath and slid the telegram out of the envelope and opened my eyes:

> WASHINGTON DC OCT 19 1943
> MRS MARGARET M QUINLEY
> 394 SANTA YNEZ WAY
> SACRAMENTO CALIFORNIA
> THE SECRETARY OF WAR DESIRES ME TO
> EXPRESS HIS REGRET THAT YOUR HUSBAND
> SECOND LIEUTENANT CECIL W QUINLEY HAS
> BEEN REPORTED MISSING IN ACTON SINCE EIGHT
> OCTOBER IN THE EUROPEAN AREA
> IF FURTHER DETAILS OR OTHER INFORMATION
> ARE RECEIVED YOU WILL BE PROMPTLY
> NOTIFIED
> ULIO THE ADJUTANT GENERAL

As I read what it said I began sobbing, then crying and saying over and over again, oh no, oh no, oh no! 'Hoddie' Wyman and Berta Mitchell heard me and came running into the room and held me tight. I showed them the letter as I cried uncontrollably. I tried to talk myself out of this when I saw the messenger, but I'd been having weird premonitions all day. Ever since that article in the paper that told about all the boys that were lost over Schweinfurt, and the sudden interruption in Cecil's letters, I could feel that something wasn't right. The dates weren't right, though, he must have been on a different mission, it said October 8th. What difference did that make? I was stunned and in shock and didn't know what to do. I didn't want to ruin Peggy's party, but there was no way I could go back in there and face the rest of the girls and pretend nothing had happened. Hoddie snuck me out the back door and took me for a walk. It was getting close to 11:30 P.M. and there was a chill in the late October air, but it felt good. We walked around the neighborhood and I must have cried a gallon of tears. On the way back to my house we stopped at Sacred Heart Church and we pounded on the rectory door until Father Christen came out. Hoddie told him what had happened and he invited us inside. By this time my crying had turned to sobbing and Father Christen read scripture to me and told me not to think the worst, as we didn't know anything yet. He said a prayer for Cecil and me and told me that he'd dedicate a prayer in mass tomorrow morning to Cecil's safe return. Hoddie walked me the rest of the way home and put me to bed. Berta must have cleared out the party, because I don't know what happened to Peggy or the rest of the girls. The next morning I was the first person in church and sat in the front row. Good to his word, Father Christen prayed and had the entire mass pray for Cecil's safe return. It was a powerful moment and I could feel the spirit overtake me. After mass everyone was so kind and promised to check in with me from time to time to make sure I was okay. I thought about calling Polly, but I didn't dare. I had no idea if the baby had come yet and I didn't want to upset her at a critical time like that. I was in shock and confused about what to do. Surely the boys were together when this happened, or maybe not. Maybe Polly got worse news than me and I shouldn't bother her, but I wanted badly to talk with her. I didn't know what I should do. I went to church every day and prayed like I had never prayed before. To God, Jesus, the Virgin Mary, St. Christopher, I prayed. I lit candles and said the Rosary. This can't possibly be happening, it just can't. Now I knew how those other girls felt that I was telling to be strong. I tried, too, so very hard to be strong. I knew that's what Cecil would want me to do. I had heard this same story from some of my friends, the missing in action letter, a long wait, and then word that their loved ones were safe in a prisoner of war camp. You can be strong and supportive for others, many times over, but when it happens to you, how do you keep from breaking down? How do you keep the faith? Father Christen and all my friends were my rock. Cecil's family was strong too. His mother was incredibly strong. I didn't know how she did it. They gave me the strength to keep my chin up, keep my faith, and keep pressing on. I decided, as a means to cope, to keep writing my letters to Cecil as though nothing had happened. I'd keep mailing them, keep going to church, keep praying, and hope that word would come soon. It just had to!

Chapter 38
Letters of Hope

October 19, 1943.

Here I am again! I received three nice letters from my darling today, which made me very happy, although a couple of them were over a month old. I spent the night reading and rereading the one you dated October 7th, and was post marked the day you went missing. Gee, honey, my hand is certainly shaky! I thought I had pretty much recovered from the shock of the War Department telegram that came tonight, saying you are missing in action as of October 8. I know you're alright, though, my darling, and I promise to keep the old chin out, as you always told me to, and I know God is taking good care of you, wherever you are, darling! You're the best pilot in Uncle Sam's Air Corps and everybody knows it, me especially. But dear, it did hit me awful hard! I think I'm alright now. Don't you worry about me, honey, just you concentrate on keeping safe and happy. I'll be praying for you every day, and night too, and surely God will listen to some of my prayers some of the time. You will always know, dearest, no matter what happens ever, that you are always in my heart, and I just know that our love will see us through. Tonight was the sorority social and there was a big crowd, 21 girls. Quite a few of the old gang came around. Henrietta was here, also Nora Castle, Faye Graham, and most all of the new kids. They had a good time, I guess. Your telegram (I mean the one from General Ulio) arrived at about 8:30 P.M. I thought it was news of the baby (Pry), I was hoping so, of course. Sure hope little Polly is doing alright, and that junior had put in his appearance before her news arrived. After the telegram arrived Hoddie Wyman went for a walk with me, then we went to church over at Sacred Heart. I lit a lucky seven candles, honey, and said the rosary and a few other prayers which I hope will be heard.

I love you, my darling, with all my heart, and miss you that much and double! Wherever you may be, May God please to watch over you, keep you from harm, and bring you home real soon. Faye just walked out (into the cold air) and made a wish on a star for you and me. She says it always works for her, bless her heart! Goodnight, honey. I'll be writing again tomorrow, and every day, 'til you come flying home. Sweet dreams, and God bless you, dear. Be seeing you soon. All my love and kisses. Your unruly, but truly wife, devotionally so.

October 20, 1943.

Hello again, my darling! Here am I again, back to say I love you and miss you, very muchly. Didn't receive a letter from sweet you today, but maybe tomorrow, I hope. You probably wrote several letters in between the 28th of last month and the 8th of this month when you were last heard from by Uncle Sam. I'll be looking for some mail every day, darling, and I'm sure I will be hearing from you regularly again in a few days, or maybe weeks. Anyway, wherever you are I know you are all right and God is taking his best care of you, I just feel that way, honey! Whatever is to be is to be and as God wills it so, it will be. We just have to keep our faith in him, knowing and trusting his goodness and grace in everything. Somehow, darling, I know that you boys are safe! Last night when I sort of dozed off after I went to bed I dreamed that you were off in some kind of thick underbrush and you and Jack had landed your ship okay. You were both having 'ants,' saying you had to get to a phone and call Polly and me so we wouldn't worry about you. Bless your hearts, both of you, for always looking after us as you do. We love you for it, and for every other little part of your make-up that makes you so dear to us.

Father Christen is saying mass especially for you on Friday morning at 8:00 A.M. and also on the following Fridays for seven weeks altogether. He is very nice, darling, and was so considerate and consoling last night. He is a close friend of Father Renwald – they went to college together. I also lit seven candles for you, honey. Hope they prove lucky for us. Honey-bun, I must write at least a note to our Polly, so I guess I'd better say goodnight for now. Well, guess I'd better sign off my dearest, until next time, which will be tomorrow. Until then, and always, I love you truly, with all my heart, and I shall be praying always for God's blessings on you. May he watch over you and keep you safe, now and always, 'cause I love you. Goodnight now sweetheart. I'll be seeing you real soon! All my love and kisses.

October 21, 1943.

Hello, honey. Just a few lines again to tell you I love you and miss you very much. I didn't get a letter today but will be looking forward to receiving one tomorrow, or soon thereafter. Faye Travis and I just got home from seeing that Army show 'At Your Service,' which was put on by the boys at McClellan Field. It was swell! I'm enclosing the program for you, darling, although it doesn't tell much. The guys and gags were pretty good, though, you would have laughed at those silly boys. They were pretty clever, all of them. June Burrell (I thought it was Brill) went with us. The show was at the Sacramento High School auditorium. I almost didn't go and then I got to thinking it wouldn't be very good spirit on my part 'cause you would want me to go, so I went. The only tough moment I had, darling, was when the orchestra blared out with the 'Star Spangled Banner' at the very beginning. But I 'sweated it out' all night, saying a prayer for you, my sweetheart.

Have to get to bed, darling, so that I can get to church on time tomorrow. It's the first of those masses I'm having offered for your welfare, dear, and I'd hate to miss any part of them. I'll be back tomorrow, though, with more news and stuff. Until then, and always, May God bless you and keep you safe. I love you, dear, with all my heart. Goodnight, honey. Love and kisses.

October 22, 1943.

Hiya, honey! Greetings for another day, and a very nice one here in sunny California. Hope it is just as nice, or even more so, wherever you are. The sun shone brightly all day today, a welcome change from the dreariness of the past three days. Darling, your mass this morning was very nice, no different from any other day's perhaps, but especially nice because it was being offered especially for the welfare of my sweetheart. Don't know whether that was the cause or not, probably so, but I have had such a peaceful feeling today, more than at any time since the telegram arrived. A feeling that everything is alright with you, that you are safe, and that soon I shall be receiving more of your precious letters. Most of all, though, honey, I know and feel that we'll be seeing each other real soon. That is how you'd like to know that I'm feeling, isn't it darling? Somehow, I'm just sure in my heart that God is watching over you and protecting you, because we love each other so very much and you are such a nice fellow.

Had a nice letter today from Esther, and one from your mom enclosed. They have their chins high, darling, your mommy especially! I am proud of her! I called Mart this morning to see how mother was taking the news and she was there so I talked to her too. You would be relieved to know how well she is taking this shock in her stride. But you should know from previous experiences what a good soldier she is! Don't you worry about any of us at home, dear, we'll keep our chins up and our spirits as high as possible. I promised you that much before you left me in Grand Island, and I'll never give up hope that you are alright, and will continue to keep my trust and faith in God, our Father. Hoddie came today and took me to the Bee office. They wanted a picture and some details about your training. I gave them the best of everything, of course. The city editor said it would be in tomorrow's paper, and also the Modesto Bee, which will be nice for everyone. I know you wouldn't mind, darling, 'cause there are lots of people who would like to know, and would feel hurt if I didn't phone them, which is rather hard to do.

Honey-bun, do you like the sweet smell of this paper? I've had that little 'Blue Grass' sachet in the box and it really gives a fragrance. Hope you like it, dear. Darling, I sure do love you with all my heart, and am trying hard to be patient and wait for the good news that is sure to come soon. It's hard to not know definitely where you are, but others have bravely survived, so I trust that I will be able to do so. I miss you more than anyone can ever say, but we'll be together soon. Then, this long separation will be just a bad dream that we can put behind us. Until that great day when you come flying home, darling, take care of yourself and God bless you always and keep you ever safe. Goodnight, my darling, I sure do love you muchly. All my love and kisses.

October 23, 1943.

Hello, honey. Another Saturday is here and I am lonely without my darling. It's more of that same old feeling, only much more pronounced, especially because I didn't receive a letter from sweet you today, but maybe Monday will be a brighter day for mail. Here's hoping! Today's collection of mail did bring forth an announcement from Polly Pry. The baby arrived on the 14th, just as Polly was sure it would, and is a girl. Jacqueline Joyce is her name and she weighed 8 lbs-9 ¾ ounces! Bet Polly was plenty roly-poly! I was very relieved to hear that it was over before news of you boys' disappearance arrived, 'cause I know it would have been rather tough on Polly right then, not that it isn't terrible news at any time. You know what I mean, honey.

I'm still trying hard not to worry about your present whereabouts; at least I'm trying hard not to fret too much. Darling, I'm trying to face it just as you would want me to, and I still have the utmost faith and trust in God that he is looking after you, and that he is keeping you safe wherever you may be. I still feel that I'll be hearing from you again real soon, and seeing you again before many more days have passed. Until that great glorious day, my darling, I'll be praying for you and loving you, as always, with all my heart. Goodnight for now, sweetheart, I'll be seeing you. God bless you now and always. All my love and kisses.

October 24, 1943.

Hello, darling. Greetings again on another Sunday. Had a very nice day today. Clarence and Helen came up with their kids and brought your mommy along, which was grand. Darling, you'd be so proud of her, as always, for the way she is taking your temporary absence. She is really being a good soldier! All of the folks seem to feel just as I do, honey, that you boys are all together and are alright somewhere, and we must just be patient and wait for the good news that is sure to come soon. Today, I have had two calls from people whose relatives are missing as of the 9th of October. A Mrs. Martin, whose husband is also a co-pilot on a fortress, was quite upset when she phoned, so I tried hard to give her some consolation. She said that she felt much better after talking to me, so I hope that I said the right things.

I love you with all my heart, always have, and always will, and I feel confident, somehow, that God is going to be good to us, as always, and bring us together again real soon. Until that day, when our world will be sunny again, and for always, I'll be praying for you my dearest darling. Have to sign off again, honey-dear. Will try to write a longer letter tomorrow. Until then, and always, be good, God bless you, and watch over you for me and all of the others who love you so very, very much. Goodnight, honey-bun. I'll be seeing you soon. All my love and kisses.

October 25, 1943.

Hi, honey. Thanks a million for those five wonderful letters that arrived today! They were dated the 30th of September, and the 1st, 2nd, 3rd, and 4th of October, so I feel much better. You see, I was very, very worried about what had taken place between the 28th of September, which was the date on your last letter I had received, and the 8th of October, the date you were reported as missing in action. Darling, those were beautiful letters. I've already read them three times and will probably do so again before I go to bed. I know I will, 'cause that is my bedtime treat. I always read the last letter(s) I have received from you every night before turning off the lights, and then I sleep on them. It sounded as though you were in very good spirits on all of those dates, for which I am thankful.

I sent Jean Noce a telegram this morning and asked her to call me tonight. She did so a little while ago and gave me some interesting information. I think I wrote you a few weeks ago when her Jack was reported missing in action. Just two weeks after her first wire she received a letter from the War Department telling her that he had been interned in Switzerland. Since then she has had a cable from him saying he is okay. I can imagine how happy the news made her. Sure am hoping and praying hard that I'll be receiving the same, or something similar, real soon. I just know that it will be good news, darling. There just can't be anything awful happen to you, 'cause I'm sure God is taking care of you. However, I realize that I can't be immune to the worst, if that is how it is to be I'll just have to take it, along with a lot of others, but I don't look at that side of the picture, honey. I'm trying to go on, living each day just as I think you would like to see me live it, praying that God will bring you back to me real, real soon, when we'll make up for this and other separations. Anyway, I have a feeling that everything is alright, darling, as I've said ever since I recovered from that first shock of the telegram, and Jean said her feeling about Jack was the same, so guess there must be something to it.

I went to see Dr. McKee today and he was swell. Told me that I had the right slant, my feeling about you. He thinks the same, but of course, admits that it could be something final, but we don't even talk about that. He was looking good, rather tired though. Guess he is kept pretty busy these days, with so many of the younger men in the service. Honey, I'm going to have to close for this time or this letter will be too fat – mine of the 22nd came back today for more postage. They check up on me pretty thoroughly these days, huh? Guess they know me pretty well. I love you, my darling, and I pray every day that God is watching over you and will bring us together again before many more days. Until tomorrow then, goodnight honey-bun. Pleasant dreams and God bless you always. I'll be seeing you darling.

Chapter 39
Kriegsgefangener

Didn't receive any letters from you today, but I did receive a package from you which naturally made me quite happy and excited to get it. I believe, though, that it was the second one that you sent, 'cause it doesn't have the contents that you said was in the first. It contains two cans, filled with gum drops, orange slices, walnuts, lemon drops, raisins, mints, and gum. I believe you said that the first one also contained peanuts and such. It all sure tastes swell, my darling, everyone else thinks so also. I was getting tired of this candy we get for rations. I don't usually eat it anyway. It is chocolate bars, which tastes about like Exlax. I always give it to someone else. Jack usually eats it, he likes it. You know how often I like candy bars anyway. But, I do like such things as what you sent, my darling.

Sure, darling, I sure would like to have some candied figs or any such things like that. I would always rather have things like that than chocolate bars and such. Those cookies, mints, peanuts, and coffee etc. are just the kind of things that I like most. You really know what to fix up to make me happy. The package wasn't crushed or anything. I will always welcome any goodies to eat from sweet you; only don't send them any more than every couple of weeks. I don't like to help crowd the mail too much. I had almost a full carton of gum that I had brought with me, and I just gave it away yesterday. I gave it to some fellows who were making up a package to take to some English boys stationed with the Air Sea Rescue. They had pulled them out of the channel and treated them so swell, and those boys don't get much to smoke, chew, or sweets to eat. I thought it was a swell idea. They had about 20 cartons of cigarettes to give them also.

You have the right idea, darling, about the information that should be written home from here. It wouldn't do anyone at home a bit of good to know all about what was going on over here, and it would only tend to worry most people all the more. The less said the better. No darling, I don't know anything about what happened to Doug. I suppose I was around somewhere at the time, but I wouldn't have known where he was or when. The only thing that I can say is that he has better than a 50-50 chance of being well off, but that's something that takes quite a while to determine. It has to come through the International Red Cross, and they usually try to make sure before sending out word.

The news is just coming over the radio and I guess everything is going okay. The U.S. troops in Salerno are being pushed back a ways, which isn't so good, but I don't think that will last long. Italy may have surrendered, but the German's haven't! The best news recently is from the Russian front. They sure are going to town lately, and I sure hope they can keep up all the good work. It's too bad that we aren't going in just as fast from this side, and the whole thing wouldn't take so long, but I don't think it will be too long anyway – I hope? Darling, I really must get to bed now, I'm rather tired tonight; these short night's sleep get me down. I always go to bed early just in case we have to get up about midnight. At least I get a couple hours sleep. Goodnight now darling. I love you very much, honey-bunch, & I'll be writing again tomorrow. God bless you darling. Cecil.

One day, about a week and a half after I was placed in the hospital, two German Captains came in. One of them spoke broken English. They took me and an American sergeant and put us in a truck. They weren't guards or from a prison camp, but I guess they were going in the general direction of where we needed to go. It all seemed very casual to me so far and that alone made me somewhat nervous. None of the Germans that I had met acted at all like the war mongering people that we heard about back in the states. I was grateful for that, and hoped that I wouldn't have to see those guys at all. They drove us down to Frankfurt. We crossed the Rhine River at Cologne. The river and the countryside was beautiful. What a shame that the war would be tearing this land and these cities apart. After a long ride we arrived at a train station late in the evening. The two officers took us inside and had us sit on a wooden bench as they handed us off to a guard. We slept on the bench, sort of, as we wondered what horrors the morning might bring. In the morning, as more civilians showed up, we discovered that we were disliked around there. Women and children were throwing things at us and spitting at us if they got close enough. The guards tried to keep them back, and would even yell at them, but there were just too many for the guards to keep track of. The guards gave us some soup and brown bread to eat, then put us on a small electric short haul train and moved us to a nearby interrogation center called Dulag Luft at Oberursel on October 20th where we joined about fifty more American and British prisoners. They put me in a dark small cell in solitary confinement that had a wooden bed in the corner. They had a loud speaker blaring with someone yelling "don't beat me, don't beat me, I'll tell you what you want to know." When they shut me in the room they turned out the light and it was totally dark in there. They turned up the heater and made me sweat in the dark for hours. I don't know how much time had passed while I was in there the first time. Fortunately, I was pretty exhausted so I was able to just sleep. Of course, any noise startled me and I would wake up, but as soon as I realized it didn't present a danger I'd drift off again.

In the morning they came and got me and processed me in by taking my picture and getting an identification card started. Then they walked me down a long grey hall to a room that had a table, two chairs, and a German colonel in it. The colonel was educated in the United States and spoke excellent English. He questioned me over and over again for six days. He kept trying to get me to fill out a Red Cross questionnaire that had way more questions on it than they needed. Besides small talk, like fishing and baseball, all any of us ever gave him was the usual; name, rank, and serial number. The colonel actually seemed quite bored, except when he was talking about Minnesota, which is where he said he went to school, just like the doctor who first treated me. I guess there must have been a large German American population in Minnesota, or they both used the same lie. He had quite fond memories of his time there. No one ever tried to torture me or get rough, but the colonel did try to scare me after a couple days. I guess he wanted me to get comfortable and get my guard down and then they'd scare me. They used two different guys. The colonel was always nice, and then a second guy would try to scare me. After the first couple of days they'd tell me that I'd better give him something or I could be shot as a spy. It worked, I was plenty scared, but I didn't know anything, so I couldn't give up anything even if I wanted to. I think, at heart, he knew that a lowly second lieutenant wasn't going to have any information he didn't already know, and they already knew plenty. It was scary how much they already knew. They must have spies all over England and the states. After the six days of twice a day interrogations they took us all out in a yard and let us wash. An English speaking guard came up to me in the yard and gave me some soap and a razor and told me to shave, that I looked like shit. I think there was a Red Cross official lurking around that made them nervous. He said they had to move us to our permanent camps because they had more new prisoners coming in and they had to make room. After we got cleaned up they told me I was being sent to Stalag Luft III near Sagan. They marched us out a gate where an officer checked our identification, saluted us, and cleared us to proceed to the train station. I found out later that it was a signal to the other prisoners in view when the German officer saluted you as you went through the gate. It meant they respected you and it was a signal to the others that you didn't talk. The officer would turn his back on the prisoners that talked, signaling to the other prisoners what had transpired.

The uncertainty of our future made us all uneasy. It was an overnight trip on a crowded rail car with urine on the floor and the stench of diarrhea from guys who were sick or just couldn't hold it anymore. The train arrived at Sagan on October 28th about 100 miles from Berlin. From there they piled us all on trucks and took us to the camp. After intake we were walked to our compound along the fenced area of another compound and I heard someone yelling and screaming my name. I looked up and saw Jack and Roger waving at me. I was glad to see that they had gotten out of the ship and were alright, it was a great relief for me, God only knew how much. The guards marched us into the south compound, a different compound than the one Jack and Roger were in. They took me into a barracks that was close to a tower and the gate that the guards always came in and out of. I was the 10th man in the barracks, and somehow I scored a bottom bunk, the last bunk in the barracks. The barracks was above ground on a block foundation so the guards could see if anyone was up to no good underneath the building. There was a guard tower about every 100 yards that had a big spotlight on it and the barracks was about 100 feet from the fence. The Germans called this camp escape proof. I learned we were called "Kriegsgefangener," which meant prisoner of war, or Kriegie for short. The fellows in the barracks were just finishing mixing up some supper on the wood stove and invited me to eat with them. It was their one hot meal of the day. They made some stew out of a can of Monterey Sardines that had come in a Red Cross package. Sounds horrible, but when all you've had is a bowl of soup every day for a couple weeks, it's like a seven course meal. The only guy I knew in my compound was a fellow named Bill Mahoney. I met him in England once. He was a good Irishman and a bombardier from Boston who used to love to talk about his Red Sox. The fellows in the barracks told me that we get a Red Cross parcel for each man every week. The parcel has things in it like powdered milk, Spam, sugar, instant coffee that they said sucked, and a few other things. They said we sometimes get Canadian parcels too, which has a bag of ground coffee in it that was much better than the instant stuff. Most of these guys hadn't been here that long but they have had, on occasion, the chance to talk with some of the guys that have been prisoners since the beginning of the war or soon thereafter. They said that Herman Goering himself ordered the building of the camp to house British and American airmen. Before that, airmen had been kept in camps that weren't so nice. Goering wanted the Luftwaffe to take better care of the foreign fliers. I guess, in theory, he thought his men who were in turn taken prisoner would get better treatment too, or he was setting himself up for better treatment after the war, which surely he knew the Germans would eventually lose. I soon learned that the Commandant of the camp was a man named Colonel Friedrich Wilhelm von Lindeiner. They said he was a former World War I officer, was personal friends with Herman Goering, and was handpicked by Goering to command this camp. He had a reputation as a fair man who believed whole heartedly in the Geneva Convention and didn't get along at all with the SS or Heinrich Himmler. Our senior officers said that he was a Luftwaffe man and did everything he could to protect the allied fliers as long as we didn't cause any trouble. That was a relief to hear as I settled in to my new digs and new life as a Kriegie as I enjoyed some fine Monterey Sardine stew cuisine. It wasn't quite the Rosemount back in Sacramento, but I'd learn to like such things and be thankful for them.

The "Polly Jo." Transferred to the 94th BG

The Crews First Assigned Ship.
Seen Here after a Wheels up Landing by Leo Jarvis

The 381st BG at Ridgewell Taxiing Out for a Mission

**Before Flying This Ship, the Crew Was Horrified by Watching
The KIA Navigator Being Pulled Out After a Mission.
Note: "Old Coffins" Survived the War**

The Pry-Quinley Crew Flew "The Hellion" to Schweinfurt

**Cecil Flew the 381st Jinx Ship "Tinker Toy" Once,
Barely Surviving a Lost Engine on Takeoff**

Eventual Ship of the Pry-Quinley Crew. 42-30009

Daniel J. Quinley

381st BG Triangle L on Their Way to a Target

Circular Contrails at High Altitude

Daniel J. Quinley

381st BG B-17's Over Schweinfurt

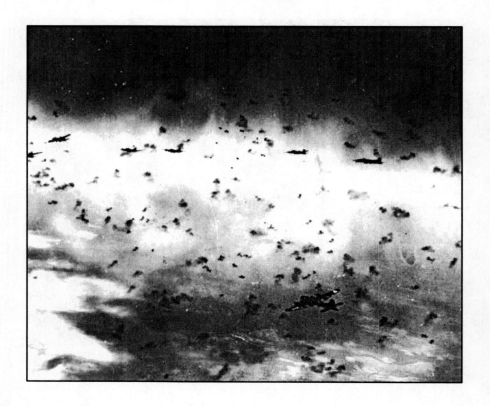

381st BG Bombs Away

Daniel J. Quinley

A B-17 under Fighter Attack

An All Too Common Scene

Daniel J. Quinley

Cecil's Stalag Luft III Registration Card

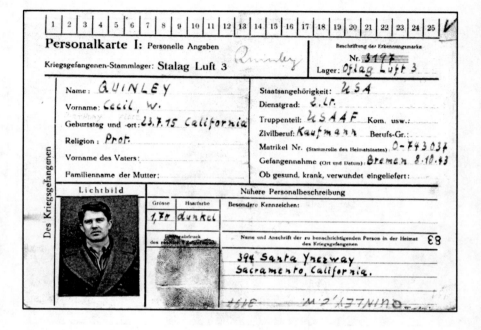

280

Cecil's POW Dog Tag.
His California License Plate Used to be POW 3197

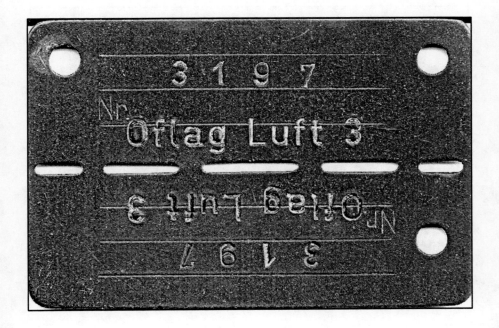

Daniel J. Quinley

Dulag Luft Interrogation Center

POW's Walking the Perimeter at Stalag Luft III

Daniel J. Quinley

The Death March out of Stalag Luft III

Vermin Infested and Overcrowded Stalag VII-A

Liberation. The Moosburg Town Flag

Liberated POW's Swarm a Sherman Tank

Daniel J. Quinley

General Patton Inspects Stalag VII-A

**Stalag VII-A POW's Being Airlifted
From a German Airfield to France**

Daniel J. Quinley

The USS General W. H. Gordon. Cecil's Ride Home

Second Honeymoon, After Repatriation.
San Carlos Borromeo de Carmelo Mission
Near Carmel-by-the-Sea, California

Daniel J. Quinley

The Quinley Family Circa 1961

Cecil Co-Piloting the Collins Foundation
B-17 "Nine-0-Nine" in 1996
Age 81

**Cecil in the Cockpit of the EEA's
"Aluminum Overcast" in 2009
Age 93**

Cecil at a Veteran's Day Ceremony
Fallon, Nevada. 2013
Age 98

The Renewing of the Vows
70th Wedding Anniversary in 2009

Mo Ghrá Eternal – My Eternal Love.

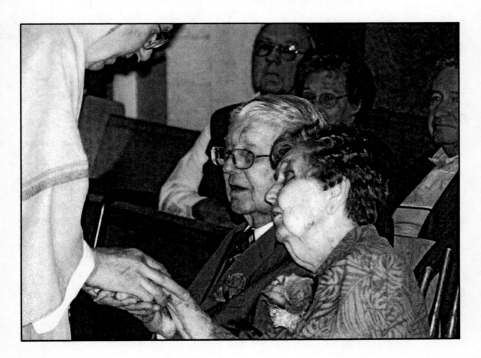

Chapter 40
A Prayer is Answered

October 28, 1943.

Greetings again from me, way over here! I didn't get a letter from you again today, but would hardly expect to do so after receiving six this week already. They're all swell letters, darling, and again I say thanks so very, very much. You are so sweet to me always, dear, and I've never appreciated you half as much as I should have, but if God will please to give me another chance I solemnly promise to make up for all past offenses, cross my heart!

Darling, you have really made headlines in our local papers! Last Saturday was the first appearance of anything in regard to your present status; it came out in the Bee. In that morning's Union, however, was a list of draft delinquencies which included your name! The F.B.I. had warrants out for the arrest of 97 fellows! Of all the nerve, huh? Boy, the Union called me last night to see if I knew how it had happened, because they would like to issue a correction. I explained to the best of my ability how you had completed all of those forms and sent them in and that I was at a loss to know why and how, etc. The morning's paper carried your picture and an article on the front page all about it. I was surprised! It certainly 'panned' the Draft Board in a subtle sort of way. The Bee had a similar article. Both papers had contacted the Draft Board and the fellow there didn't know how it had happened. He said that the statement of your commanding officer had never been received, and that the written notice from yourself, as well as mine, didn't mean a thing! I went to see them and got nowhere. The fellow who talked to me couldn't even show me what paper he claims was sent to you and not returned. He had no record of its ever having been sent! He advised me (somewhat nastily) that our written notices and the fact that you had appeared there upon enlisting and also when your orders arrived, meant nothing to them! How do you like that? Such a system. I finally got mad and told him; 'it's a crazy set-up, a fellow might even have given his life in action and they wouldn't give a damn down there! Such dumbness!' Boy, I was really feeling Irish, honey! Doc McKee said that he was going to work on the board and he was going to start at the top if they don't retract their accusation! He will too! The Draft Board wants to know if I received a wire from the War Department concerning your present status! I wonder what they think I am! Surely, nobody with even an ounce of brains would report a thing as serious as this without authority! They make me boil inside, dragging your name in the quagmire of delinquency! I talked to Mrs. McCabe, the federal Commissioner, and she told me to go to Colonel Leitch, the Selective Service Head. I shall do so tomorrow and try to get this thing cleared up. I dislike the way it has been made such an issue, but don't have much sympathy with, or for Board No. 25! Don't you worry about it dear, I'll fix it up with the colonel himself!

October 29, 1943

Here I am again! Thank you, darling, for the two swell letters that arrived today. I guess we are all caught up to date. The last one you had dated the 7th and it was post marked the 8th. It was a two part letter and I love it. Gee, I have so much news tonight, darling, that I hardly know where to begin. First of all, I guess, I'd better tell you about Polly's call from Alabama. She received the same news that I did, which I previously presumed, but wasn't sure until hearing so from her. Incidentally, her call came through just as the mailman brought me the mail, including a letter from her. She feels the same way that I do about you boys and is being the good little soldier I knew she would be. She's a swell girl, honey, and Jack should feel mighty proud of her, as I'm sure he does. She had received seven letters from him, through the fifth of October. She told me over the phone that you boys were to have gone to a rest camp on the 13th for seven days' rest! Darn the luck, when you deserved the rest so much! The baby is plenty cute, I guess, and as good as gold, according to Polly. She has her mommy's dimples, she says, and Jack's dark hair, plus blue eyes and rosy cheeks. Bet she is darling! The doctor didn't tell Polly the news about you boys until Saturday. Jack's folks had left on Wednesday, and Mrs. Pry turned right around and flew back to be with Polly, which was plenty nice of her I think. She apparently is doing alright now and the baby sounds plenty healthy. I'm glad that she is keeping her spirits up, 'cause that means a lot at a time like this. She feels the same as I do, that hoping and praying, and placing our faith and trust in God, are the only things to do. Knowing that God will in turn take the best of care of all of you and bring you back to us very, very soon. We're hoping hard that you aren't worrying too much about how we are taking this news, darling. Polly also wrote that Jack had mentioned the presentation of your medals; purple hearts, etc., and she is equally as proud as I am of all of you! Jack had bought his cigars for 'Junior' and Polly feels sort of bad that he will have to change them to candy, maybe, not that it makes any difference what a new father passes out to the fellows. Cigars are preferable, probably, to a bunch of you boys. Don't get sick on them, any of you! Just the same, I'll bet neither one of those two would want to change their dimpled darling girl for a boy! Did I tell you the other day that I had picked out a cute gift for the baby? I think that I did. Anyway, I sent a very cute 'Snuggles' doll, and hope she and Polly will get a kick out of it. I'm sure Polly will before the baby does.

I went to see Colonel Leitch of the Selective Service System today, he is the top guy, I guess. He was swell and is going to see that Board No. 25 clears their files of the charges against you. He was very apologetic and told me during the course of our conversation that Dr. J.R. McKee had talked to him at noon and told him that he'd better clean up that mess or he'd be ready to shoot him at sunrise! I guess that they are very good friends. Anyway, he told me that he wished there was more he could do under the circumstances and even offered to send a formal letter of apology to be published in both papers, if I wanted him to do so, but I told him I'd rather that it wouldn't be made an issue of any longer 'cause you wouldn't enjoy so much publicity, and besides, everyone knows it's the Draft Board's fault and not the colonel's – why cause him embarrassment? So he had his secretary make a copy of the telegram from the War Department for their files and is going to see that the case is closed right now. That's good, I'm glad that I went to see him. I told him how stinky that fellow on Board No. 25 treated me the other day too. He accused me of insinuating that his board filed important papers in the waste paper basket. Could be, huh? Anyway, I guess it's all cleaned up now, darling. Your name is clear, and they had better keep it that way or Doc and I will be on their necks again. He was really mad at those guys on the board. You know he thinks an awful lot of you, darling.

The west coast has ceased its dim-out regulations, we are once more ablaze downtown, I guess. It will be quite a change. Remember how dark it was when we got in from Walla Walla, honey? It will probably mean that lots more people will roam the streets at night and will no doubt make more business for the stores. The news has been good from all of the war fronts during the last few days. Your boys have been doing a lot of good work, darling.

Gee, honey, it's been a month today since your last letter and a month tomorrow since you were last heard from at your base. I'm still hoping and praying that everything is going swell with you and that it won't be much longer till I'll be hearing the good news that's bound to be coming. I tried last night from 5:30 on to get Polly and finally reached her at 9:30. It was her and Jack's anniversary. I had planned to call her sooner but was afraid I might scare her. Then, in her letter that came yesterday, she said she was waiting for that phone call, so I tried right away. She is feeling swell now and is able to be up most of the time. The doll I sent her for the baby arrived okay and seemed to make her very happy. She spoke of having received a letter from Burwell's mother in which she mentioned having met a major who just returned home on leave from one of the English bases. He was on that mission with you fellows and told Mrs.

Burwell that headquarters records over there show that 240 of the 300 of you boys who went down on the 8th are safe. That's really good news and a plenty good average! We're both still anxiously awaiting that good news that you are safe somewhere over there, and I still feel that it will be here pretty soon now. In the meantime, I lay awake reading your last letter to me each and every night. I thank God you had the time to finish it before leaving your base that last fateful morning. I read one of the letters that I wrote to you from Fallen Leaf Lodge. Gee, I was kind of silly, huh? I loved you, though, honey, just the same as now which is more so, if that makes sense. Those were swell letters that you wrote to me, honey, too. I enjoy them every time I read them. Sure wish that I'd get a telegram with good news about you, then I'd be very, very happy. My news should be arriving soon, I think. A man came up the walk this morning with a telegram for Louise and Bill and I was actually disappointed to see it wasn't for me, although I know that the next one I receive will probably have me in an awful dither before having the strength to get it opened! Such is life! I'm certainly becoming more and more impatient as time drags by. I just can't help it sweetheart. I'm so sure that you are safe, and yet I want the proof that a telegram from the War Department (like Bonnie's and Maxine's) will bring. Until it comes I guess I'll just be on edge. I can hardly wait for the day when you'll come flying home. It seems so terrible long since I told you goodbye that day in June. Pardon my wishing mood, darling, I just can't help it. I miss you so very much. I'll be seeing you soon, though, and then this bad dream will be all over. Until that lovely day, and always, I'll be loving you and praying for God's blessing on you. May he keep you ever safe and bring you home real soon. All my love and kisses – from your Mrs. Margaret.

On Sunday, November 14th I attended morning mass, as usual, and went through my whole routine. When I got home and walked through the door I saw a telegram leaning up against Cecil's picture on the mantle above the fireplace. Mac had left it there when it was delivered while I was at mass. I wasn't sure if I had the courage to look at it by myself, but I slowly went over and picked it up. Goosebumps filled my arms as I felt chilled and faint, and with my trembling hands I pulled the single page telegram out of the envelope. He was alive! My God, he was alive! My prayers had been answered, he was alive! I broke down and cried just like the night I got that first telegram, only this time I was crying tears of joy and relief, he was alive!

WASHINGTON DC 1943 Nov 14
MRS MARGARET M QUINLEY
394 SANTA YNEZ WAY
SACRAMENTO CALIFORNIA
REPORT RECEIVED THROUGH THE
INTERNATIONAL RED CROSS STATES THAT YOUR
HUSBAND SECOND LIEUTENANT CECIL W
QUINLEY IS A PRISONER OF WAR OF THE GERMAN
GOVERNMENT
LETTER OF INFORMATION FOLLOWS FROM
PROVOST MARSHAL GENERAL
ULIO THE ADJATENT GENERAL.

Chapter 41
Stalag Luft III

Oh, happy day! I received my good news this morning! You are alive and safe, even though you are a German prisoner of war! I'm so happy, honey! I don't think that I ever really gave up hope, but there was always that little shadow that maybe I was taking too much for granted in thinking everything was alright! Gee, it is such a relief to know for sure! I didn't call Polly, thought I should let her call me to be sure she has had the same good news! Oh, gee, I haven't calmed down all day, no fooling! I've been about walking on air! I got up this morning feeling so awfully low and blue and when I went to mass I prayed extra hard for God to give me patience to take the next few weeks in stride without worrying too much. My wire came while I was at 9 O'clock mass. All of the way home, though, I was thinking (and wishing) how nice it would be to have good news here waiting for me, and there it was! Oh darling, I'm so glad you're alright! Thank God for being good to us again, as always. Guess I'd better not mail any more letters to you now, till I hear my details from the War Department. Bonnie says that the letters all come back. I'll save them all and keep on writing too, just the same.

I love you darling, just in case I neglected to mention it in a while. It's different now, writing to you and not mailing the letters. Until today I have mailed your letters to your A.P.O. address, but guess they'll be coming back soon. I'm surely glad that I kept writing, 'cause it helped to keep up my spirits. Those 25 days were awfully long ones, though! Had a letter from Esther, and Corky called to say how happy she was to hear the news of your safety. I still haven't calmed down, darling; I'm so happy and thankful to know you're alright. Just finished reading a good article in 'Read Magazine' about our prisoners of war. There was quite a detailed account of Stalag Luft III, which is the airman's camp and where Bob Pelton is. I certainly absorbed the details, 'cause I sort of feel that that is where you are too my darling. I surly hope that I'll be receiving your address soon so that I can mail you a letter or two now and then. I hope you won't be too lonesome in the meantime. Gee, you are probably seeing a lot of the fellows who went down on previous raids, some you have known and trained with. Maybe good old George and Win Gredvig, plus lots of others. You will have lots to tell me when you get home.

Holding the letters I write makes it harder to write things of interest. I guess because they'll be old stuff by the time you receive them. Anyway, the most important fact is that I love you truly, and with all my heart, and I'm so thankful that God has kept you safe and is even now watching over you for me. I'll be seeing you one of these days soon too, dearest darling, and we'll be happy again together for always. Until that great day when we shall greet each other again, I'll be loving you and awaiting your return with open arms. Goodnight for another day, darling. I love you, dearest. May God bless you and continue his loving care of you always. All my love and kisses. Margaret.

He's coming around, he's coming around! Shoot Ted, shoot! Smitty! Smitty! Eddie, get back there and check on Smitty, I haven't heard from him since that last hit we took! Never mind, get up here and help me with Lieutenant Quinley, I think he's hit! Jerries, 9 O'clock! Diving down on us! I'm hit, I'm hit, shit, I'm hit. Who is that? Slow down, who's hit? It's Carl, he's hit pretty bad! Eddie, never mind, man your guns, man your guns. Shit, they're all over us! Quinn! Quinn! God damn it Quinn! Wake up! Quinn! Cec! Cecil!

I opened my eyes, but this time I wasn't sitting in the pilot seat with Jack yelling at me and pressing his oxygen mask onto my face. This time I awoke in a smelly room staring at the bottom of a wooden bunk bed above me. It wasn't Jack yelling this time. George Rawlins, my bunkmate from the top bunk, said I was yelling and rolling around in my sleep. He said not to worry about it, that it happened to everyone in there who had gone through what we all went through. I told him I could hear everything. All the voices, the yelling, even when I was half conscious. I could still smell the gunpowder and hear the guns. I asked him if it would get any better. He said no, not really, and he went on to say that we were being roused for a roll call. As I began to roll out of my bunk I realized that I had been sweating badly, even though it was only about 45-50 degrees in the room. We went outside and formed a loose group that could hardly be called a military formation, but the guards didn't care. Roll call was called "appel" and I soon learned that we would stand there for as long as it took to get the count correct. As the guards began their count a most curious thing happened that had me pretty confused and, frankly, scared me because I wondered how the guards would react to it. Some of the guys thought it good sport to mess with the guards during the count. As the guards went down the line counting, some of the guys, after already having been counted, would sneak down to the other end so when the guards completed the count there would be too many men. Pretty funny, I guess, but I wondered how the guys with the guns would react to it. It must be a common game because they didn't get mad. They had to do three counts in all because, each time, the Kriegies would do some variation of their game to screw with the Goons and each time they would yell a little louder to knock it off. Finally, they completed their count and we were released back to our barracks.

Back at the barracks I received more instruction on how the camp was operated and who our commanding officer was. The ranking officer in the south compound was Colonel C.G. "Rojo" Goodrich. I was informed that no escape attempts would be permitted without being authorized by a committee that had been put together to organize such activities. The reason being they didn't want someone trying something on their own and ruining a better and more organized plan that might be in the works. I didn't think that I would be trying anything that would get me shot, but you never know what the future holds. As American fliers we were never really trained on what to expect from being captured. We were told to give only name, rank, and serial number of course, but that was the extent of our education. The Brits had a very different education and I was told it was expected of them to attempt escape. They were always up to something. It was rumored that they were up to something right now, but no one really knew what they were doing, not in south camp anyway. We Americans were not required to try and escape and we were left to our own ambitions. My understanding was that anything we did know about escaping was learned from the Brits before our compound was built. It must not have been much because I don't think anyone had ever been successful up to that point. I had heard that one day the Germans brought a horse drawn wagon into the compound carrying coal or something heavy and the wagon broke through the ground into a tunnel that was obviously being dug too shallow in the sandy soil. If not for the consequences I'm sure that was a hilarious sight to see. No, I thought, I'll just wait out the war here. It's not an ideal situation, but we're a long way from anything and I just didn't see how getting killed was going to help anyone or anything. It was just plain stupid if you ask me. The conditions at the camp were just not that bad, compared to how they could have been that is. Eventually the allies were going to whip Germany and, hopefully, we would then be able to go home. I suppose the big question in everyone's mind was what the Germans might do to us once they are faced with defeat. Would they surrender, simply leave, or kill us all as a last final option? If our treatment deteriorated, or we got wind of some sort of SS takeover, then that could change things and make escape or fighting necessary, but for now self-preservation was the right idea I thought. The Brits had this idea that by escaping they were somehow tying up German forces to force them to search for them. That didn't really hold water, in my opinion, because the troops that were hunting for them were obviously not being recalled from any front lines and were running about the countryside already. No, I reasoned, my main job now is to survive all this and get home to my wife and family.

Later in the day I was given more information during an informal tour by George Rawlins. He was a captain and bombardier who hadn't been there very long, but long enough to know the ropes. He pointed to a wire that was running parallel to the fence, about a foot off the ground and about thirty feet inside the fence. He told me not to ever-ever cross that wire, no matter what. The area between that wire and the fence was called "no man's land" and was a kill zone for the guard towers. Anyone found in that area would be shot. There were German fellows running around the camp all the time that were called "Ferrets." These Ferrets had the job of basically spying on us Kriegies to make sure that we followed all the rules of the camp. They also looked for evidence of escape plans, tunnels, and the like, and it was not unheard of for them to pop up into a barracks from the crawl space underneath. Sometimes they would even crawl around under the building and just listen to what was going on. We kept a log close to the gate and we kept track of who entered and who left. Every Ferret had a nickname, so the Germans didn't know what we were talking about on the log. They didn't know we were keeping a log of their coming and going. If someone noted that not all of the Ferrets had departed and been checked off the list, all activities were halted and a search was done to find the little bastard. I was pleased to hear that Germany had signed the Geneva Convention agreement and we were fortunate enough to have three international organizations looking after our well-being as prisoners of war. The thought was never far from our minds that we could be shot at any time, especially if some overly distraught officer went nuts and did something stupid to get us all punished. But, it was nice to know there was someone out there watching over us, even if they were thousands of miles away with very little leverage. The International Red Cross supplied care packages consisting of food, clothing, blankets, and medical supplies. The Swiss Government watched over the camp conditions and rules of the Geneva Convention and investigated complaints. The International YMCA provided recreational equipment such as; musical instruments, sporting equipment and things like that. George showed me around our barracks more after appel. The barracks, or blocks, consisted of several rooms that held ten men each. On each end of the barracks there was a semi-private room that held the ranking officers for that barracks. Our end held two lieutenant colonels. Each barracks had a central kitchen with a coal or wood burning cook stove that each room took turns using and each room had its own smaller coal stove that we could also use for cooking things, like that sardine stew they were making when I arrived. The hard part was finding coal or wood to burn. I prayed that my good fortune would hold out and we would continue to be treated well until Germany's defeat. My dream of flying hadn't included this.

Chapter 42
The Great Escape

Here I am again to tell you I'm thinking of you and loving you, as always. I surely do miss you lots, too! Had a nice letter from Polly today. She had received Jack's address and he is where Bob Pelton is, Stalag Luft 3. Sure hope you are there too, honey, 'cause that is the most widely publicized German prisoner of war camp, especially for airmen. Sure hope I'll be hearing more soon. I keep hoping and praying every day, so my turn will come soon. Once again I must be patient. This is a cold night in Sacramento and I'm hoping that wherever you are you are being kept warm. I received two prisoner of war bulletins (put out by the Red Cross) today and they have lots of encouraging items in them.

Just finished balancing our bank account statement for this month and everything is now under control. Our liabilities are practically all erased from the books now. I hope to have the records clear by February 1st, 1944, at the latest. I feel bad that I haven't been able to save much lately, but as you say, we can always start at scratch if our bills are paid. I know that it's all my fault that we have had so many, but I promise to be a better manager from now on. I hope to have at least a three or four figure savings account when you come flying home to me. It will be swell to have enough saved so that you won't have to take just any job and can even have a vacation before hopping back into harness again. I'll keep trying hard, honey-dear.

Surely hope I receive your address and prisoner of war number pretty soon 'cause I know how you must miss not having any mail. I can't figure out any logical reason for the 'detaining government' not reporting your number and address with Jack's and Burwell's! Maybe the Germans don't recognize the letter 'Q.' I'll get this in the mail as soon as I do hear, honey, as you probably realize, so keep the chin up till then.

Bonnie got another letter from Bob at Stalag Luft 3. She also told me of Marcia's having received word from her (Bob's) commanding officer that he is a prisoner of war in Germany also. Maybe you'll be seeing them too, darling. I just mailed a letter today to Marcia and tried to reassure her that her husband was probably with you boys. Once again all of our prayers have been answered. Our 'carload' of boys has been very lucky, in spite of everything!

Father Christen called to say he would offer 8:00 A.M. mass for my intention tomorrow. I had planned to attend that one anyway so am quite happy that it will be especially for us. I'll pray extra hard for God to bring me your number and camp name tomorrow, or soon after. I'm going to Holy Communion also, so maybe that will help. Until tomorrow then, and for all time, I'll be loving you and praying for God to bless you and watch over you and bring you home real soon. Till we meet again and forever, I love you dear, with all my heart. G'night for this time. I'll be seeing you. God bless you, my darling. All my love and kisses. Margaret.

And so the day dragged on and on. I found myself getting bored often and missing Margaret more than I ever thought I could. I had to tell myself to snap out of it from time to time. I'm sure there were fellows at other camps that were far less fortunate than we were. After a while I could understand why some guys tried so hard to escape, even knowing that to get caught could mean death. We had twice daily appel, morning and evening. Morning appel was at 0800. If you were sick the guards would come to your room and count you there. After appel we were released and we could head back to our rooms to scrounge up something to eat. We were constantly hungry, but we managed to have enough food to just get by on. The Krauts gave us German black bread and we had a couple slices in the morning that we put on the stovetop in the rooms to make into toast. It wasn't much, but I got used to it. Often it was made with sawdust as a filler. I was a pretty small guy already, so I fared pretty well with the food we got. Some of the bigger guys didn't fare as well and they lost a lot of weight from the meager rations we had. After breakfast and clean up George and I headed outside and walked the perimeter, usually 3-5 times. It was important to keep exercising as much as we could stand with the food we were taking in. You never knew if you'd have to be able to get out and run in a hurry. There was a lot of standing around and watching the Goons, which is what we called the guards. Colonel A.P. Clark was the officer in charge of security in the south compound and he had us keeping pretty close track of the guards all the time. It was as much to keep us occupied and sharp as it was for security. At lunchtime we had a canned meat of some kind, usually corned beef or spam. It was common to make a soup and eat light for lunch, saving the meat and as much lunch as we could to add to our dinner rations. That way we could eat more at dinner and go to bed with a full stomach. It helped us get through the night. We were also given one head of cabbage per day that we had to split amongst all ten of us, and some sort of sausage or beef. After lunch our routine would start all over and we would walk the compound again. It seemed like it got dark awfully early where we were at. The rumor was that the Germans set their clocks two hours ahead. It sure seemed like it was dark at 4:30 in the afternoon. After about a month George and I volunteered to do the dishes and clean up. We did this because some of the guys weren't cleaning stuff very well and everything was disgustingly filthy and people were getting sick. A week later we decided we would do the cooking for our room also, because some of the guys just couldn't cook to save their own lives. It kept us busy and we were able to make what we wanted with the very limited supply of what we had. Every once in a while we could bribe a guard with cigarettes to get us seasonings or spices or something to help make things a little more tolerable. American cigarettes were plentiful from the parcels we received, and from packages sent from home, and they were extremely popular with the guards because their cigarettes were pretty lousy.

As I settled into my life as a Kriegie we gained more and more privileges. Don't get me wrong, it didn't make up for being a prisoner of war under constant threat of being gunned down by a guard, or being half starved to death, or being all but cut off from our loved ones, but it made life in the camp tolerable. I have to admit, though, I had no desire at all to attempt escape. That being said, the escape committee still existed and was kept busy, and we were kept busy keeping an eye on the Goons as much as they kept an eye on us. I was assigned the job of watching the guards after lights out for half the night. There was a knot hole in our window shutters and the windows did not have glass in them. I hung a blanket over the inside of the window and stood between the blanket and the shutter peeking out through the hole. It was a pretty monotonous task, but I did it as ordered and made notes of all the guards comings and goings and their habits if I noticed any. One night, though, a Goon was walking by and he noticed the knot hole and he poked something sharp through the hole. I looked away just in time and it hit me in the cheek. I wanted to yell, but I managed to keep my cool, even though whatever it was it hurt like hell and set me to bleeding all over myself! I tried my hardest to not make a sound so the Goon wouldn't know that he hit anyone. The next morning at appel, however, I saw a Goon staring at me, pointing and smiling with his buddies. Ass hole, I thought! Most of the time the guards kept with decorum; checking in with the ranking officer when they entered the barracks or rooms. But they would surprise us every once in a while. It was common practice to yell "Goon on the block" if a guard was noticed coming in the door. We would yell it nice and loud so the other rooms could hear as well.

In February, 1944, the camp theater opened in the north compound. It was a very nice theater, all things considered. It was heated and held 500 people and even had an orchestra pit. The seats were made from the wooden boxes of Red Cross parcels and were actually quite comfortable. I didn't attend many plays, but I went to as many motion pictures as I was allowed to and I always loved to hear the camp orchestra play. On its face it sounds like a summer camp or something. Don't get me wrong. We made lemonade from the lemons and the German philosophy was to treat us as good as possible and it would deter the want of escape. We were still surrounded by barbed wire, guard towers and machine guns. There was no place to go or hide. Even with all our privileges, it was no summer camp. The orchestra received their instruments from the YMCA and many of the fellows in camp were very good; having had previous experience. Of course, some of the brass instruments disappeared from time to time and were turned into stills that were hidden in various barracks. The camp brew made in these stills was usually made from raisins and prunes. Sometimes it was very tasty. The south compound jazz band was allowed to make visits to the different compounds and put on performances under the leadership of a musician named Dusty Runner. One time, however, the band was being escorted back to our compound and noticed that the Goons were conducting an appel of the Brits. The band stopped and started playing "God save the king." Every British soldier out there suddenly turned toward the band and saluted. The Goons got real upset and stopped the band from playing for a month. There was also a fine record player in the theater and we were able to play records every day. It became a nice way to escape the day to day boredom and brought a sense of home to the camp. The winter was cold until I received some extra clothes from the Red Cross and from Margaret. Some guys were driven to risk themselves to try and keep warm. One fellow on our block, named Wes Corson from Alabama, took advantage of an unguarded horse in the yard that was pulling a wagon full of supplies. He stole the blanket off the horse to try and help keep himself warm at night. The Goons were awfully upset about that and did an extensive investigation over the whole incident. Finally, not having made any progress, they let the word out that they would be cutting food parcels until they got the blanket back. Wes threw the blanket out in the yard one night where the Goons could find it on their rounds. He was never caught over the ordeal, as far as I know.

There were several officers in camp that were school teachers, some university instructors, who volunteered to hold classes on various subjects. A fellow could get pretty educated in camp if he wanted to and many took advantage of the opportunity. I didn't care to attend classes, but I did take advantage of the camps extensive library and I read every day of my captivity. Reading was a great way to escape my surroundings and place myself in the world of the book in which I was engrossed in. Some of the British authors, I thought, carried on way too much with details and filler talk that slowed their story down, but I learned to love those books too. It took me away, if just for a while, to a better place. It took three months but I finally began to receive mail from Margaret and we were able to continue our back and forth letters once again. I had to be even more careful with what I said here than what I said at Ridgewell because the slightest mistake could place someone's life in jeopardy. For that reason all outgoing mail was censored before it was given to the Goons for mailing. Margaret's letters, however, were not censored and, really, there was no need to anyway. I was glad that she knew I was safe, but I knew it was tearing her up worrying about me. I felt so sorry for her and what she must be going through.

March 25th, 1944, we were awakened for appel in the early morning hours. There was a lot of yelling going on by the guards, enough so that we could tell that something serious had happened. When we went outside we were surprised to find trucks in the compound with machine guns on them being pointed at us. It was very disturbing and I wondered if the SS were taking over the camp and if they were going to shoot us all. It appeared as though most of the activity was over at the British compound, but there were plenty of guards surrounding us as well. Quietly, up and down our ranks, we asked each other what was going on, but no one knew. Our theory quickly became that there must have been an escape attempt. I figured that's where my bunk rails must have gone. By this time I was sleeping on a blanket that was nailed to the sides of the bunk in a hammock fashion. Our bed slats had been taken, we supposed, for tunnel support. Eventually, we were allowed back into our blocks but all privileges were suspended until further notice. That night a guard got nervous and fired a couple shots into a barracks in our compound but no one was hit. Over the next week and a half we were called out for surprise appels at all times of the day and night. It didn't take long for word to get out that there was a massive escape attempt by the Brits. The word was that 76 men were able to escape through a tunnel. They weren't all British men, but they were all members of the Royal Air Force. While we were out on the sports field being counted the Goons would search our rooms. Then, on April 6th, the Commandant spoke to us about the escaped prisoners. It was a powerful moment, words delivered sincerely by a man that was truly ashamed of the behavior of his fellow countrymen, the SS. The Commandant had tears streaming down his face as he told us that fifty of the RAF men were "shot while attempting to escape again." He said that they were in a rail car and an SS guard said that they were trying to get out again so they shot them all. We would later learn that information was false and they were all shot two or three at a time in the back of the head by the Gestapo on the side of the road as they were being allowed to relieve themselves. The news infuriated everyone in the camp, but it also stopped everyone from trying to escape, at least for a while. The cremains of the RAF escapees were returned to the camp and a formal memorial service was held with full honors on April 7th. It was that quickly that we were all reminded where we were, what we were doing there, and the very real dangers that surrounded us always. Every day after April 7th the thought of our fifty slaughtered men was on everyone's mind. Our situation was very real, and death could be at hand very quickly.

Chapter 43
Psalms 23:1-6

The Lord is my shepherd; I shall not want. He maketh me to lie down in green pastures: He leadeth me beside the still waters. He restoreth my soul: He leadeth me in the paths of righteousness for his name's sake. Yea, though I walk through the valley of the shadow of death, I will fear no evil: For thou art with me; Thy rod and thy staff they comfort me. Thou preparest a table before me in the presence of mine enemies: Thou anointest my head with oil; My cup runneth over. Surely goodness and mercy shall follow me all the days of my life: And I will dwell in the house of the Lord forever. The Lord is my shepherd; I shall not want. He maketh me to lie down in green pastures: He leadeth me beside the still waters. He restoreth my soul: He leadeth me in the paths of righteousness for his name's sake. Yea, though I walk through the valley of the shadow of death, I will fear no evil: For thou art with me; Thy rod and thy staff they comfort me. Thou preparest a table before me in the presence of mine enemies: Thou anointest my head with oil; My cup runneth over. Surely goodness and mercy shall follow me all the days of my life: And I will dwell in the house of the Lord forever.

Words I'll remember for the rest of my life. Words spoken by Padre Mac at the memorial service for the fifty murdered RAF officers. It was a somber, powerful ceremony that brought us all back down to earth and reminded us how fragile our existence really was as prisoners of the Third Reich. A fragile existence that was again displayed to us a few days after the service when the camp air raid sirens sounded in the middle of the day. It was a flight of B-17's passing over, and what a beautiful sight it was to see them this far inside Germany. Unfortunately, one of our corporal's was working in the south compound kitchen area and he stepped out into the yard to watch the formation pass by. A shot rang out as a guard from outside the fence placed a bullet between his eyes. He was dead before he hit the ground. Other guards would later tell us that the guard who shot our man was newly arrived from the eastern front. He was nervous and trigger happy.

The next day there was a warning posted that we should know that the rules say to stay inside during air raids or we will be shot. There was no such rule before our man was gunned down. At least the corporal's last vision was of American B-17's and his last thought, possibly, was of a future freedom because of it.

I was never a very religious man, although since marrying Margaret I'd been attending services with her. In camp I began attending Padre Mac's services to help myself cope with everything. Padre Mac, Murdo Ewan MacDonald, was a Scottish ordained minister who was rumored to have been a commando who was captured during a mission. Some American airmen managed to convince the Goons that he was an American flier so he was sent to Stalag Luft 3 with them. His sermons were tremendous and were delivered in his wonderful Scottish accent. I felt as though the Padre was one of us, a man who understood us, our fears, our guilt, what we had been through and what we were currently going through. Padre Mac was indeed one of us and that was what brought me and many others to his services. It was sometimes hard to understand that there is a God when you are in a war surrounded by death and destruction and ugliness. Now we are at the mercy of a people who you don't know whether they will murder you or treat you humanely. Padre Mac helped to restore some of my faith and to understand that it wasn't God that allowed all this wretched evil to continue. God gives man free will and it's man who wages war and kills his fellow man, and it's through the hands of good men that the evil will be destroyed and goodness and peace restored. It will take time to accomplish that and our faith in God will guide us along the way. His sermons were indeed a source of comfort for me throughout my stay in the camp.

Life began to get back to normal in the camp. A new Commandant was brought in to replace the temporary officer who was left in charge when they court martialed Colonel Von Lindeiner because of the escape. The head Goon sergeant, Oberfeldwebel Hermann Glemnitz, remained in his position, which was good for us. He was a master at tunnel finding and could be strict, but he was also fair and sometimes tolerant of our escapades. One night he was in our block and one of our fellows was bad mouthing him terrible. The sergeant was losing his temper and our man just wouldn't stop. I thought the sergeant was going to kill our man and we had to separate them, a dangerous task in itself because we weren't allowed to touch the guards. I managed to convince Sergeant Glemnitz that our lieutenant was crazy and we'd take care of him if he could see his way not to hurt him. He was still mad, but he left and didn't do anything further. In June we had a huge morale boost. I was awakened by shouting and men running through the block. Some were shouting in a barely recognizable Gaelic "Thainig iad! Thainig iad! Thainig iad!" My Gaelic was restricted to what I had taught myself when I proposed to Margaret so I asked someone what the heck they were yelling about. I was told that Padre Mac had received word through the wire from the north compound and Gaelic was one of the ways they coded their conversations to keep the Germans from knowing what they were saying. In this case it meant "They've come!" I still had no idea what that meant but everyone was certainly excited about it. Finally, I learned that it meant the allies had invaded. At last there was hope. In the following days the German news broadcasts and papers talked about the allied invasion of Europe. The German news said that our forces were being beat back and were losing. We knew better, though, through getting our news from clandestine radio sets that had been built piece by piece from parts that had been either smuggled in or purchased from guards with cigarettes and chocolate. The Goons couldn't understand why we were yelling and cheering when our forces were being thrashed, but we knew the truth. The beginning of the end was at hand. We got a new officer assigned to our barracks. He was one of two colored fliers from the 332nd fighter group in Italy who recently arrived at Stalag Luft 3. Some of the guys called them "night fighters," an obvious nickname based on their color, but most of the guys didn't mean it in a derogatory way, even though, I imagine, that's the way it was probably received. Most of the guys that were from bombers had a deep respect for the 332nd fellows because of their reputation as fighter pilots in the bomber escort role. I had not flown any missions where they escorted us in the 381st, because there were no deep penetration fighters flying with us at the time I was shot down. The lieutenant that was assigned to our room was well received by all except for one fellow who was from the Deep South in Louisiana. He made such a fuss that we told him to just shut up or move out, that this officer was just as good as any of us and had earned our respect. He didn't agree and made arrangements to move across the hall into a room full of like-minded fellows from the Mormon faith. One of their guys, who was not like that, moved into our room in the personnel trade. In fact, this Mormon that moved into our room cursed, smoked, and drank coffee and booze if we had it. I used to tease him that he wasn't going to get to heaven if he kept that up. He would say that, yes, he'd get to heaven, he just wouldn't get to be as high up in status as the other guys, and we'd laugh while we lit up another cigarette.

"Blue Boy" was a Goon Ferret that we used to bribe all the time to get extra food or contraband of different sorts. We called this fellow Blue Boy because of the blue coveralls he wore when he was in the camp. One day he was getting a pass to go to town and he had a big date with his girl. In the process of coming around looking to get chocolates or other contraband gifts he could take to her, he inadvertently stumbled upon a distillery operation. He tried to use that information against the fellows he caught to get more booty for himself and his girl. He threatened to blow the whistle on the distillery operation. The Americans said, wait a minute, let's have a drink and talk this over. I'm sure we can work something out. A couple hours later they had Blue Boy falling down stinky drunk on raisin hooch. They loaded his pockets up with contraband and kicked him out of the barracks. He staggered to the gate, obviously quite drunk, and was detained by the guards. After that incident we never saw him again. Our thought was that he was probably shipped off to the eastern front, which was actually getting closer and closer to where we were. Of course, the still was taken apart and hidden for a while, but not for long. It was sometimes a fight over the raisins that we'd get in the food parcels. The booze hounds wanted them for the still, but we'd developed a nice recipe of cut up corned beef, or spam, cooked in a raisin sauce that was actually pretty darn good. Most of the time the booze hounds won, but we'd get our raisins if we had a nice meal planned where we needed them.

I fared pretty well health wise while in Stalag Luft 3. Many guys would get recurring diarrhea because of their lack of precautions with cleanliness or preparing their water properly. Having grown up on a farm my parents taught me about those things and George and I were careful about cleaning and cooking. I didn't mind doing it, and it meant that someone else was doing my laundry, since we divided up all the tasks like that. There were also some problems with appendicitis from time to time, and gall bladder attacks. We had some medics working inside the compound that were in premed when the war started, so they weren't full-fledged doctors, but they had a better knowledge than the rest of us. If there was something that they couldn't handle there were a couple British doctors outside the fence that we could be taken to. One time I had a terrible pain and itch in my ears. In the summer we had talked the Goons into letting us use a fire pool as a swimming pool and they agreed. The fire pool was a diked area that held water for firefighting purposes. It was awfully dirty but we cleaned it up real good and then had a place to swim and cool off, or so we thought. I managed to get athletes foot in my ears. The medic's, thankfully, were able to diagnose it and treat it properly until it went away, but I think it drove me half-crazy until it was gone and it undoubtedly damaged my hearing. Toward the end of 1944 things weren't going good for the Nazis. With our clandestine radios we had all the latest news. Generals' Patton and Montgomery were having their way with the Krauts, and the Russians were moving fast toward our position. There was nervous talk about the Goons maybe killing us all and taking off before the camp got overrun. Word was passed of plans being put together to resist the guards at all cost since we had so many Kriegies in the camp. There were just too many of us for them to be able to kill us all. They'd get a lot of us, but we'd eventually be able to overrun them if we had the fortitude to keep up a charge. It was an unpleasant thought and the nervousness around the camp was palpable. Padre Mac did what he could to keep the calm. Then, on January 27th, 1945, the word came right in the middle of a fresh snow of about six inches. Pack up what you can carry and insulate yourselves as much as possible! We're moving out by forced march! You have one hour to get ready!

I love you and miss you very much. I sure do feel low tonight, honey. Wish I'd hear from you, mail takes so long to come. I know you must be feeling equally as bad without any mail at all to come for some time yet. I think that there is something to that 'mental telepathy' or 'psychic transaction' or something. You are probably feeling as blue as I am and that's why I'm this way. Sounds crazy, but seems quite possible.

Darling, I know wherever you are you certainly are in more dire straits than I am right now and I pray for you every day. It has been a long crazy and stressful month here and I don't mean to burden you with my bad news, but I feel that by the time I am able to get this correspondence to you all will be right again. In a short period of time I was fired from my job at the Dentist office. The doctor had more in mind than just having me type, and honey, you know I'm not that way. He told the office manager to get rid of me because I refused his advances. I'm not sore about that, I wouldn't want to work there under those conditions anyway. Then, a few days later, I was notified that our house had sold and the new owner wants to live on our side and we have to move out. It's okay, though, we have 90 days to move under the agreement. If that wasn't enough, soon after I learned of you being missing in action. It has been a long hard month, alright, and I hope that stuff doesn't add to your stress. Things started looking up already when I learned you were safe. It isn't an ideal situation, I know, but think how much worse it could have been. I thank the Lord each and every day that he saw fit to protect you boys from further harm and has provided for your safety, wherever you are. Guess you are probably feeling about the same over there 'cause you haven't had any letters for almost two months. That's how I look at it when I feel bad about not hearing from you. Here's surely hoping hard that your address will be here soon. I've already decided on how I may send you a wire, honey, but I guess the War Department will probably have special instructions, at least that's what I have heard from some of the other gals who are in the same boat as we are.

I'm going to 8:00 A.M. mass in the morning just for you again and it's almost 10:00, so I'll be closing for now. God bless you and keep you safe 'til we meet again and always, my darling. I'll be loving you forever and always. Good night, darling. I'll be seeing you soon 'in all the old familiar places.' All my love and kisses. Margaret.

Chapter 44
Gewaltmarsch

To Parents, Wives, Loved-Ones, and Friends of P.O.W's in Germany. I hope you will forgive me for this form letter, but as I am receiving thousands of letters asking for news of the German camps, and all are anxious to hear quickly. I am doing this in order to relieve your minds as soon as possible. I am glad that my news of the officers camps is so good and that I can truly assure you of the safety and care of your loved-ones.

Our camps in Germany are very well organized and are run by the senior American officers, our only contact with the Germans coming through them. The Red Cross has made arrangements through Switzerland so that each week we receive a Canadian, English, or American Red Cross food parcel, which is sufficient balance for the full week. I may add that they do contain excellent canned foods, fruits, cigarettes, and candy. With the Red Cross food, we officers could hold our own weight, and some are even gaining weight. There is no need to worry about their diets.

Our bedding and clothing are also given to us through the Red Cross, and I am happy to say that no one goes without or is cold. We are given coal briquettes each week by the Germans and we do manage to keep warm.

Our entertainment comes from theater productions in our own theater which we built in the camp. We have lectures on all subjects, all forms of amateur hours, a top notch orchestra, etc. We have a complete and large library with research and fiction books. They are available to all and all have time and do read.

Strangely enough, in our camp we have very little sickness. In a camp of over 1,000 we have a sick call of 8 to 20 each morning, usually scratches, colds, and minor ailments. Our dental service is good though limited, but we do take care of all emergency and routine work.

As you know, we are allowed to send three letters and four cards per month, but we can receive as much as is written. I encourage the sending of snapshots and mail as often as possible. We do look forward to the mail each day. Parcels from home are coming in regularly. As with the mail, it takes some time to receive them, but they do come and bring joy and pleasure to all the boys.

Many people have asked of the coming downfall of Hitlerism and the safety of the camp. Although I can't say more, don't worry. I doubt if any trouble would come, but we are prepared for any unexpected thing. The boys will be home in good health, in good mental condition, and we're all praying it will be soon.

Perhaps the most outstanding thing in camp is the morale. It is unimaginably high. The fellows are all well of mind and health, and naturally enough, morale is high. They say if a man has a full stomach he is happy, and they are as happy, really, as can be expected, being away from home and family. People have asked for reports on the religious services. We do have them every Sunday morning, and throughout the week in the evening we have open forums on religion and evening prayer hours.

The camp is located about 80 miles from Berlin (south) and is charted by all allied forces as well as German forces. There is no danger of any place being bombed within a radius of 50 miles of the camp, and I doubt if any bombs fall closer than 80 miles (Berlin).

I really appreciate all of your kind thoughts in regard to my injury and my coming home. I was repatriated, for I was considered a permanently disabled soldier. That is the only condition under which we are exchanged. Most of our boys are in good health and very few injured, so I don't believe many more will be coming. However, it won't be long before all my friends and your loved ones will be home.

Strangely enough, most of the information you receive in your letters from the camp is true. The censorship is very lax and we are not compelled any special thing. We write as we please. I wish I could talk to you all personally and

know all the fellows you ask about, but that is not possible.
I hope I have given you a little of what you wanted to know,
and that I have eased your minds from worry.

I am truthfully and sincerely yours,

Lt. A.G. Irish

0227220

Tourney General Hospital

Palm Springs, California.

An hour to get ready! To get ready for what? Where were we going? No one knew what was in store for us, other than we were leaving Sagan. I had gotten somewhat used to life in Stalag Luft 3, but things had been deteriorating in the latter part of 1944. Our room that held ten men when I first got here now held eighteen in triple bunk beds, with no wood slats. Our parcels weren't distributed as often, now had to be shared, and the Goons gave us less food and less coal for heating. As bad as we thought we had it, it was about to get worse. Wherever we were headed most of us were ready to get out of Sagan. The Russians must be close. We had been hearing artillery in the distance off and on for a couple weeks. I had a British pullover sweater that I decided to make into a kind of sling rucksack. I hurriedly sewed the bottom of the sweater closed and then sewed the end of the sleeves together. I packed as much food, D-bars, and cigarettes into the pack as I had. D-bars were a ration that we all got in our Red Cross parcels. They were made with chocolate and oatmeal. Kind of an instant meal in candy bar form. I placed my letters and photos from Margaret inside some extra hidden pockets I'd sewn into the lining of my jacket. It also added some insulation to the jacket. I had just received a new pair of shoes in the mail from Margaret but decided to wear my old shoes to start out, so I tied the laces together on the new shoes and slung them over my shoulder. I tore up the blanket that was holding my mattress up and wrapped the strips around the bottom of my pants and shoes. There was fresh snow on the ground and the temperature was well below zero Fahrenheit. I rolled up two nice thick army blankets and slung them over my shoulder figuring I'd need them sooner or later. At 11:00 P.M. the word came. Time to leave, line up at the gate.

South compound was the first to leave. George and I moved out as we trudged through our compound gate; then out the main gate as our identification was checked. As we walked past the north compound we could see a raging out of control fire. The word spread fast that it was the block where tunnel Harry had been dug. We surmised that the Brits had torched the place. Finally, at about midnight, all 2,000 of us from south compound were out the gate, checked, and ready to go. We began our march down the road as the snow began to fall again. It was an uneasy feeling being outside the camp walking in a blizzard at 20 below zero, especially not knowing what was in store for us. To push us this hard the Germans must be real afraid the Russians might catch up with them. We marched all through the night on that frozen road until about 10 O'clock the next morning! I have no idea how far we had gone or where we were. After daybreak we began to see a lot of refugees headed in the same direction we were. Most of them were a sad looking bunch that appeared to be worse off than we were. Several times we were ordered off the road by the Goons because of passing military convoys, some heading toward the fighting, some heading away. Once they had passed we got back on the road and kept on going. During a short break, after several hours of walking, I was sitting on the side of the road smoking a cigarette and noticed an old German sergeant standing a few feet away resting his head on the butt of his rifle with the barrel stuck down in the snow. I recognized him from the camp and knew that he spoke English.

"Isn't that going to make it so you can't fire that rifle?" I asked.

"It doesn't matter, the rifle is already broken and I have no bullets. But don't get any ideas, their guns work and they have bullets." He said.

He pointed at a few Goons standing a short distance away. I just chuckled a bit and smiled, taking another draw on my smoke. I don't know why, but that interaction and the sight of seeing that sergeant in such despair made me feel better and gave me hope that the war would end in our favor. After a few minutes we were up and moving again. The pace we kept was very fast for the condition some of the men were in, but our column stretched for a mile and the word swept through the column that the Russian Army was only about twenty miles from Sagan when we left camp. We came upon some houses and barns and the Goons finally allowed us a good break. There were a bunch of kids running around asking the Kriegies what they could get for us. When one of those kids asked me I said in my best German,

"Heiβwasser bitte."

The kid ran off and a while later he came back with a tin full of hot water and handed it to me with a smile. I handed him a pack of cigarettes and he ran off to the next Kriegie he could find. The event reminded me of a comical scene when I was first taken prisoner and being transported from the hospital to the interrogation center. We had stopped somewhere and a boy asked me then, also, if he could get me something. I saw a sign on a wall that said HeiBwasser, but back then I thought that meant ice water and boy was I hot at the time and that sounded too good to be true. It was too good to be true, as the boy soon returned with my tin of hot water. In this case, though, hot water was exactly what I wanted and I mixed some of that terrible instant coffee from our Red Cross parcels, but today it was the best coffee I'd ever had. Those kids worked their tails off while we were there because it looked like everyone had the same idea. Looking around it appeared to me like everyone was sipping hot coffee, even the Goons. I ate a few dried prunes I'd packed in my bag and sipped my coffee, making sure to enjoy every last drop while it was still warm. I enjoyed another smoke and nearly drifted off to sleep where I sat. I got up and went into one of the barns, laid down on some hay, and closed my eyes for a couple of hours.

Shortly after noon the guards rousted everyone and we were off down the frozen road again. Our column stretched farther than we could see and everyone was exhausted beyond belief, but we kept going. I decided the best way to keep moving forward was to just look at the back of the man in front of me and walk at my own pace. Every once in a while I saw a Kriegie or two run off into the woods but eventually they came back. I guess they ran out of ideas on where to go and how to survive in the frozen wilderness. They figured out that as lousy as our situation was it was still their best chance of survival. We marched until close to 2:00 A.M. on the morning of the 29th and came upon a town called Muskau. There, we were allowed to enter a tile and glass factory to seek shelter. The locals were saying that this was the coldest winter in years. Great, I thought. Not including our short breaks, and the two hour break at the barns, we marched for 26 to 27 hours, 35 miles through blowing snow, packing down the road for the columns that followed us! At the tile factory their furnace and boilers were still hot so we were allowed to pile into those buildings to get warm. We were trying to find a place to lie down but some colonel went and stood up on some platform and commenced to try and direct everyone and give us a pep talk. If that was the goal they could have selected a better officer to do it. There were two guys with me that used to be stationed with him back in the states. They told me that he was under investigation for embezzlement there because he was taking money from the officers for "base improvements," but he was keeping the money for himself. They didn't know how, but he managed to end up on combat duty maintaining his rank. Finally, I turned to some other colonels that were standing nearby and asked them, can't you just make him shut up so we can get some rest? They nodded and went and got him off his soap box. I spread my blanket down on the concrete in that nice hot room, closed my eyes, and woke up twelve hours later not having moved an inch. I think the Goons were concerned for their own soldiers in Muskau. It was obvious that they weren't handling the march very well. Many of them were not fit for combat duty, either because of prior war injuries, or their advanced age. This march was really doing them in too. They decided to keep us in Muskau a while longer. Our stay would turn into a 30 hour break that was badly needed. We were fed black bread and soup while we all recuperated. During our rest I saw Padre Mac going around checking on everyone. I remembered seeing him during the march hurrying to the rear of the column. I asked him what he had been doing. He said word was passed to him that one of our men could not go on any longer and had just sat down in the snow. He said that by the time he got to him it was too late. He was still alive but had given up. He said he sat and talked with the man for a short while, learning that he had been an All American football player before the war. I wondered aloud what chance the rest of us had if a man like that could not go on. Padre Mac said the man died in his arms and he closed the man's eyes and recited last rights for him, that there was nothing else he could do and he left him there. I think he felt terrible about it, not being able to help him or even bury the man. As we were ordered to pack up and reform our column for the remainder of the march, I wondered in silence if that was a fate that awaited us all. I asked the Padre how many men fell during the death march.

"Too many, leftenant, too many."

Chapter 45
Three Days in Hell

Greetings wherever you may be. I had a nice day but have been awfully lonesome without you, more so than ever, if possible. It just seems like no day is right without you, darling, especially holidays. Don't think I'm griping, honey, I'm not. I feel a very great thankfulness knowing that you are safe and well, and that means so very much. I just wish we could be together, that's all. But there will be lots of other holidays and we can make them up. My work at the hospital was okay and I was glad to help out. I saw Merta Caswell and Georgianna Fabian (she works for Cal-Western also) and wished them well. I took Dr. Savesien his dinner. He was rather low in spirits, but I imagine he will be alright soon. He's been very sick this time, Dr. Hale removed three kidney stones last week, and this trip to surgery coming so soon after the bad time he had last summer has been pretty hard on him. I talked to him for a little while, while his nurse went to eat, and he was asking all about you, how you are, and if I've heard any more news. Jeanie had told him about your being a prisoner. He assured me that you would be well taken care of over there, which I feel is true, but just the same I'm lonesome for you and wish you could be right here with me.

I miss you heaps, but it won't be for many more months, at the rate your pals have been bombing away at the Axis. Your buddies surely did a good job of bombing Berlin last night! Sure hope the bombs don't come near where you boys are. Berlin was in ruins today, so it was reported. Nice going! Bet you wish you could have helped! Polly wrote of Carl Baird having been wounded. Sure hope he gets along okay and that the rest of you are well. Just finished letters to Pat Mutschler, Polly Pry, and Vince and Mildred so guess I've caught up a little bit once more. I like to receive letters so am trying to keep up on my correspondence. Sure wish I'd be hearing from you, honey, so I could mail you another letter. It seems to take so long for mail to come through. Four letters a month just isn't enough, but I guess it will have to do until we are once more together after this old war is finally over. In the mean time I sure hope that everything is alright with you. I went to 8 O'clock Mass this morning and lit ten candles for you and your boys. Just five years ago we celebrated our engagement, honey. We had such a good time! We'll do it again, huh? Gee, this is surely a lonesome letter. I must be missing you. We've surely a lot to make up for when you come back home, darling, and we will too. That's a promise! I am writing here in front of the fire place and have your handsome face before me. You are handsome, you know!

Must close for now dear, but I'll be here again tomorrow with more chatter. Until then and always, May God bless you and keep you safe and please bring you home soon. Good night, my darling, I love you with all my heart now and forever. All my love and kisses. Margaret.

We were just finishing up what little black bread the Germans had given us when a fellow I knew came up to me and told me that a good friend of his was having a real hard time and might not be able to finish the march. He said that his shoes were falling apart and the snow and ice was just going right through the holes and the soles were falling off. He noticed that I was carrying an extra pair around my neck and asked me if he could have them for his friend they called "The Russian." He was an American flyer, but they called him that because his father was a Russian tank commander. My shoes were holding up well so I gave him the new pair and one of my blankets too. Soon we were off again. Our mile long rag tag column of stinky limping men, many moaning as they walked on bloodied and frozen feet. We marched on through the cold and ice for another fifteen miles to a town called Spremburg where a rail line would take us on to our final destination. By the time we got there many of the men were sick with pneumonia or dysentery or both. Helplessness, hopelessness, and despair ran through everyone. Finally, our captors told us we would be getting something to eat. More black bread. God how I learned to hate that black bread, but for now it was keeping us all alive and I was thankful for it. This time they also gave us a barley and rabbit soup that was darn good, under the circumstances. I went back for seconds, and to my surprise, they gave it to me. I made sure to eat slowly so as to not shock my system into rejecting the food. The problem with the soup, I would soon learn, was it was very salty and the Germans had no intention of giving us water.

Soon we were being forced into box cars, holding as many as 60 men in a car that should hold 40 comfortably. The cars were called 40x8, meaning they could hold 40 men or 8 horses. If that wasn't bad enough, the floor was covered with recent cattle manure. Not long after the door was shut and locked from the outside we began to move. It became obvious real fast that we were going to have to figure out a system by which we could take turns laying down. To start with there were about 60 of us all bunched up and standing with barely enough room to turn around. The air was acrid with only a small vent at the top of the car on each end. Soon, men began to vomit and lose control of their bowels. The stench was unbearable, but we went on, locked in our own private hell. We came up with a system where we took turns sitting and standing. The floor was the stinkiest disgusting thing I had ever seen and it made me vomit to sit down, but we stood as long as we could until the pain in our legs and backs was too much to bear. After a day the train stopped and the guards started allowing fellows out one car at a time starting from each end of the train. Our car was in the middle of the train and before they got to us the engine whistle blew and they loaded everyone back up and we started rolling down the track again. The dysentery was horrific as we were all wallowing in shit in various stages of runniness or dried on our clothes and floor, mixed with the cow shit, urine and vomit. The moaning went on and on. Men were reduced to crying like babies, begging for death to come get them because of the continuous extreme pain brought on by muscle spasm from the dehydration caused by the diarrhea and lack of water. Every muscle in a man's body would cramp at the same time, from his legs to the muscles between his ribs. The pain was excruciating. The train stopped again in a rail yard next to a large city. Some of the guys thought it was Schweinfurt and some thought it was Regensburg. The engine disconnected and went and hid in a fortified building, leaving the 2,000 of us out in the open as we could hear air raid sirens blaring. The sound of hundreds of bombers nearby filled the sky and we all thought we had gotten this far only to be bombed by our own men. Oh the cruelty of our captors, it seems it knows no bounds. We were all in agreement that if we must go out this way we only hope it is quick and we no longer have to suffer, but as soon as it started, it was over. Sometime later the guards again started letting prisoners out to stretch their legs and urinate, but again they started at each and, and again before they got to our car the whistle blew and we were off. For three nights it was the same story, rocking back and forth down the tracks, in more pain than I had ever experienced, listening to the moans, reduced to wishing for death to come. Instead of death we finally arrived at a town called Moosburg. The guards let us out but kept us crowded in a small area. They didn't get too close to us. They couldn't stand the stench. We saw a hand pump sticking up off a well and made our way in a near mad rush to the water. The Goons were yelling at us to stop, but no one listened. Shoot us if you must, but we're getting water! Each of us drank and drank until we vomited and then we drank more. I don't know if it was brought on by our weakened condition and pre-existing dysentery or if it was a bad well, but everyone after that couldn't stop shitting for several days. The guards brought us some timbers and some shovels and we made a trench to use. It was horrific.

After about one and a half days the Goons gathered us up and marched us a short distance to Stalag VIIA. They led us to some showers where we were able to get cleaned up and wash our clothes a little. I washed and washed but it didn't seem like the smell of shit was ever going to go away. Many of the fellows were nervous about using the showers because there were rumors about the Gestapo tricking people into going peacefully into showers and then gassing them to death. With great trepidation we slowly went into the showers and were relieved when water came out of the shower heads. The water was ice cold, but it was water, thank God for that. Fortunately I had a change of clothes in my homemade rucksack. I'm glad I didn't get rid of it on the march. At times I wanted to lighten my load and throw it away. Many fellows did just that and they regretted their actions later but they did what they had to do to live through the march. Even guards threw away their heavy ammunition and in some cases their guns. They had it bad too, I guess, but at least they had food and water and didn't get stuffed into the box cars from hell. I never did find out how many men didn't make it. I heard that some men just sat down in the snow and waited to die. If a fellow American didn't help them they were just left behind to die. The Goons didn't bother to shoot them. For the fortunate ones, we had finally arrived at our new camp, somewhere in lower Bavaria. The camp was extremely overcrowded because the Germans were moving men from all over to this camp. They housed me and several others in tents for a while until they could find a barracks to put us in. After a couple of days we were led to a delousing area where we showered again and were deloused with chemicals before returning to our tents. After a few more days they ushered us to a barracks that had been occupied by Russian soldiers. The Luftwaffe guards had ordered the Russians to vacate the barracks and put them in tents. They liked us a lot better than the Russians and thought of them as little more than dogs. I felt sorry for the men we displaced, but I was glad to have a roof over my head. The barracks was cramped with 300 men in a space intended for 100. After a few more days and our constant complaining to the guards they temporarily moved us back to some tents because the barracks was infested with rats, fleas, crabs and bed bugs. They deloused the barracks for us. I'm sure on orders from the Luftwaffe officers. Once again we went through the delousing procedure before going back to the barracks. I lost track of George and hadn't seen Jack, Roger, or Ted yet. This was going to upset Margaret a great deal, I thought, as I lay there wishing that sleep would overtake me. Once again, she's not going to be able to get mail from me. The word here was that the Red Cross parcels were few and far between because of the sad shape of the German infrastructure thanks to the 8th Air Force and the RAF. The Red Cross was having a great deal of difficulty getting the parcels in from Switzerland. There were over 100,000 men in the camp and our captors were having a hard time feeding themselves, much less us. At least I was out of that damned box car, I thought, and I hoped that I could hold out until the end of the war, which looked like it was coming soon. The biggest question on everyone's mind was what would the Krauts do when faced with another potential move? Would they move us again, and if so, where? Or, would they just shoot us all and be done with it. Most of the Kriegies were of the same mind. We couldn't handle another move like that and live.

Chapter 46
Fighting the Blues

Gosh, it's been simply ages since I've heard from you! Are you alright? Let me know quickly. Have you heard from Cec yet? Gee, I do pray you have. How is he? I had a letter from Jack two weeks ago, dated Sept. 6th POW farm. Why do you suppose he did that? He evidently meant Nov. 6th. Said he was fine. Etc. Wants to know all about Jr., and says to remember, no matter how far apart we may be there is always one who can bring us closer together. Hopes to see us soon, needs heavy clothes.

Mrs. Burwell and Mrs. Snyder wrote that Roger is wounded – piece of 20 mm shrapnel in him – torn ligament in his diaphragm – says he'll never be the same after being a POW. Mrs. Snyder writes that Ted said 'I was wounded,' and the rest was censored. Jack said neither of them were wounded, I wonder if he, too, has a few slight wounds.

Margaret, I'm going to tell you something. I've debated, ever since Jack first wrote, whether or not to tell you, and I've decided it's best. I'd want to know if it were Jack. He said Quinn was wounded, but he didn't know how badly, as he hadn't seen him since they bailed out. I'm sure it isn't serious or you would have been notified, please don't worry, and don't be angry with me for not telling you earlier, I did what I thought was best.

Have you moved? The Pry's moved yesterday, our new address is on the envelope. Have you gotten Quinn's things yet? I haven't heard anything about Jack's things. Think we should write? Jay and I had planned to go home earlier, but we're to be presented Jack's medals, an Air Medal and two clusters, 'for exceptionally meritorious achievement while participating in aerial flight against the enemy.' Tex Brandt, tail gunner, was awarded the Distinguished Flying Cross (DFC), or rather, his family was. Ray Everett is a major now, and was also awarded the DFC and a Purple Heart. He is expected home in September, Janie's gong to meet him in

Houston. I had dinner with his parents Sunday – fun! Annie Cooke had a letter from Bill Sunday; it was the first he'd gotten through. He said not to worry; they were well fed and well clothed. Gosh, on bad wet nights like this I often, in fact always, wonder whether or not our darlings are sufficiently clothed and fed. God take care of them for us and send them home to us soon.

80 bombers were lost today, so in a way I'm glad our boys are where they are. God keep them safe. I was so sorry to learn of D. Mutschler's death. Please give Pat my sympathy – please! Mrs. Smith, our ball turret gunner's mother, sent me a copy of a letter she received in May. Her son, Lieutenant Russell Smith, (Irvin's younger brother) was killed in a plane crash in Cuba May 13th. He piloted a B-24. She's never heard any more of Irvin, and it's been ten months now, poor thing. She has what it takes, though, faith in God. Good night. Write me soon, and keep your chin up. Cec will walk in one of these days, along with my Jack. Wonderful thought, isn't it? Let's pray it won't be long. Jay sends her love. Give our regards to Quinn. We love you. Polly & Jay.

Waiting at home for some word of where Cecil was, and how he was doing, was tearing me apart. I tried to occupy myself as best I could with my work. In a one week span I was fired by a dentist who made it clear he only hired me because he wanted me to be his play thing and I shut him down right quick. He didn't even have the nerve to fire me himself; he made my friend do it. She was so apologetic, but I understood and I didn't want to work there anymore after that anyway. Then, I got the news that Cecil was missing in action. Shortly after that, while I was still waiting for news on Cecil's fate, I was informed that the duplex I was renting had been sold and I was given 90 days to move out. Finally, good news started coming in-in response to my prayers. I got the news that Cecil was safe, and the new duplex owner wasn't going to make me move right away. I still went about looking for a new place, but affordable apartments weren't in great supply in Sacramento at that time. I got a lot of that off my chest by writing letters to Cecil, even though I had nowhere to send them. The stress was nearly more than I could stand but I managed to keep my faith by visiting my church almost every day. I got rehired at Cal-Western Life Insurance and that kept me busy in the day. At night and on weekends I volunteered as much as I could as a nurse's aide. My favorite location to work in the hospitals was labor and delivery. The nurses' liked me a lot and I got on well with the new mothers'. Being able to be there when a new baby came into this world helped keep my faith. The pure magic, blessedness, and innocence of the new arrivals took my mind off of my own troubles, if only for a while.

I wrote Cecil all about the trouble I was having with the stupid draft board in Sacramento. He had been having issues with them when he was stationed at Luke Field in Arizona, but he had always sent them back every letter or piece of information that they had asked for. Still, they just either ignored his correspondence or lost it, one or the other. One day here at home one of the local papers carried a list of men wanted by the F.B.I. for draft evasion, and Cecil's name was on it! Can you imagine? Your loved one is not only in harm's way, but has been shot down and is a prisoner of war and they publicly defamed him and our family due to their own mistake! I was furious and went to the board to get them to correct their mistake but the man there was absolutely rude, unapologetic, and, in my opinion, disrespectful of an American missing in action and his family. My next stop was to the newspaper and they questioned the board too, but didn't get anywhere. They ran a small story about the problem.

Flier Missing In Europe Is Listed As Draft Evader.

Second Lieutenant Cecil W. Quinley of Sacramento, reported by the War Department to be missing in action in the European area since October 8th, was found today to be listed as delinquent by Sacramento Local Board No. 25 and a warrant for his arrest on a charge of failing to report for induction is in the hands of the Federal Bureau of Investigation.

Wife is Disturbed.

Lieutenant Quinley's wife, Mrs. Margaret M. Quinley of 394 Santa Ynez Way, declared 'it is a little bit disturbing' to find her husband is listed as wanted for draft evasion. She said following her husband's enlistment in the air corps in February, 1942, the draft board was notified. She stated continued communications from the draft board were returned with the notification Quinley already was in the service.

Notice Not Sufficient.

Local Board No. 25 announced, however, it has 'nothing officially' to show Quinley entered the service, stating the local army officer neglected to file a required statement from his commanding officer. 'All we had was word from the family,' the local board clerk stated. Assistant United States Attorney Thomas O'Hara said dismissal of the complaint against Lieutenant Quinley will have to be requested by the draft board. Lieutenant Quinley was manager of a local service station before entering the air force. He has been overseas since July 4th as a copilot on a Flying Fortress.

Another newspaper ran a similar story and called for an apology, but an apology never came from the draft board. On advice I went to see the head of the Selective Service, Colonel Leitch. I went into his office with my Irish blood ready to boil but he disarmed me right off the bat with his charm and apologetic statements. He was genuinely apologetic and said he had no idea how something like that could have happened. He asked me for a copy of the telegram from the War Department which stated Cecil was missing in action, which I gave him. Dr. McKee, our dentist and family friend, is good friends with the colonel and he had already been to see him about the issue. I don't know if that rude board member was ever disciplined, but I didn't care as long as Cecil's name was cleared. It took over three months before I received a letter from Cecil and that waiting sure took a toll on me. I couldn't understand why, if he was a prisoner of war, there was just no word on his condition or whereabouts. Communications from Polly Pry informed me that she was already in contact with Jack and so were Roger and Ted's wives. Polly told me that Jack had seen Cecil, but I still had no contact with him or from the Red Cross telling me how to write him. One of Polly's letters disturbed me when she said that Jack thought Cecil had been injured. There was no word about that from the War Department or the Red Cross, but could it be true, since I wasn't hearing from him? All these things played ugly tricks on my mind and continued to stress me every day. I tried to keep my chin up, but the lack of communication was horribly stressful and made me think, at times, that maybe my beloved husband was dead somewhere. It's easy to think ugly thoughts like that when other wives are getting killed in action notices almost every day. On November 18th, 1943, I received a telegram from the War Department stating:

RE: 2nd Lt. Cecil W. Quinley, American Prisoner of War, Camp Unstated, Germany. Dear Mrs. Quinley. The Provost Marshal General directs me to supplement the information recently forwarded to you concerning the above named prisoner of war. Since the report received did not state the exact place of his internment, it is impossible to correspond with him at this time. It is believed that the accompanying circular #10 contains all information now available. When further information is received, you will be informed immediately. Sincerely yours, Howard F. Bresee, Colonel, C.M.P., Chief, Information Branch.

Then, finally, eleven days later on November 29th, I received another telegram from the same colonel that confirmed for me that Cecil was at least safe, but there was still no word on whether he was actually injured, or if he was, how bad. The telegram stated,

RE: 2nd Lt. Cecil W. Quinley, American prisoner of War #3197, Stalag Luft 3, Germany, VIA: New York, New York. Dear Mrs. Quinley: The Provost Marshal General directs me to inform you of the transfer of the above named prisoner of war to the camp indicated. You may attempt to communicate with him by following the enclosed mailing instructions. One package label and two tobacco labels are enclosed with instructions for their use. Parcel labels are forwarded to the next of kin every sixty days without application. Further information will be forwarded as soon as it is received.

I went down to Sacred Heart church and with tears flowing from my eyes I showed the letter to Father Christen. He has been so emotionally attached to my fear of losing Cecil that he openly cried with me, then we said a prayer of thanks. He said he would announce the news at mass the next day and dedicate the mass as a thank you to God for keeping Cecil safe. I don't know what I would have done through these trying times without my faith and without Father Christen.

It was late January when I finally got a letter from Cecil and my heart felt like it was finally going to heal. He was only allowed to write a few letters each month, three small one page letters and four post cards. The letters were censored by fellow airmen in the camp, so he didn't say much at all when he wrote. That was okay, though, our communication had been re-established and I could do all the talking, I was good at that. I supported him the best way I knew how, through my words of faith, love, and encouragement. I sent him things he needed such as food items to supplement what he was getting from the Germans and the Red Cross. I also sent him some clothes and a nice blanket. In one letter he asked for a new pair of shoes and I sent those to him as well. I was sad to learn that two of the men on his ship were killed when they were shot down. Staff Sergeant Al Johnson and Staff Sergeant Irvin Smith, who Polly had talked about in one of her letters. Smitty they called him, had a younger brother that was a B-24 pilot and had been killed in an accident over Cuba. Smitty was the ball turret gunner and by all accounts was killed by machine gun fire and flak before the rest of the men bailed out. Poor Mrs. Smith, she has lost two sons to this ugly war. What a terrible-terrible thing to have happen, not one son, but two! How badly I felt for her. She deserves our undying gratitude and respect for her loss. I couldn't imagine such pain.

Chapter 47
Stalag VIIA

Office of the Embassy

Union of Soviet Socialist Republics

Washington, 8, D.C.

Gentlemen:

This letter is being written with the hope that you may be able to give me some assurance regarding the whereabouts of my husband, 2nd Lt Cecil W. Quinley, U.S. Army Air Forces, Army Serial No. 0-743087. He has been held a Prisoner of War of the German Government since October 8, 1943, at Stalag Luft 3, Germany. His Prisoner of War number is 3197.

Since the recent Russian onslaught and terrific drive through that particular part of the country, namely the vicinity of Sagan, where Stalag Luft 3 has been reportedly located, I have naturally become more than a little anxious concerning his safety. Of course I fully realize that I am far from being alone in this state of anxiety, but I have thought for several weeks that your department might be able to give me some assurance regarding my husband's safety and also perhaps advise me how soon I may expect to hear from him directly after his ultimate liberation by the fast-advancing Allied Forces, from all present indications, those of the Russian advance!

On February 13, 1945, there were several radio broadcasts in which it was stated that Allied Airmen who had been held Prisoners of War in camps in Germany, the territory surrounding which had been penetrated by the Russian Armies, had been released and then transferred to Poland, where they were awaiting transportation home. Of course this was a very exciting and thrilling day and was most encouraging! However, on February 15, 1945, the International Red Cross issued a statement quite contrary to the above good news, and even went so far as to mention the names of the prison camps, Stalag Luft 3, included, from which our men had been forced to march, on foot, deeper into the Reichland, ahead of the Russian advance.

If there is any chance at all that you may know or hear of my husband's arrival in liberated territory, please be so kind as to notify me as soon as possible. Enclosed is a self-addressed, airmail-stamped, envelope for this purpose.

Thank you for any service you may be able to render in the above respect. Very truly yours, Mrs. Margaret M. Quinley.

Mrs. Margaret M. Quinley

2210 "I" Street

Sacramento 16, California

Dear Madam.

In reply to your letter of February 16, 1945, please be advised that we do not have any information as to the whereabouts of your husband.

You, however, may be assured that if and as soon as your husband is liberated by our troops he will be given the opportunity to proceed to the United States as soon as possible. Very truly yours.

E. Tumantzev

Chief

Consular Division.

Stalag VIIA was a hell hole and looked more like a hobo camp than a military prisoner of war camp. The whole place was infested, so I didn't know how well the delousing would take hold in our barracks. There was not near enough food to go around because the Red Cross parcels weren't getting through. I guess the Krauts were having a hell of a time on all their fronts, which were shrinking in on them every day. I quickly learned that if I rubbed lye soap all over myself from head to toe right before bed it was a fairly good way of keeping critters off of me. The soap stung a little at first but I got used to it. It was better than waking all night long with that itchy feeling from bugs crawling all over me in every nook and cranny. In the daytime I wandered about the camp looking for food and people I knew. I wasn't very successful at either. I don't know what the camp used to be like, but now it had boxes, mattresses and whatever, strewn about the place with men laying everywhere. Dysentery was still a big problem and some men were getting so sick that they didn't get around much. They just laid there shitting themselves until they either died or were taken to an outside hospital. That, in and of itself, was rumored to maybe be a one way ticket to a crematorium. There were enlisted men, below NCO status, working outside the camp here. They went out and refilled bomb craters and repaired roads and such, under guard of course. One day I was out by the fence soaking up some early morning sun. Anything to get out of that bug infested stinky barracks. I called one of the enlisted work detail guys over and made a deal with him. I gave him a pack of Chesterfield cigarettes and asked him to please-please see what kind of food he could scrounge up while he was out and about the area. He took the cigarettes, thanked me, and told me that there was no guarantee, but he would see what he could find for me. I stayed close to where I was in case he came back early, keeping warm in the sun. Occasionally, I would go to the nearest tent and sit in there for a while. While I was in the tent I heard the roar of some aircraft overhead. I came outside with everyone else and we all stared into the sky as two twin engine planes with U.S. markings buzzed the camp a couple of times. Everyone yelled and applauded with excitement, which made the Goons mad and they yelled at us to be quite. I didn't recognize what type of planes they were. They had a twin tail like a B-25, but it wasn't a B-25. Several of us were discussing the matter when one guy said,

"Well, it's not a flying prostitute either."

"What the hell is a flying prostitute?" I asked.

"It's a B-26. Because of their short wing span."

I didn't get it at first and I just stared at him wondering what he meant.

"Ya, there's no visible means of support on a B-26 because of the short wings. A flying prostitute!" He said laughing.

Even in our depressed filthy situation we all had a nice laugh with that one. One fellow walked up who hadn't been locked up as long as the rest of us and said the planes that buzzed us were P-61's and went on to tell us they were originally intended to be used as a radar guided night fighter but had been pressed into service as a ground attack plane toward the end of the Ardennes offensive and had proved to be pretty successful at that, so they kept at it.

Later in the day that fellow I gave the Chesterfields to came back and I ran over to see what he had accomplished. That nice young chap had managed to scrounge up a couple of eggs from a local civilian's chicken coop. I couldn't recall having been that excited in a long time as I walked carefully back toward my barracks. I had to resist the urge to run so as not to fall and break my precious cargo. I pulled out a little homemade miniature stove that many of us had assembled to heat food. It consisted of little more than a couple empty tins that were saved from our ration packages. With mine I had it set up so I could cook over direct heat (a little fire) or indirect heat. In this case one of the cans served as a holder for the small fire and I had a small pan that I had also fashioned from cans. It took a while to cook my eggs this way, but this was a real important project for me at this point. I don't recall ever being so careful with eggs before. I gingerly cracked them into the little pan and heated them up slowly. At the perfect time I placed a small amount of water in the pan and covered it, just like my dad had taught me to do back in Ceres. The steam finished off the top of the eggs without the bottoms getting overcooked, and the yolks turned a beautiful pink color. I think I was the envy of whoever spied what I was doing, but these were all mine! Those were the best eggs I had ever eaten! Man alive, I couldn't recall eggs ever tasting that good. It made me think of home and I wondered again if I would ever see home again. I continued to give some of my cigarettes away to the work detail guys to find me food. Finally they made the discovery that there was a black market bakery in Munich. A couple times they brought back some pretty good bread. That was a longer trip and they didn't go there often, but when they did they managed to bring back some stuff. We tore it up and passed it around as far as it would go, which was never far enough. Hunger was always the order of the day. The last time those fellows went to Munich they came back with bad news. The bakery had been hit in a bombing raid! There would be no more black market bread for us. Moosburg was suffering too, not like us of course, but there wasn't any food there for these guys to liberate. That meant our source of extra food had dried up and we found ourselves right back in the starvation boat again. When Red Cross parcels did come in we had to share our package amongst a lot of men, meaning it didn't go very far. The French finally managed to get some kind of cheese to us on a regular basis that came in little round chunks. It was very strong tasting and rich and carried a long aftertaste. I figured out that if I saved it until right before bed, then ate it, the aftertaste stayed with me all night long and kept me from getting too hungry.

There were several escapes from the camp, nothing organized, but men would just take off. There were too many of us for the German's to watch. It was a dangerous game to play. We were primarily still guarded (close in) by Luftwaffe personnel, but there was regular Army and SS people all over the place here. I'm pretty sure that everyone who managed to get out was either caught in short order or they returned on their own accord from near starvation. The thoughts that preoccupied our minds were hunger and food, illness, bugs and rats, and will the Krauts eventually kill us? Lastly, we wondered if our own troops would come and get us. We must be closer to them here at this camp than we were at Stalag 3. The Russians got real close, of course, but there was always that question of whether they would shoot at the camp or even care if we got in the way. I didn't have Padre Mac's services to attend anymore. He was placed with the British prisoners here, so I attended the Protestant services mostly, but went to the Catholic services once in a while. I figured it would make Margaret happy and it reminded me of the times we sat next to each other in mass back in Sacramento. There wasn't any mail coming in here, or going out, so I'm sure Margaret was fit to be tied. One morning in early spring, after church services, I went back to my spot by the fence to think about my wife. There were some old timbers there that I had arranged in a way that I could sit on the ground and lean against them while staying warm in the spring sun. I noticed something happening a short distance outside the fence, so I sat there and watched. Some Goons marched five black men to a work area near-by. The black men had heavy French accents. The Goons were trying to communicate with them to make them dig some post holes so they could move the fence farther out. It was obvious the French troops knew what the Goons were asking but they kept playing dumb. The Germans thought that black people were of below average intelligence. Of course that's not the case, but the Goons thought that, which made the French troops plan work even better. A French soldier would take the shovel and mess it up, then a Goon guard would yell, nine, nine, nine, take the shovel back and dig some more. The French guys kept acting like they didn't understand and they would mess the job up every time they had to dig. The guards ended up digging every post hole. By the time it was all over there were fifty of us standing there laughing our heads off at the Goons. Oh the little things in life that bring us such joy, and right then we needed that relief, it was much appreciated.

April 13th, 1945, there was a commotion out on the yard. I went out to see what was going on. The Goons were all acting strange, walking back and forth talking to each other, some pointing toward the prisoners. Soon, a Luftwaffe major flanked by a few guards came into the yard and spoke to one of our colonel's. The word soon got around that President Franklin Delano Roosevelt had died the day before of natural causes. The mood in the camp was one of astonishment and disbelief. No one knew what to do. He had been our president for a long time, since 1933, and, like him or not, had led us through bad times. Everyone kind of just wandered around talking in low tones. I wasn't exactly a Roosevelt supporter, but I still felt like I lost my own grandfather.

Chapter 48
Liberation

I'm back again to tell you I'm still in love with you and missing you as always. I just came home from a Nurse's Aide Corps meeting. I was elected president for the coming year! Aint that something? I defeated Mrs. Wilson Craven, can you imagine? She wasn't present. Anyway, I should appreciate the honor, which I do, and hope that I'll be worthy of the re-election. It was nice of the girls to want me again. Outside of that there isn't much to report from this point of the globe. Had another nice letter from Marcia McCowen today. It was rather sad, she hasn't heard yet about her Bob and he's been missing since early in August. Poor girl, I feel so sorry for her! No news is good news, though, I still say.

I got a new job, honey, at Cal Western Life Insurance again, so things are looking up already, just like I said they would. I'll be keeping the books there and I'll have two full months of paid service as the Red Cross Nurses Aid Corps President while we hold a fund raising effort. It will be my job to supervise the counting of the money, keep the books on it, and make the bank deposits, with a police escort again of course. Isn't it all exciting, darling? Now all we need is for this old war to be over. Gee, the way the news is coming in it won't be long until we'll be seeing each other! We might be able to keep that Christmas date yet, darling. Here's surely hoping hard! We had a swell time in Ceres, but missed you, naturally. The whole gang was there, even John and Thelma. Earle went pheasant hunting and bagged us a nice meal. I'm off soon tonight to our Alpha Sigma meeting. It's a party for our new pledges at the Copper Lantern Tea Room. It's a costume party and Berta is Chairman, so it should be pretty good. Faye Travis is coming by for us in a little while. Red Skelton is on the radio and as funny as ever! He is 'helping' his mother at the butcher shop and rationing is interfering. It's a good show, as usual.

I surely miss your letters, darling, and pray that as soon as you are able you will write me once again. It would be plenty wonderful to have even just a card from sweet you. I sure do love you, sweetheart, and wish this old war will hurry up and get finished so that you can come home! Don't know much more news tonight, there's nothing new here. Gotta 'sign off' for now, but I'll be thinking of you always, and praying that you are safe and well wherever you are and that God will bless you and take care of you now and always. I'll be-a-seeing you real soon, honey-dear. Good night for now. God bless you, darling. All my love and kisses. Margaret.

The rest of April 1945 was quite eventful. Everyone was talking about the President's death and how it would affect the war. One day I was out in the tents having a smoke after wandering around thinking about food. All of a sudden I heard a loud boom that sounded like a bomb was dropped nearby. I ran outside to see what was going on and got the fright of my life as a Luftwaffe jet went screaming over the camp as he was pulling out of a dive. Seeing something like that, the speed of that aircraft, compounded by the death of the President, made us all wonder if this was a turning point in the war. A few days later we had our confidence restored when the air raid sirens went off. The Goons allowed us to go outside and seek shelter in some slit trenches that had been dug in the camp. As I laid there on my back I saw an amazing sight. It was an entire wing of B-17's going to bomb somewhere, I presumed Munich. Many more ships than we were ever able to field. That sight was something I'd never forget. I'd been in those battles in the sky before, after all, that's how I ended up where I was, but to be on the ground watching it all was something. There were Luftwaffe ME-262 jets streaking through the formations firing their guns while American fighters tried to fight them off. Other fellows in the trench told me the American fighters were P-51 Mustangs. I hadn't yet seen one of those, but had heard of them and knew they were capable of escorting the bombers all the way to their target. Boy, I wish they had been around for our missions. It looked to me like the German jets that were going through the formations had very little time to shoot because of their speed. That also meant that the B-17 gunners had very little time to shoot back. Soon, things were falling on the camp from the battle thousands of feet over our heads that must have happened well before we could see them, considering their altitude. Empty ammo boxes from the bombers fell in and near the camp that were thrown from the planes. Empty shells from the fighter's guns dropped in some places, as well as pieces of the bombers that had been shot off. Then, as quickly as it began it was all over as the formations droned off into the distance. When we were sure nothing else would fall out of the sky we made our way out of the trenches. Thousands of prisoners began cheering and hollering, which upset the guards quite a bit. They shot a few rounds into the air and yelled at us to go back to our barracks and be quiet. As much as it made us feel good, and gave us renewed confidence that the war would soon be over, it had the opposite effect on the Goons. Many of them were war weary, you could tell, but they didn't like seeing their country and their cities torn apart. Some had wanted the war to end while there was still some of Germany left. This was evident in an assassination attempt that we heard about through our clandestine radios back at Stalag Luft III in mid-July, 1944. Someone had tried to blow up Hitler by planting a bomb. The attempt was unsuccessful and the war continued on, but it showed that not all of Germany was behind their leader at that point. Most of the guards just wanted the whole thing to be over so they could get back to a normal life and I think that's why many of them treated us with kindness. They were stern and followed the rules, but there was no cruelty in their actions.

The food was still an issue, but had gotten a little better. We had been making soup from string bean hulls. It always had weevils in it, but we got tired of picking the weevils out and figured they were a source of nutrition, so we just left them in. Eventually, the Russian prisoners were put in charge of cooking and the food seemed to get better. They were pretty good at putting together recipes with nearly no supplies to work with. One day we were sitting there eating a watery stew, or soup of some kind. It was salty and had some meat in it. No one knew what the meat was, and no one cared at that point. The guy next to me bit into something hard and pulled it out of his mouth and said,

"What the hell is that?"

"That's a horses tooth, haven't you ever seen a horses tooth?" I said.

He got nauseated a bit, but overcame his feelings and continued to eat. Funny what hunger will do to a fellow. Eventually, also, some British volunteers managed to get some Red Cross parcels through from Switzerland. They were life savers!

349

April 28th, 1945, I could tell that something was happening, but no one knew for sure what it was. All the guards were acting extremely nervous and there were SS patrols around the outside of the camp. At bedtime I ran through my normal routine of washing up as good as I could in the water I had saved throughout the day, and covered myself in the Lye soap to try and keep the bugs off of me. I fell asleep that night staring at a large rat that was in the corner staring back at me. That fellow was there almost every night waiting to scrounge around for whatever he could find. I'd seen him so much since arriving there that I named him Patrick, after St. Patrick. I know the legend states that St. Patrick rid Ireland of snakes, but even though this Patrick was a rat it still seemed appropriate. I called him Patty Boy for short. If the Russians saw him he'd be in our pot for supper. The morning of April 29th I awoke to a slightly brisk barracks room. Most of us got our little homemade cookers going to heat up some dirty water to make coffee. Most of the grounds were used but we mixed them with what little fresh grounds we divided up from the limited rations we had left. It was about nine O'clock as I sat there having a smoke while waiting for the coffee to get strong enough to taste like coffee. Patty Boy was nowhere in sight by this time. After the coffee was done I slowly drank it to wash down the moldy black bread I'd been saving. By this time it no longer made me sick to eat such things. Shortly before ten several of us walked outside to have another smoke. As we approached the fence all hell broke loose. Some SS officers with a squad of troops came into the camp and demanded that the Luftwaffe turn over the prisoners to them. The head Luftwaffe sergeant told the officer no and they yelled back and forth at each other but the sergeant said he had orders to only turn the prisoners over to the Americans. We didn't know what he meant by that and we stood there confused as hell. The SS officer and his men were getting real mad, but the Luftwaffe sergeant held his ground and he had many more men backing him up than the SS officer did. Then, all of a sudden, there were explosions very close to the camp followed by a lot of shooting and the SS men ran out of the camp hollering at other troops running up and down the road. Some flares were shot over the camp and scared the hell out of us before we realized what they were. Soon, someone yelled that he saw a Sherman tank off in the distance, that the U.S. Army was here, and the flares were being used to mark the camp location so no one would fire this way. That didn't stop the SS from firing our way, though, as bullets came zinging through the camp hitting a couple guys. I ran back to our barracks and a bunch of us sat down around our table discussing what to do as a bullet came through the wall and bounced off one of the fellows and just landed right there on the table. We all scattered to find a place to hide. I ran to the barracks shower area where there was a concrete wall and I crouched down low behind it while listening to the battle that was drawing nearer to us. There were five or six of us who squeezed into the small space for protection. A P-51 was diving over the camp shooting at nearby German positions while prisoners yelled their approval. In a building across the road from the camp we could see an SS soldier on the roof shooting at prisoners with his rifle. Everyone was trying to hide, but there was not enough room, and this soldier would shoot at anyone he saw out in the open in the camp. I thought what a coward this man must be, shooting at unarmed prisoners instead of battling the American forces coming up the road. He managed to hit one of our guys in the hip. He was one of the Doolittle Raiders, reassigned to the 8th Air Force and shot down over Europe. Now, shot in the hip by a coward! A short time later a tank came rolling close by and its machine gunner obliterated the SS sniper as everyone who witnessed the shot erupted in cheer. Then the tank fired a round into a guard tower and obliterated it. Almost as soon as it started it was all over. The shooting suddenly stopped at about 10:30. We slowly and cautiously walked out into the compound and as I looked down the road toward the town of Moosburg I saw something. We all saw something that brought shivers down our spines and tears to our eyes. No one tried to hide their tears or emotions as we watched the Nazi flag slowly being lowered and a United States flag being raised in its place! My God, nearly all of us said, is it really over? The rush of emotion was overpowering.

"We're going home," I cried out loud, "we're finally going home!"

I soon took notice that all the guards were gone. As I looked around I could see that they were in an outer area, about 250 of them, with their sergeant. A couple Peeps (Jeeps) drove right up to the Goon guards, one with a mounted machine gun on it, and all the guards surrendered. This was all happening so fast it was unbelievable. Then, just when we thought it couldn't get any better, a Sherman tank came busting through the main gate and into the compound. Hundreds of men, including me, ran toward the tank hollering. So many men climbed onto the tank that you couldn't even see it under the mass of humanity. Behind me I heard someone yelling and crying that he'd been a prisoner for six years and has never seen a tank and could we please let him see it. He was a little British fellow, about five foot two. The tank commander yelled to come on up and several of us lifted that excited young man onto the tank where he broke down and cried without shame. A lieutenant that had come with us from Stalag Luft III came running up yelling that he had made a flag at the old camp and smuggled it here during the death march. He said he wanted to run it up the pole. I watched as the Nazi flag was again lowered, this time in our camp, and that fellow's small homemade United States flag was raised in its place. Another cheer filled the air. Again, just as it was a few minutes ago, chills ran down my spine, tears filled my eyes anew, and I thought again; it's really over, I'm really going home!

Chapter 49
Camp Lucky Strike

Hello, my darling, on a nice spring day from Sacramento. I just got home from Mass at Sacred heart. Father Christen said a nice prayer for you again today and sends his thoughts to you, wherever you may be. It's been a long while since I have received mail from you and the letters I mailed to Stalag Luft III have been returned by the War Department with the notation 'not deliverable.' There have been some reports that your camp has been moved, but that is all the information that we have been told. No one knows what has become of our dear boys and I fear that I may go crazy with worry having to go through this all over again.

My job is going swell and everyone at the Life Insurance Company sends their prayers to you too. You are quite the celebrity there. I have been assisting with more births at the hospital and it sure is a swell feeling to be able to participate in that. I pray that someday it will be our turn to start a family as well. Don't let the tone of my blue letters get you down, darling, 'cause everything works out for the best. I probably shouldn't write at all when I feel so low, but I hate to miss a day of writing to you. I know you understand my moods, though, so I guess I really am wasting space apologizing.

Most of all, I love you with all my heart, darling, and I know that the minute you walk in the door, or even the minute I hear the news that you're coming, everything will be just right. It's only because I miss you so that all of these little problems seem so big. I'll be back again tomorrow to talk to you on paper, and every day, of course, 'till you come flying home. Until then, and always, May God bless you and watch over you 'cause I sure do love you, truly and devotedly forever! Good night, my darling, special pleasant dreams to you. I'll be seeing you real soon, honey-bun. All my love and kisses. Margaret.

Several tanks of the 14th armored division sat in and near the camp with prisoners climbing all over them. General Karlstad was on the tank that busted down the main gate and symbolically freed the camp. The word around camp was that just a few hours ago the 14th didn't even know we were here. A guard told me that what we witnessed this morning was the SS trying to get control of American prisoners so they could use us as cover for their escape after a negotiation with General Karlstad earlier in the morning had failed. Thank God the Luftwaffe officers and guards held their ground against those guys. Who knows what may have happened if the SS had managed to gain control over some prisoners. As the day went on we went about our normal business of trying to find something to eat. The 14th Armored Division fellows gave us as much food as they could spare, but they were still on the move and didn't have much, especially considering the number of prisoners that were now in the camp. General Karlstad ordered that food be brought in as quickly as possible, but that was going to take some time. That lieutenant that raised his own homemade flag eventually lowered it to save it for posterity and a regulation size flag was raised in its place. Later in the day George and I, who I had reconnected with, decided to go for a walk outside the camp. We walked toward Moosburg, looking for food to eat, but didn't find anything. I saw an SS helmet lying on the side of the road and I thought that would be a swell souvenir to take home, so I kicked it over and reached down to pick it up. The sight that I saw startled me as I stared into the helmet at the partial head that was still inside it. We decided maybe it wasn't safe enough to be outside the camp on our own yet so we went back to the safety of our barracks.

The next day we began to see some Red Cross parcels roll into camp on trucks. Still not enough, but the Army was assigning a support group to come to the camp to help with everything. It was a waiting game now. It was obvious that the Army was not prepared for finding a POW cap of such magnitude. Their primary focus was on advancing toward the enemy as fast as possible, which means minimal supplies, except for ammunition. The next day George and I tried to venture out from the camp again. We walked into Moosburg and looked around the town and stood at the base of the pole that held old glory. We stood there for a few minutes and stared at the American flag flying there and talked about how we got to where we were, our wives, and looking forward to getting home to the states. Then, after a fleeting glance and shrugged shoulders we walked on to investigate the rest of the town. We found a fairly nice looking farmhouse on the outskirts of the town where there were a couple Kriegies sitting on the porch drinking coffee. We stopped and talked with them for a while and a handsome woman named Hanna in her 30's came out and said hello to us in broken English. We had been in Germany just long enough that between her broken English, and our broken German, we were able to talk together. She said her husband had been killed on the eastern front, at least that is what she believed, and she was there alone with her four year old son. She hadn't heard from her husband in almost a year. She was very apologetic about our situation and asked us if we could stay with the other two airmen and she would cook us supper. Of course we agreed and thanked her profusely. Supplies were short for the civilian population too, but she managed to cook up a very nice chicken schnitzel with brotchen. Oh man, was it heaven having a home cooked meal but it was so good and rich that it almost did us in. Our systems weren't used to rich food like that, but it was wonderful. After supper we helped clean up and we all sat in the front yard and had a smoke while her son ran around playing. She said she was glad that the war was almost over and that life might be getting back to normal. We told her that it has been hard on everyone and we were sorry that we had bombed her cities but it had to be done to win the war. She was understanding and sad all at the same time because of the human toll it had taken on everyone. As the sun began to get lower we had to excuse ourselves and head back to the camp. I suppose we didn't have to, but if we didn't get back to the camp we may miss something important. As hard as it was to leave Hanna and her hospitality we went back. The weather was just getting warm enough that there was no way we were going to subject ourselves to the bug infested barracks any longer. We packed our blankets out next to the fence and made a lean-to shelter to sleep under. It was one of the best night's sleep I had since arriving at the camp, but my stomach was beginning to cause me some pain. I figured it was because I had real food for a change, but I would soon find out it was worse than that.

On the second day after our liberation I convinced George to go back to our barracks for a card game. I was standing about halfway inside the room when we all heard a commotion outside. All of a sudden a man who looked like he was seven feet tall stepped through the door. He wore two hand guns with ivory grips and had stars on his uniform. I called the room to attention and everyone, more out of surprise and conditioning than anything else, snapped to. There he stood, General George Patton himself, flanked by several colonels. He stood there for what seemed like an eternity, looking around the room at our living conditions, our raggedy uniforms, our underweight physical condition, and I'm sure he noticed the foul odor of the room, which was normal to us. Then, his glare focused on me as I stood there shaking, feeling almost half his size, and he said,

"Lieutenant, come forward."

I walked forward and stood at attention in front of the general and before I could salute him, he saluted me, which I returned smartly. After the salute he held out his hand and shook mine.

"Thank you lieutenant, thank you all. I want you all to know that I'm going to drive this army all the way to Berlin and personally shoot that paper hanging son of a bitch for what he's done to you men, you can count on it."

He looked around again, turned, and left the room. We all just stood there looking at each other wondering if that really happened. Wow, I thought, I just shook General Patton's hand, and he saluted me! It was a moment I wouldn't ever forget. But now life in the camp had to go on until we were out of there. As quickly as the general had entered the room he was gone. A short time later we saw him coming back from the direction he had gone after inspecting our barracks. It was a comical sight. General Patton was walking at a brisk pace with his long stride and all his colonels and other staff officers practically running to keep up. None of us had any doubt that the general intended to keep his word.

It took two more days and George and I were evacuated by truck on May 7th to an airfield. As I was being transported in the big troop carrying truck the pain in my side got worse. Every bump in the road caused excruciating pain so I laid down on the floor of the bed and closed my eyes to try and ignore the pain, but it was impossible. The cool air that rushed by as we drove down the road chilled me to the bone. I didn't know what could be wrong. I asked myself if it was the schnitzel that I ate. Could it be having normal food after all this time was a shock to my system? I discounted that because George didn't get sick. Perhaps it was just the flu, I thought. Whatever the cause, I managed to endure the ride to the airfield. Once we arrived we noticed that the troops and other liberated Kriegies there were running around hooting and hollering and hugging each other. Our driver asked what was going on and we were told that Hitler was dead and Germany had surrendered. The war in Europe was over! My God, it was over. We were instructed that C-47 transport planes would be arriving to ferry us all to France. I couldn't believe how lousy I felt and how much pain I had. My God, did I endure all this just to die here, right at the point when freedom was at hand and the war was over? George helped me slowly hobble to a building next to the flight line that must have been a ready room of some sort for Luftwaffe pilots. I couldn't walk or stand fully upright and had to be hunched over to tolerate the pain. There were beds in the room, so I made myself at home on one of them. George went and got a medic who nursed me there for three days while I lay there sweating and moaning in pain. There were no doctors available at the time and I was told that there would be doctors at the airfield in France, but there was just no way I could tolerate getting on that plane and flying out. I ate nothing for those three days and sipped water when I could to replace what I was sweating out. Finally, on the third day it felt like the fever had broken a bit and the pain had lessened so I walked, hunched over, to a waiting C-47 and climbed in with George. The plane filled quickly and the engines started with a sputter and shake. We taxied to the runway and began our takeoff roll. That damn plane shook and rattled like it was going to come apart and it made my insides feel like they were going to do so as well. I asked one of the crew if we were going to come apart and he said not to worry about it, C-47's were always like that, that's why they called them chatter boxes. After what seemed like the longest flight of my life we landed at Camp Lucky Strike, located in a town in France called Saint-Sylvain, about 40 miles from Le Havre. At the camp I was hustled off to the hospital area where I recuperated for a few more days. The pain slowly subsided and the fever went away. The doctor had me eat carefully rationed bland food while I was there for fear that rich food would be a shock to the system. His impression was that something had happened with my appendix, but since I was getting better it would be best to deal with it back in the states if that remained necessary. Eventually, after getting out of the hospital, I found myself a nice big juicy steak and chowed down on that, slowly savoring the taste like I had never eaten one before. During the second week in May they loaded me and George into a troop truck and drove us in a convoy down to Le Havre where we boarded the nearly new troop transport ship USS General W.H. Gordon. May 19th, 1945, at long last, I was on my way home!

Chapter 50
USS General Gordon

Reginald West, Editor

Y Monthly Courier

Sacramento District

Relatives of War Prisoners

Young Men's Christian Association of Sacramento

505 Jay Street

Sacramento, California

March 23, 1945.

Dear Mr. West.

Congratulations on the fine work you are doing in the interests of relatives of prisoners of war in both theaters of operations. So many of us wives, mothers, sisters, and other relatives, who have dear ones in prison camps, appreciate your untiring efforts to help ease the worries we have at this time. I have missed attending the monthly meetings of the relatives group; but hope to be able to come to the next one – my work and night school courses have interfered in the past. Even though I have had to miss meetings for a while, I haven't forgotten you and the group who were so enthusiastic to start a Sacramento Group of Next of Kin. I only wish that I could have taken a more active part. Here is a little poem which appeared in the Saturday Evening Post recently – if you haven't already received it from other sources, I thought you might like to use it in the 'Y-Monthly Courier.' Wishing you continued success in all of your inspiring activities in the community, I remain, sincerely,

Mrs. Margaret M. Quinley.

Dare Not.
By Alastair Panton.

I do not know the horror of this time,
When, sharp, frustrated thoughts are rife.
I do not know, because I dare not think
How bitterly I hate this life.
The sanctuary of home will give my mind
Release to think untrammeled thought.
There I shall face the bitter sense of loss
Distilled in prison's crude retort.
In light-dimmed theaters, by my whispering fire,
Beside a tree-ringed cricket field,
In country bars, in lighted, thronging shops,
To happiness this hate must yield.
Promotion, war's excitement, laughing men,
My love's earned company on leave,
The pride of service which is pride of self-
I long for these without reprieve.
I dare not hope to be returning soon,
For hopes too long deferred must die.
So, coward-like, I say, 'It's two years more,'
And in the speaking trust I lie.

Stalag Luft 3.

Dear Mrs. Quinley.

Thank you for those kind words, and the poem which has been used in this issue. Ye Ed wishes to emphasize that much credit for the Courier belongs to a relatively small, but loyal group of relatives who assist clerically. Mesdames Chas. Grooms, Bette Johnson, Grace Schwartz, Marie Swenumson, Dena Ricketts and Helen Silva are certainly among the number entitled to 'citations' and we thank them for their generous and helpful cooperation. Following is an article you will find in the next issue, I'm sure you will find it interesting.

WAR PRISONERS AID

Many prisoners of war will leave their camps at war's end, better equipped to face life than when they were captured. Some of them, indeed, may make important contributions to the post-war world.

In their grim struggle to maintain their morale, to grow mentally and spiritually, rather than succumb to the frustration and despair incident to long imprisonment, such ambitious prisoners work with a determination seldom found in civil life. These men are the honor students of that great barbed wire university whose buildings are barracks and whose campus comprises the dreary camp compounds on all the continents.

Of special help to American prisoners are the many courses of the United States Armed Forces Institute, designed for enlisted men, but made available for American war prisoners through the cooperation of War Prisoners Aid of the YMCA, a participating service of the National War Fund. The men are encouraged to register their study preferences with the YMCA's Geneva office, which then sends the necessary textbooks and all supporting educational materials to the camps.

Some of these men also discover their true relationship to the Source of Life and to their fellows, and the YMCA assists in this spiritual revaluation, regardless of race or creed.

Sincerely,

Reginald West, Editor.[5]

Hurry up and wait, we all joked, or complained, or both. Hurry up and wait. It was, of course, the Army motto I supposed. We departed Le Havre on May 19th. We thought we were getting on the ship to go home, but the military had other plans. I guess we would just enjoy the ride while it lasted, but taking a vacation on a troop transport ship wasn't my idea of a vacation after being locked up in a prisoner of war camp for over 18 months. I was in a hurry to get home to Margaret, and everyone else who was in the same situation was in a hurry to get home to their loved ones too. They had me on the third deck down and our cabin was over one of the boiler rooms. It was nice and warm while we were in the waters off France and England, but it would get too hot later in our voyage. We set sail and passed through the English Channel out into the Atlantic Ocean. The seas were very rough and vomiting was common. We rendezvoused with an American destroyer and were assigned to refuel her, but the swells were too rough for the sailors to perform the necessary procedures. The refueling had to happen, however, no matter how long it took, so we sailed at low speed side by side waiting for the ocean to cooperate. On the second day of waiting the ship was lurching up and down from bow to stern and back again. She was moaning and creaking and loose items rolled back and forth on the deck. I was lying in my hammock on the 3rd deck down, in the afternoon, when all of a sudden there was a tremendous sound and vibration as the stern of the ship rose and the bow sank very low. Then, as suddenly as it began, the stern came crashing down hard knocking everything off the shelves that hadn't already been thrown, including us from our hammocks. I was sure that we had hit a mine or had been torpedoed by a renegade U-Boat that didn't know the war was over. As fast as I could, I got to my feet and ran up the stairs to the top deck, followed by nearly everyone from our cabin. No one wanted to be caught inside a sinking ship just as we were freed and going home. As we reached the open deck we were greeted by laughing sailors, U.S. Coast Guardsmen, actually, as it was a Coast Guard crew that manned the General Gordon. It was a puzzling sight to see them laughing and not being worried at all or in a state of readiness. I asked them what the commotion was and they said that we went through a huge swell and the stern rose so far that the

---

[5] "Y – Monthly Courier." Sacramento District. Relatives of War Prisoners. 1945.

screws came out of the water and vibrated the whole ship, then slammed back down into the water. They said not to worry about it, that it happens from time to time in rough seas. They all had a little chuckle at the fly boys, then we went back to our cabin to try and ride out the rough sea. Later that day we were told that the Captain decided to pass out ice cream to help calm our nerves. I don't know if it calmed nerves or not but it was like heaven on earth. I couldn't even remember the last time I had ice cream. They even shot a cable over to the destroyer and passed some over to them also. It was safe enough to do that, but still not safe enough for a refueling operation. Since the war was over there was no urgency to the refueling and, therefore, no need to risk the ships and men. They would wait out the weather. Finally, on the third day, the swells subsided enough to complete the refueling and then we headed toward the Port of Spain in Trinidad. The farther south we got the better the weather and the smoother the seas became and the cruise became much more pleasant. We docked at the Port of Spain on May 29th and the Army troops we were carrying got off the ship. They were to hop boats over to Venezuela to relieve other U.S. troops that had been there too long already and were ready to go home also. Under those circumstances none of us minded the detour. The thing we hated about being docked at the Port of Spain was that none of us were allowed to get off the boat for the three days that we were there. Of course, however, the Coast Guard fellows went into town and whooped it up the whole time we were there. Those guys were hooting and hollering and drinking all three days while us POW's laid around on the deck wishing we could either go to town too, or get headed for home.

Finally, on June 1st, our ship set sail for the states. We headed up through the Caribbean, and what a beautiful voyage it was. Wow, it was the most beautiful, relaxing, and at the same time exciting boat ride I'd ever had. The Captain allowed us to sleep up on deck if we wanted, so many of us crowded out into the open air. I laid there looking up at the clearest evening sky with millions of stars and a beautiful quarter moon to boot. During the day the dolphins raced alongside the ship and flying fish flew everywhere out of the water. The water was very clear and the only thing that kept us from seeing through it was the foam and wake of the ship as we raced for home. Our course took us into the Caribbean and through the Windward Passage at the south east tip of Cuba and into the Bahamas. From there we continued on through the many islands toward the southern end of Florida and straight up the east coast of the United States toward New York. Then, at long last, on June 4th, 1945, we entered New York Harbor and were escorted by fire boats to our dock. They sprayed water all around us and blew their horns as we crept past the Statue of Liberty and into our proper space at the port as crowds hollered and waved from the dockside. What a wonderful welcome home this was. If only Margaret could have been here, but as far as I knew, she didn't know yet that I was on my way home. There had been no opportunity to tell her. After our arrival in New York we got off the General Gordon and there were throngs of people gathered there to meet the sailors, soldiers, and airmen who arrived. Many of us were taken to a ferry that transported us over to New Jersey where we were billeted at Fort Dix. After I got my room secured the first thing I did was find a phone and call Margaret. I was informed by the operator that she had a new address and phone number and it was supposed to be on file with them, but no one could find it. Talk about frustrating! I figured I'd try again later, but that night was the first night that I had slept in a normal bed since the night of October 7th 1943, and sleep I did, for twelve hours.

On June 5th me and a couple other fellows from Sacramento took the ferry back over to New York and we went to Times Square because it was the only place in New York we knew about from books. We passed by a telephone company building so we went inside and asked if they'd be so kind as to help us get in touch with our families back in Sacramento. They were very kind and enthusiastic about helping us and in no time at all they found Margaret's new number and got her on the line for me. Gosh it was nice to hear her voice. It took a while to have a conversation with her because she initially screamed in excitement and then cried. I cried too, and when I looked up, expecting to be embarrassed, I saw that everyone standing nearby that knew what was going on was crying too. One woman passed tissues around. After a nice long talk I told her that I'd call her back in a day or two when I received my next set of orders and knew exactly when and where I'd be going. She wanted to drive out to New Jersey and get me, but the Army was still in control and I had to convince her to be patient for just a little while longer until we had more information on my status. She reluctantly agreed, but we were so close now it wouldn't be long. The other fellows managed to get their families on the line too and had similar experiences. It was a stroke of luck finding that building and those nice people. Now, the three of us could rest easy knowing our loved ones knew we were safe and almost home. We left the telephone building looking for a place to eat lunch. There was a great big restaurant near Times Square called Craft's and we all agreed it looked like a good place to eat. We all went in the main entrance and there was a businessman who came up to us because he noticed our uniforms. He struck up a conversation with us while we were waiting to be helped and he asked us all about where we had been and what we did and how we ended up in New York. We each told him briefly about flying missions, being prisoners of war and being repatriated here while awaiting transport back to California. He finally said, come with me, and he took us up to the fourth floor, wrote something on a piece of paper, handed it to the waitress and told her to take care of us. As it turned out that businessman was the manager of the restaurant. We sat and ate steaks that rivaled the Rosemount back home. The guys I was with were both jokesters and they had everyone in the room in stitches for the hour we were there. Finally, the waitress came up to me with the bill and asked me to sign it. She said the manager had covered our meals and drinks and he thanks us for our service and sacrifice for our country. I didn't know what to say, that was such a generous act from someone we didn't even know. Everyone we had met in New York so far had been nothing but nice and generous to us. We found a nightclub in the Waldorf Astoria so we went in and looked around and yet another guy came up to us and said, let me buy you guys a drink. We enjoyed a couple drinks with the man and he left. When the man left a second man came up to us and asked,

"Did that guy just buy you a drink?"

"Yes," I said.

"Well I'll be damned. I've known him for years, and I've never known him to buy anyone a drink."

We laughed as we left the bar and headed down the street to do some shopping. I saw something in the window of a jewelry store and went inside. It was a very nice Rosary that I wanted to get for Margaret, but it was very expensive. The proprietor was a Jewish fellow and some of his family was in the store. They said they knew about the concentration camps in Germany where the Jews were murdered and asked me about the war and if I knew anything about it. All I could say was that I had heard rumors about the camps while I was a prisoner, but that was all. They let me argue them down on the price until I could afford it, so I made the purchase, thanked them for their kindness and the three of us went back to the port to catch the ferry to New Jersey and a ride to the camp. I was still full from the huge lunch we enjoyed, so I headed off to bed. Life was getting better and better, but I longed to see my wife and thought about her while looking out the window at the moon as I drifted off to sleep. I knew she was doing the same, I could feel it.

Chapter 51
Need a Ride Soldier?

Margaret.

I just got home from mass on the morning of June 5th. I stayed a little while after the mass so I could talk to Father Christen. The stress of worrying about Cecil was taking its toll on me. I felt like God had intervened for us and kept him safe all this time through his many missions, his being shot down, the medical care he received in Germany, and the better than average prison camp he was sent to. But after the Russians overran the area where the camp was located I hadn't heard from him again. There were rumors that Hitler was using the prisoners as hostages and that prisoners were being executed or starved. Then I'd see news about how well they were being treated. If that was true, then why haven't I heard from him? Bad thoughts raced through my mind every day. I wanted to believe, I wanted to have faith, but it was getting harder and harder not to collapse and cry. Perhaps allowing the reality of the inevitable to finally sink in. It was my visits with Father Christen that gave me the strength to keep my faith. He never gave me false hope, rather, we talked about the possibility that Cecil could be gone. We talked about, if that were true, then it is God's will and I must have faith that there is a bigger plan for the two of us. It wasn't something that I wanted to hear, but it was something that I had to hear. Of course, we mostly talked about having faith and the fact that the prisoners are being moved and the Germans are being soundly beaten so Cecil is more than likely not in a position to be able to write. I knew, through reading the newspapers, that there were thousands of POW's being repatriated and shipped back to the states. The hardest part of life for any military wife is the waiting and the not knowing. I suppose it's true for every family of every service member, no matter the branch of service. I talked with Father Christen for about an hour and felt much better. On my way out I went back inside Sacred Heart and lit a candle for my darling, then went home. I took a leave of absence from work because I knew that if Cecil was one of those boys on the ships heading for home that I needed to be ready to hear from him. It was frustrating sitting at home by the phone all day. My mind would want to wander back to the darkness but I made a conscious effort to keep my chin up, bolstered by nearly non-stop praying. I sat on the couch that morning wearing Cecil's Army sweat pants re-reading several letters that I had received from him when he was at Ridgewell before he was shot down.

Hello, my darling, and a happy anniversary to you on our 51st month wedding anniversary. This is our first one with an ocean between us, and I hope there won't be very many more of the same. Not more than five or six anyway, I hope. Anyway, I still love you, and more as each one passes. I have been playing softball for a couple of hours a day for the past couple of days. It's about time I was getting some exercise of a little more strenuous nature, not that playing softball is very hard, but it helps. I know that tonight my legs are a little stiff from doing it. I guess I aint used to running. If you go to town over here they are more particular about how you dress than they are in the states. If you were caught in town without your class 'A' uniform on I think they would consider shooting you. I guess they want to make a good impression on the 'Limeys.'

I received a letter from Esther today. I found out for the first time what Milly's new baby was named and such. I imagine that you wrote me all about it at some time or another, but as yet I haven't received that particular letter. As long as they were giving him part of my name I'm glad they picked on the middle name for it. It was nice of them to put it in there though. Now you have a niece named partly after you, and I have a nephew named partly after me, aint that something?

I got paid this morning and also bought myself a bicycle. It is a pretty good one. I paid six pounds for it, which equals about 24 dollars. I think it will be worth it 'cause it will save a lot of walking. Even if we can't go riding together now, we will probably be riding at the same time. Of course, I would prefer to be riding with you. A lot of people over here have bicycles built for two. They put racks on them and you see them riding down the road going out for picnics or camping and such.

It took me a long time to figure out what you meant when you mentioned the flannel fatigue suit that I sent home in the bag with the other stuff. It finally dawned on me that you were talking about my sweat suit. I had to figure out everything that I had put in there before I could figure out what you meant. You are perfectly welcome to wear them to sleep in this winter if you wish. I imagine that they would be quite warm to sleep in at that. I used to wear them while flying in primary.

I didn't see the picture 'Bombardier' that you mentioned, but I don't imagine that I would have enjoyed it so much anyway, from what the fellows said who saw it. Most of those pictures are alright for someone who doesn't know anything about it, but if you know what it's all about it all looks too much like a farce and a lot of foolishness. I guess they make them up for the civilian population.

You sounded like you must have been in a mood when you wrote one letter there. You were wondering if I wanted to go out on dates and stuff over here, but darling I think that I can really assure you that you won't have to be doing any wondering or thinking along such lines, 'cause I think that you are pretty sure that I wouldn't do such a thing, and know for sure that I will never do such a thing. I'm just not in favor of doing such things, and especially when I have someone as swell as you at home sweating me out. I am devoted to you my dear. You shouldn't suppose such things of me – as out painting the town red and especially with some blonde or brunette and of all things a red head (if you have any good friends who are red headed don't tell them what I said). But just the same they don't appeal to me and from the time that I fell for sweet you, neither does any other woman, so you needn't wonder what kind of a skirt I'm out with cause it won't be anyone but you my darling, At least not as long as you will allow me to stick around you. You're the honey and I'm the bee, you just draw me near you and I stick right to you.

Right in the middle of reading a stack of letters the phone rang and it was Cecil on the other end. I started bawling out loud I was so overcome with emotion and I think I heard him sniffling too. He kept saying, "It's okay darling, don't cry, I'm fine and I'm back in the states now. It's okay, don't cry, I love you too!" But I couldn't help myself and I just kept on crying and telling him I loved him over and over again. He was safe and almost home. He said he was in New York and hadn't been assigned a train yet but he would call me back when he knew when he was leaving for California. I was shaking all over and it was so hard to hang up the phone when it was time to go. After his call I telephoned everyone I knew and the whole family to let them know that I finally heard from him and he was okay and almost home for good. I ran to Sacred Heart and pounded on the rectory door until Father Christen answered. I told him, in near hysterics, about my phone call and he cried too. I guess I'd spent so much time leaning on his strength that he had become emotionally invested in Cecil's return also.

Cecil.

The morning of June 6th I awoke slightly to the sound of revile. I hadn't heard that in a long while; since flight training. After it was over I drifted off to sleep again for a half hour but jumped from my bed when my thoughts became coherent enough to remember that I needed to go find out when the troop trains were leaving for California. I cleaned up a bit and went over to an area that they had set aside for us fellows to check on orders and such. There was a train leaving around noon so I signed up for it and put my papers in for departure approval. I hurried back to my barracks and packed up my bag, which was nearly intact still, and went over to the chow hall for some breakfast. After breakfast I went down to the departure area and waited around to make sure I was going to be able to get on that train. At 11:30 I checked with the official again and was told that everything was a go, so I went to the nearest phone and called Margaret again to let her know that I'd be arriving at Camp Beale in Marysville, California, in three days-time. It was a quick conversation because I wanted to make sure that I got a decent seat on the train. It was fully packed with GI's heading west and reminded me of my days riding the train to the different assignments in California and Washington before my deployment to England. There were fifteen cars on the train with a great big dining car. Right on time we pulled out of the station and I sat there with my eyes closed listening to the clatter of the wheels and the engine whistle as we picked up speed. Soon, I would find out there was a difference between our troop train and the troop trains at the beginning of the war. When I was riding the rails to and from cadet schools on commercial trains we had to pull over onto side rails and let the troop trains pass. Being a bunch of repatriated fellows heading home I guess we didn't have as high a priority now that the war in Europe was over. Our troop train pulled over onto the side rails to let the commercial and freight trains pass. I thought we'd never get to California at that rate. Even so, it was a grand party all the way. I still wasn't much of a drinker, but most of the fellows on board were, and did!

The conductor said the engineer planned to take it easy and we stopped at almost every town we came to and they'd let everyone off the train until he blew the whistle for them to come back. Most of the guys ran off to bars and drank as much as they could, then ran back to the train when the whistle blew. We stopped in Moberly, Missouri, for an hour because General Omar Bradley was there celebrating his homecoming. I only walked around the train station to stretch my legs, but most of the fellows did their usual routine of running to the nearest bar. There seemed to be a lot of festivities in town because of the general, but I wasn't interested in that, I only wanted to get home. I worried a lot about what I was going to say, how she would react to seeing me, what we would do. I don't know why I was so nervous, but I hadn't seen her in two years and it was almost like starting over on our first date again. Some of the other fellows I was traveling with talked about it and many of them felt the same way. We shared some wine that some of the guys bought in Moberly while we played cards, poker and blackjack mostly, and it helped to ease my mind a little. I wondered how much I had changed and how she would accept me now. Everyone changes in war, there's no way not to. She will want to know everything I did and saw, everything I experienced, I'm sure. I wondered if I should tell her everything, or hold back the worst parts. There will be nightmares still, what will that do to her? I don't want her sympathy. I just want everything to be like it was before. The closer I got to California the more nervous I got and I had to calm myself down. I did that by napping, playing cards, and listening to the musicians that played during the trip. There was always someone who had their instrument with them and played popular band music of the day. Normally, if they packed their instrument around with them they were good and easy to listen to. The trip took three days, but was actually quite relaxing and pleasant, except for the eagerness to get there. On the third day we rolled into camp Beale, which had become an airbase since I last saw it, and I disembarked the train twenty-five dollars richer from my blackjack winnings and checked in with the officer in charge. After checking in with the OIC I set about trying to find a phone but they were all busy with a long line of fellows calling their loved ones. About an hour later I decided to go back and sit in the terminal for a while and was just starting up the steps when I heard a car horn honk. I turned around and there was Margaret driving a red 1939 Plymouth convertible and she yelled,

"Hey soldier, need a ride?"

"Heck ya, where did you get this?"

"I rented it."

"Move over beautiful, I'm driving."

After a long steamy embrace and kiss, with an accompaniment of cat calls from the other fellows nearby, I drove down the long road to the gate and pointed us toward Sacramento-and home.

Chapter 52
Carmel-By-The-Sea

Cecil had been soaking in the tub for quite a while. A luxury that he now had the opportunity to enjoy. The last two years, and especially the last four months, didn't afford itself to luxuries like a nice hot tub of water with no time limit. We arrived home late in the afternoon on June 9th and, of course, spent some much needed time catching up throughout the evening and on into the night. I was really worried about getting to know each other again. Since we had been apart for so long I worried about his feelings and how his experiences might have changed him. On the outside he looked just like I remembered, except for being thinner. I did notice that he sometimes seemed to disconnect during a conversation or I'd find him staring off into the distance. It wasn't a day dreaming type stare, but a scary blank frown like stare. When I would call out his name he would snap out of it and be his old self. His demeanor wasn't any different and he was still as gentlemanly and sweet in nature as he always had been, but I could tell things were bothering him. I didn't want to press the issue and I figured that he would open up when he was ready. June 10th found us at Sacred Heart Church and we received a standing ovation from everyone there. Father Christen welcomed Cecil home and the congregation said a prayer in thanks. Cecil was a bit red faced. He was always a very modest man and was uncomfortable with attention aimed his way. There was a lot of hand shaking after mass and we thanked everyone for their prayers and encouragement since that awful night when I received the missing in action telegram. Cecil got to know Father Christen a little after everyone had left and he thanked him for being the rock that I could lean on when I needed it. It was a pleasant morning for sure.

We went for a nice stroll through the park and talked about what the future would hold for us. Cecil didn't know if he would be receiving orders or not, but right now we didn't care. This was our time and we intended to make the most of it. Personally, I didn't care if the war was still going on in the pacific; I was of the opinion that my husband (and me) had already done our duty and paid a high price. There were plenty of fliers out there that could hold things down. Cecil, of course, had a great sense of duty and would go wherever he was told to go, and do whatever he was told to do. He was a loyal and dedicated officer that loved to fly. When lunchtime was rolling around he had one request, to eat at the Rosemount. We had prepared ourselves by not eating breakfast. Cecil was determined to get one of their famous two pound steaks with French fries that took up the whole plate. No vegetables, no bread. Just a juicy, medium, char-broiled, giant steak with fries. He said it's something he's been thinking about for two years. Not as much as me, he added, but food was something they thought about all the time. It was okay, I told him with a smile, I understood. When the manager at the Rosemount heard who we were he said he remembered reading about Cecil in the paper because of the draft board debacle and he told us the meals were on the house. What a wonderful thought that was. Everyone has been so nice to us. That afternoon we walked off our meal down by the capital building and sat around on the lawn. That's when I sprung my big surprise on him. Dr. Hopkins, who I had worked with extensively while Cecil was overseas, wanted to give us something special for Cecil's homecoming, as thanks for his service and sacrifice and for what I had to go through with the draft board. He got us a room in Carmel-By-The-Sea for ten days with Champaign, tickets to a dance in Monterey, and a round of golf at Pebble Beach. The man was a saint and when I told Cecil about it he was so surprised he almost passed out right then and there. That lifted his mood quite a bit as we drove home and spent another afternoon and evening getting reacquainted like newlyweds all over again. Our first day in Carmel was supposed to be Monday, and we would make the reservation, but not until late. We decided to take in the morning mass at Sacred Heart and then head down to the draft board for a little visit. We got up at the crack of dawn and Cecil wanted to take another soak before starting the day. While waiting for him I decided to read more of his last letters from Ridgewell again. I had already packed and there wasn't anything else to do, and I guess I was a little addicted to those letters. For two years it was all I had to keep him fresh in my mind.

> Hello, my darling. So sorry, here, that I have missed a couple of days of writing to you, but I've been on a 48 hour pass and went down to London, and we can't mail any letters in any town so I had to wait until I got home, which I just did. I didn't know in advance that I was going to get off, they just up and said to take off when we got through on Friday. We only had about an hour to get ready and catch our transportation to London. I felt like a couple of days off so I didn't waste any time. I had a pretty good time in jolly old London. I got around and saw a little bit more of it.

There is really quite a bit there. It is a lot larger than I thought it was on my first impression and it really is probably a lot bigger than it still seems. I really didn't do very much while there but I enjoyed it. I went to see a couple of different shows besides looking over part of the town. Someday when I go in I will have to find a sightseeing tour and go on it. I stayed at one of the American Red Cross clubs there in London. It was a nice place, called the Princess Club. It is in Princess Gardens. They have several clubs there in London, and this one is more or less out of town. There are a couple officers clubs and an enlisted club up near Piccadilly. I ate all my meals in the Reindeer Club, which is one of the officers clubs uptown. They have better meals there than they have anywhere else in town. They only charge about 40 cents for meals and 60 cents to sleep there. The Red Cross is pretty good over here; I don't know what all the fellows would do without them. They will do most anything for you. They are supervised by the Americans and have British volunteers working there.

You should have seen the spill that I took on my bike today. I was riding along without using hands and going back and forth and I skidded in the gravel. I'm still picking little rocks out of my hands, which I skidded on. I guess I won't try that anymore. To ride without any hands I have to sit way over on one side and then lean that way also. The bike isn't very well balanced, I imagine. At least I didn't get hurt 'bicycle jousting' like some of the fellows do here. The colonel isn't at all happy when that happens.

Pardon me darling if I sound a little English once in a while, or don't you mind? As for the term 'sweating it out' goes, though; don't think that it is 'English' 'cause that is a good old American G.I. phrase, which means exactly what you figured. That's one thing you do plenty of in the Army. As far as I know they never call me Cecil, it's always 'Quinn,' or like the guys in the barracks call me 'the little man' or 'short stuff.' That's what I go by around here. Getting mail from you is the only thing there is to look forward to over here, 'cause there sure isn't anything else to expect. I sure do love you, and I sure do miss you like everything. May God bless you, darling, and take good care of you while I'm away. Love and kisses. Cecil.

I had a good cry going when Cecil came out of the bathroom and he stood there looking at me asking what was wrong. I said,

"Nothing. I was just reading some of your letters while I was waiting.

"Oh what do you want to go and do a thing like that for? If those old letters are going to make you cry, then let's just get rid of them."

"Oh no we won't! For two years these letters were all I had of you. They kept my spirit alive when I didn't feel like I could go on. I'm not crying because I'm sad. I'm crying because these memories remind me of what we have and how much we love each other."

He didn't really know how to respond to that, he's not a touchy feely kind of man. He just walked over and sat next to me on the bed and took me in his arms and held me. That, more than words, was the perfect thing he could have done. After a several minute long embrace I got up and went into the bathroom to collect myself and get straightened up so we could leave. We attended the morning mass as planned and then drove down to the draft board for some unfinished business. We didn't go into the regular draft board office, we went in to see Colonel Leitch of the Selective Service System. He recognized me right off and since I had the arm of a nice 2nd Lieutenant he knew right off the bat that it was Cecil and he grinned from ear to ear. Cecil saluted him, which he returned, and then the colonel held out his hand to shake.

"Lieutenant Quinley, how wonderful it is to see that you made it home okay. This pretty young lady was worried sick about you. You're lucky to have such a lady, you should see her when her Irish blood gets boiling mad. She's quite the fighter you know."

The colonel asked us to follow him and we went into the draft service office where he called everyone out into the common office area. He said,

"Ladies and gentlemen, let me introduce to you Lieutenant Cecil Quinley, repatriated prisoner of war and veteran of 14 combat missions over enemy territory in the European theater of operations."

Everyone cheered and crowded around us to shake Cecil's hand and hug me. Even the lieutenant that gave me such a hard time sheepishly came forward and shook Cecil's hand. They all asked Cecil questions about flying in combat and being a prisoner, which he graciously answered for a few minutes, then he politely excused us so we could get on the road.

The car was packed already so we started south out of town toward San Jose, then over the Santa Cruz Mountains on State Route 17 and down into the town of Santa Cruz where we got on State Route 1. After catching a quick meal in Santa Cruz we continued down SR1 stopping every once in a while to take in the breathtaking scenery of the Pacific Ocean. We continued south through Monterey and into Carmel-By-The-Sea, or Carmel for short. It was a lovely and quaint village type town. We checked into our cabin and headed immediately for the beach. The Pacific Ocean is cold water and if you've never set foot in it-it could shock you. But, being from Ft. Bragg I was ready for it. It takes some getting used to, but we waded around in the water for a while. Long enough for our feet and lower legs to go numb, but that's part of the fun I suppose. We had a nice time watching the waves and cuddling up in a blanket after eating some cold fried chicken that I packed for this well planned evening alone with my husband. It was one of Cecil's favorites that we had packed on numerous picnics to William Land Park in Sacramento. Cecil started a fire on the beach with some driftwood and we sat on a blanket, with another blanket around us, watching the sun set on the ocean. What a beautiful and romantic evening it was, and it was so very extra special because of the two year wait. We cuddled for a while next to the fire until the ocean breeze became just a little too chilly and we made our way back to the Plymouth. When Cecil opened the trunk he discovered the next big surprise that I snuck in there for him before we left Sacramento. Since Dr. Hopkins was kind enough to also arrange for us to play golf at Pebble Beach, I bought Cecil a brand new set of Wilson Sam Snead Blue Ridge Model golf clubs. A whole set of irons with a driver, 3, 4, 5, 7 woods, and a putter and bag with shoes. He was genuinely surprised, excited and speechless while he took them from the trunk and examined them in the headlights of the car. He said he didn't know what to say, except thank you, but the look on his face was enough said. He added,

"I'm going to put these back in the trunk and look at them again at the cabin. Thank you so much, darling. It's going to be another real nice day tomorrow. I love you dear, thank you."

His raw emotion was the most I had seen since he came home and I started to cry a little while he was thanking me, but he said,

"Oh, now don't start that again. Save your crying until tomorrow. When you see me golf you'll cry from laughing so hard."

He always knew how to lighten the moment. Cecil drove us back to our cabin with me sitting beside him with my arm around him, whispering in his ear how much I love him, and we settled in for the night as the fog rolled in and enveloped our cabin in its romantic embrace.

Chapter 53
Pebble Beach

The morning found our cabin still enveloped in a thick pacific coast summer fog. The air was wet but fresh from the salt air, and free. No fences here. No guards, no flack or fighters. I sat on the small porch sipping a hot fresh brewed cup of black coffee. It was just a normal cup of coffee to others, but it was fresh percolated heaven to me. It kept my hands warm as I looked into the glowing white air and listened to the crashing waves and fog horn in the distance. Margaret was still sleeping. It was still early. I thought about what the future held and what the Army may have in store for me. I had a thirty day leave before I had to report for duty again. The war was still going on in the pacific and I figured that I'd probably be sent there. The good news was that they weren't using very many B-17's at this point in the Pacific Theater. They were using a new larger bomber called a B-29 and it would take a few weeks of training in that before being deployed, and the war might be over by then. Of course, they could just plop me down in a B-25, or B-26 or something with minimal training. I surely didn't want to replace this peacefulness, this tranquility, with war again. But my butt belonged to Uncle Sam and I'd go where he told me to go. That didn't mean I'd have to be happy about it, but I'd go. Sooner or later I'd have to have this conversation with Margaret. I'm sure she was aware of it. We talked briefly about it back in Sacramento, but it was a subject we had for the most part avoided so far. This is our second honeymoon, so to speak, and that subject isn't something I wanted to bring up while we were having so much fun and rediscovering intimacy. When I heard Margaret stirring I went inside and prepared a nice bacon and eggs breakfast for her. It was nice having real food at my disposal in a good American made ice box. After breakfast we showered and got ready for the world outside and this time walked to the beach. It wasn't the same stretch of beach we visited the day before. This one wasn't as much of a tourist area, but we did see a couple there letting their two big Alaskan dogs play in the surf. It was entertaining to see the excitement the dogs had. Their innocence as they turned their backs on the ocean only to be plowed over by a wave, or one of the dogs having a sand crab latch onto its lip. It kept us laughing for an hour. The beach was at the base of some steep cliffs but someone had built a nice wooden staircase over the tougher spots where the trail to the sand was steep. I carried a blanket and two Thermos', one with coffee for me, and one with hot cocoa for Margaret. We sat on the beach watching the waves in the mist as the fog burned off and rolled back out to sea. The quiet times were the best. We just sat there enjoying each other's company and talking about our day ahead. Today would consist of playing a round of golf at Pebble Beach Country Club. It was a wonderfully thoughtful gift of Margaret giving me a set of clubs. She had been practicing while I was overseas, so I probably wouldn't be able to keep up with her, but that wasn't the point. I had no intention of even keeping score at this point. Just hit the ball, walk, and enjoy the fresh green grass, the salt air, and each other's company. When the fog rolled all the way out we packed up and walked back to the cabin, jumped in the Plymouth, dropped the top down and drove to the golf course with our hair blowing in the nice cool fresh air.

It was a beautiful day for a round of golf. When I gave the man our name at the clubhouse he was already expecting us and said the day was arranged by Dr. Hopkins. Of course, we already knew that but what he said next surprised me. He said the doctor had explained that I was a prisoner of war and Margaret and I were on our second honeymoon after my repatriation. He said that the club would like us to come back as often as we wanted, on them, while we were in Carmel. I was speechless and the words kind of fumbled out of my mouth as I thanked him and blushed at the same time. I was always a bit bashful when it came to getting attention or accolades. I thanked him kindly as we went out to the first tee. It was a bit breezier than what I was used to from playing in Sacramento, but the point of the day was to have fun and enjoy each other and the scenery, so I really didn't care how many balls I hit out of bounds. I told the fellow at the clubhouse that I usually played in the 70's. He said,

"Wow, have you ever considered turning pro?"

"No, because if it ever gets any hotter than that I don't want to play."

He got a good laugh out of that, and then I added that in all honesty I hadn't played in a while, so I was going to be chasing balls every which way. He said he understood and told me to just have a good time. We had met the nicest people every day during our trip and it was making the trip that much more enjoyable. The sea air was indeed fresh, and the temperature was cool with the ocean breeze blowing in. Margaret was beautiful as always and the day couldn't have been any better. Much of the course is right along the cliffs with the crashing wave's right below. There was a beautiful blue sky, seagulls, magnificent green grass, fairways with that just cut smell, which I must confess reminded me of baseball more than golf. Of the days I spent at the ball park in Sacramento watching the games there. The day went just as I thought. Margaret hit the ball straight, but not as far as me. I hit my shots farther, but not very straight. The day was classic, though, as we held hands while walking from shot to shot for the rest of the afternoon. We would spend nine days in Carmel and we golfed at Pebble Beach on six of those days. Hand in hand, enjoying life, each other, and getting a little sunburned in the process.

The morning of our third day we moved over to the Pine Inn, right in Carmel. Doc McKee had arranged for ten days at the Pine Inn but I wanted a little seclusion time before heading to the touristy area. I really didn't want to be around other people just yet, only my wife. I wanted some seclusion and quiet moments as we spent time together. I was still a bit nervous and kind of felt like we were starting all over again. It was a giddy type nervousness, but scary too. Plus, not having had any privacy for the last two years, I just wanted to stay off the beaten path for a couple days. By the third day I was ready for the hotel. It was beautiful and the good doctor spared nothing. We stayed in a suite with a view of the ocean. The staff was wonderful and saw to our every need. I'd never been so pampered in my life. I was a bit uncomfortable at first, but by the end of our stay I was thinking I could get used to this. We had a nice big claw foot bathtub in our room and we both managed to fit in it nicely, soaking up the hot water in the dim candlelight while the radio played in the outer room. This would be our nightly routine for the duration of our stay. On the fourth day the weather looked a little like rain so we drove around looking at the sights. We made a quick pass into Monterey and back and the drive along the coastal highway was majestic. Margaret wanted to go see the Carmel Mission, or San Carlos Borromeo de Carmelo Mission, to be exact. On our honeymoon we roughly followed the missions of Father Junipero Serra, but we didn't have time to stop at this one. This time we made it a point to go see the mission that became his headquarters, so to speak. He founded it in 1770 and he died there on August 28th, 1784. He is buried under the sanctuary floor, which gives this mission an air of importance as you walk around inside. It's a wonderfully handsome place with a walled compound, beautiful flora and green trees, just like the rest of Carmel. I wasn't disappointed with the visit and we spent most of the day there, even attending a mass. I love attending masses in the old missions and churches we've visited and I have enjoyed the formality of the old world feel to the Catholic style mass. While I had attended other more spirited services, much like Padre Mac's readings and discussions, I felt more spiritually fulfilled, or more genuine, I guess, attending the Catholic masses with Margaret. There was an obvious old world history to their services. I'm sure Margaret shares the credit too, since she had been urging me since we got married to convert. I don't know how to explain it. I guess I just felt more peacefulness, more spirituality, like I belonged there, like my wife's faith had something to do with my surviving the last two years. I decided during our visit to the Carmel Mission that I would convert and when I told Margaret she jumped into my arms and hugged the breath out of me and, of course, cried. When the war is finally over we will reignite our plan to adopt a son and begin our family. We decided that it is then that I will convert and be baptized at the same time as our son.

We attended one more mass at the mission on Sunday the 10th. Throughout the week mornings would find us at Pebble Beach chasing a little white ball around. I figured we did pretty well because we found more balls than we lost. I decided that the ball count was the best way for a guy like me to keep score. I couldn't get over the short seventh hole and its majestic beauty with the Pacific Ocean as its backdrop. Lunch and dinner found us dining at the Pine Inn, and sitting by a fire on the beach as the sun set. Some days the fog went far enough out to sea that we could watch the sun set all the way into the horizon. Other days the sun set into the rolling mist and became a large orange glowing spectacle. Either way, we became lost in the moment, lost in the absence of distraction, lost in each other. It was a magically romantic time that neither of us would ever forget. The night of the 19th found us back at the beach for the final night of our trip to this heavenly place. We toasted with a bottle of wine as we sat by the fire draped in a blanket. We had the whole beach to ourselves. The fog was absent as the sun slowly and gently lowered itself into the sea. It was a perfect evening as the cool breeze delicately lifted Margaret's hair and the fire flickered gently as its glow reflected off of her face. We would spend our last night on this beach, our beach, as the distant remnant of the sunset faded into darkness and the sky came to life with the sparkle of millions of stars, each one there just for us. As we finished our bottle of wine we reclined to the softness of the sand, wrapped in our blanket, wrapped in each other's embrace, covered by our stars, with our waves playing their music just for us.

Chapter 54
The Long Road

April 18th, 2009, two days after their official wedding date, Cecil and Margaret celebrated their 70th anniversary at St. Patrick's Church in Fallon, Nevada. The happy couple celebrated by renewing their vows in front of family and friends, many of whom were surprise guests. The ceremony was conducted by Father Oliver Curran, a good Irish priest, as Cecil would call him. Each of the three sons and two daughter's-in-law read select "Prayers of the Faithful" during the ceremony. They were never more satisfied with what they had accomplished in life and where they had arrived, through all of life's twists and turns. Father Oliver blessed them and re-introduced the "newly-weds" to everyone as Mr. and Mrs. Quinley. The surprise was not over, as everyone adjourned to the local American Legion Hall for a surprise reception, where a life-time video presentation set to the popular tunes of their generation had been prepared by David, the first son. Everyone sat quietly in wonderment as the video displayed a life-time of photographs and love from 1939 to 2009. When the video ended the hall erupted in applause as Cecil sat, somewhat uncomfortable being the center of attention, and Margaret cried a few tears from her feeling of graciousness and love that was being sent to them from everyone in the room and from long absent family members who could not be there. The long lived couple had become the Elders of their respective families. Both are the last remaining siblings of the Quinley and Farley families from their generation, and both lived a modest respectful Christian life, sharing good values with family, friends, and all who they came in contact with.

It indeed has been a long road. A road that started in 1936 and endured a world at war with all its ugliness, fear, lonesomeness, and personal sacrifice. Margaret and Cecil were two of the lucky ones who would be reunited in 1945 and were able to pick up with their lives almost where they had left off. After their second honeymoon in Carmel-by-the-Sea they returned to Sacramento where Cecil reported back for duty with the expectation of being sent to the Pacific. Instead, he was told to take another thirty day leave because there was a huge surplus of personnel having come home from Europe and the Army hadn't made plans for them yet. Even if they wanted to send the B-17's and their crews directly to the Pacific the logistics involved in such a huge shift would take time. After his thirty day leave Cecil reported in again, only to be told to take another thirty days and to stay in contact in case things changed. Before that second thirty day leave was up the Japanese surrendered on September 2nd, 1945. World War II was finally over. Lieutenant Quinley decided to get on with his life, although he didn't want to completely give up his dream of flying. He reverted to the Air Force Reserves and sought employment in Sacramento to begin his renewed life as a civilian and with his beloved wife Margaret. They obtained a home loan through a veteran's guarantee program and built their first (owned) home at 145 Tivoli Way in Sacramento. Cecil gained employment at the Home Bakery as an engineer and they renewed their efforts to start their own family. Two months later they traveled to St. Elizabeth's hospital in San Francisco to accept the adoption of their first son, two month old David Michael Quinley. A short time later, in 1947, Cecil was finally promoted to 1st lieutenant through a program initiated to remedy a flaw in the system in which POW's were placed in limbo instead of receiving their promotions. In April of 1949 they repeated the trip to San Francisco and adopted their second son, six month old Dennis Patrick Quinley. Margaret was ecstatic, having finally achieved what she'd dreamed of so many times while working with the mothers in labor and delivery and having witnessed first-hand the miracle of birth. Having helped so many mothers and fathers with their newborn gifts from God. The happy family suddenly had their dreams realized and Cecil worked his way up in his new position at the Home Bakery until it was purchased by Rainbow Bakery. In 1950 Cecil was offered a position as the Chief Engineer at the newly established Rainbow Bakery in Chico, California. A small college town 100 miles north of Sacramento. They traveled to Chico to see the bakery and the town and fell in love with it. Chico is situated along state route 99 approximately 10 miles east of the Sacramento River and has a (then) 2,500 acre park where they took their sons on regular outings to swim in the creek that ran through the park and picnic at its many picnic sites located along the creek. Cecil's job went well and Margaret spent her days taking care of the home and the boys.

David and Dennis enrolled at Notre Dame School, part of the St. John the Baptist Catholic Parish in downtown Chico. This would prove problematic as the school and Cecil's job were both about two and a half miles from their home on Sarah Avenue. Cecil was finding himself on call 24/7 and they only had one car. They sold their Sarah Avenue home and moved into the downstairs portion of a duplex on West 5th Street, across the street from Notre Dame School and about three blocks from Cecil's workplace. On Easter Sunday, 1953, Cecil finally converted to the Catholic

Church, as he had promised Margaret so many years before. He was baptized along with both of his children. Both David and Dennis were born in a Catholic Hospital so, undoubtedly, they were baptized at birth. But there were apparently no official records of the baptism, therefore, under those conditions, the church allowed the rebaptisms to take place again. All three were baptized together, bringing the entire family under the same church. In 1955 Cecil was promoted to captain in the Air Force Reserves, but learned that he would never fly again. His eyesight had deteriorated too much. Whether it was from the lack of oxygen in 1943 or just a normal symptom of aging, it didn't matter. His busy schedule at work and his lost interest in the reserves because of his lost flying status kept him from attending his reserve days, even though he hadn't actually flown since October 8th, 1943. He separated from the reserves in the early 60's.

In November, 1958, Jeune Addy, a friend of Margaret's, who she worked with at Cal Western Life in Sacramento, asked Margaret if they would consider adopting another child that wasn't due until January. Jeune was working in an attorney's office in Chico who handled adoptions and she was aware of the upcoming birth. Margaret and Cecil agreed and asked the two boys if it was okay with them. They were both excited to have a new baby coming and in January, 1959, the family accepted Daniel Joseph Quinley into the family. In 1960 Cecil lost his mother, Cora Belle Quinley, formerly Cora Belle McCoy, at the age of 82 in Ceres, California. A few years later the family decided to buy a larger home and they moved a few blocks   to 627 West 2nd Street. Cecil survived a scare as a boiler at his plant exploded near him, causing second and third degree burns to his hands, arms, and face. He recovered completely with no visible scars, another testament to his hardiness. Margaret spent a lot of time entering sweepstakes of various types. Her hard work at putting together multiple entries, which was allowed under the rules, paid off and she found herself very lucky indeed. Her winnings included a 19" black and white television (fancy for the time), a hair dryer, different foods and deserts, and for the grand slam, his and hers 1968 Ford Mustangs, which weren't even first prize. The grand prize were his and hers airplanes! Cecil sold one of the cars to pay the taxes but the second Mustang remains in the family to this day. David and Dennis entered the Air Force in the 1960's and Daniel followed in 1978. During the 1960's and 1970's the couple remained strong in their faith while they struggled to make ends meet. Margaret would at times take clothes in to wash and press and for a couple years they housed college students in the bedrooms on the second floor of their home. Margaret took a job working in the parish rectory as a secretary and things began to improve.

In the late 1970's they grew tired of living so close to the university with all its noise and activities. They moved to El Monte Avenue, east of town, in what was a country setting at that time, surrounded by horse property. Rainbow Bakery decided to close its Chico operation but offered Cecil a position in Stockton, California. Neither one of them wanted to leave Chico, so Cecil retired with 35 years of service to the company. Soon, he would find, however, that the union had mismanaged the retirement fund and he would never see a penny of his retirement. He was forced back to work again and he took a job with a new rice cake company in Chico which would end up moving a few miles south to Gridley, California. They sold their country home and moved to a mobile home park in north Chico. Cecil was forced to work until he was 80 years old to recover a resemblance of security from his lost retirement. As time rolled on Margaret and Cecil became grand-parents and great grand-parents. In the 80's Margaret became actively involved in a "shut-in" program where she traveled to all the different retirement homes in the area and provided entertainment with a "Kazoo" band. Margaret's band dressed in barbershop quartet style garb with straw hats and performed for the elderly shut-ins. In 1991 the family celebrated the 100th birthday of Margaret's mother Ella Farley-Himanka. A little over a year later they mourned her death as she passed away peacefully in her sleep. It wasn't unusual to see Cecil, as an 85-90 year old man, out playing baseball with his grand-kids, running the bases as his older children yelled at him to slow down. His physical health and stamina was astounding.

June 4th, 1996, Cecil was surprised with an early birthday gift. Stick time in the Collins Foundation's B-17G "Nine-O-Nine." Captain Quinley took the co-pilot's seat once again for his 15th mission, this time with no enemy fire raining up at him. As an 81 year old he said he found the yolk a little harder to steer than he remembered, but he was ear to ear smiles as the old bomber powered its way from Chico, over Oroville Dam and Lake, then back again. His son, Daniel, accompanied him on the flight and videotaped the experience. Cecil would only get 15 minutes stick time during the 50 minute flight, but it would be an exciting experience he talks about to this day. The rest of the flight he walked the aircraft and looked at the view from the various gun positions. He sat in the bombardier seat and imagined what Ted saw that fateful day over Bremen. He pointed out the exact spot where he dove trough the bomb bay doors. Cecil suffered nightmares for a long time after returning home, but it wasn't common for the men of that generation to seek help for such things. Eventually, the nightmares faded as their lives took other turns and they raised their family. In the 1990's Margaret pushed Cecil to become more active in the Veterans of Foreign Wars (VFW) and they put together a large display that they showed in the Chico Mall on Veterans Day and Memorial Day. Their display primarily covered Cecil's service and other WWII units. Other VFW members began to put displays together and soon the Korean and Viet Nam wars were represented as well, and the very nice display attracted the attention of local media and politicians. The display brought back a lot of memories that were better left buried, in Cecil's opinion, as he began to suffer the nightmares again. Soon, however, the nightmares would fade as he consciously confronted the memories through his active involvement in the displays and through granting interviews with reporters and local school projects. One hour and a half interview was so popular that it was accepted into the Library of Congress and remains there today. He has attended a few reunions of the 381st Bomb Group over the years, and reunions for Stalag Luft III veterans, where he once again met Oberfeldwebel Hermann Glemnitz, and Padre Mac. Margaret became approved to assist in taking the Blessed Sacrament to shut-ins in the Chico area, and it was a mission that she cherished. They sold their mobile home and moved into an independent living retirement complex in Chico that Margaret had her eyes on since she had been making her rounds with the Blessed Sacrament. In 2001 Cecil lost his beloved brother John, who he spent so much time with throughout his life, including at the Donner Trail Ski Lodge and Treasure Island. John died at the age of 95 and his obituary read as follows:

No services will be held for John C. Quinley, who died Saturday in Santa Cruz. He was 95. Mr. Quinley was born in Copperopolis. He lived many years in Moraga before moving to Aptos four years ago. Mr. Quinley worked at the San Francisco Ship Yards during World War II. He was an electrician at the Lawrence Berkeley National Laboratory. He was honored with a 60-year pin from the Electricians Union. Mr. Quinley was a member of the Moraga Country Club. He enjoyed golfing, traveling and many outdoor activities including, skiing, hunting, fishing and golf. He is survived by Brother Cecil Quinley of Chico; sisters Martha Zimmerman of Modesto and Corabelle Hawkins of

Alameda; and many nieces and nephews. His wife, Thelma A. Quinley, died in 1992.

Cecil and his son Daniel met Phillip Quinley in Santa Cruz where they sailed out onto the bay and spread John's ashes into the sea. A celebratory shot of Patron Tequila was enjoyed back at the dock, just as John would have liked. In the next few years Cecil lost his last two siblings Martha and Corabelle, leaving him the last offspring of John Winson Quinley and Cora Belle McCoy. He is also the last surviving crew member of the "Feather Merchant." Margaret had already lost her two brothers Ray and Ken and is the last child left in her family as well.

Requiring more care in their advanced years, Cecil and Margaret once again packed up their home and moved. This time to Fallon, Nevada, to be near their youngest son and daughter in law, who are both in the medical profession and aid in their care. Cecil drove his beloved wife everywhere they needed to go in Fallon, but refrained from driving out of town. He said his Buick was smaller and was easier to steer than a B-17. The decision was made eventually, however, and at long last, to hang up his car keys at the ripe young age of 97 years. While mostly confined to wheel chairs now, both Cecil and Margaret still enjoy their undying love and companionship with each other. Their memories of their World War II days are still sharp, and greatly contributed to this book.

Chapter 55
Epilogue

With mom and dad now living in Fallon, a (first cousins) reunion was organized in Modesto, California. My wife and I drove them down to the reunion and we met my brothers there, along with many of the cousins we hadn't seen in years. Some, I was too young to remember when I saw them last. During the course of the event people were scattered throughout a small clubhouse at a mobile home park chatting. I don't recall if the conversations were about politics, or another patriotic theme, but suddenly dad stepped to the center of the room and said he wanted to say something. The room went quiet, recognizing that he was the elder Quinley now and deserving of the respect of all present. He told the story of his liberation from Stalag VII-A, and how scared everyone was because of the battle occurring right outside the camp fence. You could hear a pin drop in the room. With everyone's complete attention he went on to describe seeing the Nazi flag lowered in Moosburg and the United States flag being raised, and how it was at that time that they finally knew they were safe-and free. He said he looked with pride at the stars and stripes as tears welled up in his eyes. I don't think there was a dry eye in the room and the silence was deafening. I had lived with the man my entire life and I had never heard that story before. It had only been recently that he began to talk about his war experiences in detail at all.

After hearing the Moosburg story my wife Leslie and I talked about it and agreed that his story has got to be told. It was at that time that I decided to write this book. There is too much history to ignore it and it shouldn't be lost, but rather, documented for the generations that follow to see what our fathers and grandfathers did to earn our freedom and safety that we enjoy today. Some have said that we have inherited our freedom, and I think that's exactly true. I don't think the sacrifices that this generation made to earn our freedom can truly be appreciated because we have inherited it and taken it for granted that it was always there, but that's just my opinion. There have been skirmishes and other wars since then, but WWII was the last war that threatened to change the entire world as we know it, and quite possibly could have led to the end of the United States had the Nazis been successful in creating the atomic bomb first. The generation that fought and won the wars in the Pacific and in Europe truly fought for and earned our freedom and safety with their blood-with their lives. The sacrifices that were made by the soldiers, sailors, marines and airmen. The sacrifices that were made by the families here at home and how the country came together as a whole, as a dedicated unified country, has never been achieved since, and probably never will again. I've read a lot of material to verify facts and faded memories to put this book together and one of the things that impressed me most was that, while this is my father's story, it could very well be one of thousands of airmen's stories and I'm thankful for the sacrifices of each and every one of them. Until doing research for this book I had no idea of the staggering losses that were suffered by the airmen of "The Mighty Eighth" over Europe.

Dad is 98 now, and mom 96, at the time this book was completed. They are both still living in Fallon, and are currently in decent health, although they both have scary bouts of illness from time to time. Although their memories are fading somewhat, concerning the events of 70 years ago, their recollections are remarkable and have been verified through other sources and through the hundreds of personal letters they kept all throughout their years together. Many of the letters were used throughout this book and in some instances stand by themselves because of the historical information they contained and their powerful message. Through the course of my investigations I had the pleasure to contact a Mr. Burt Carter in England. I'd found a letter from him addressed to dad asking him if he was the pilot of the "Feather Merchant" when it made an emergency landing in mid-June, 1943, at a new airbase near Bert's home. Bert was a young man at the time and was quite excited with the situation. Dad hadn't arrived until mid-July, but we were able to discover that the pilot in question was dad's eventual friend, Leo Jarvis. Bert told me an amusing tale that he found a large bullet hole in the tail section of the "Feather Merchant" and placed a rolled up piece of paper containing a good luck prayer in the hole when no one was looking. Perhaps it was that prayer that kept the old gal flying just long enough for the boys to get out, for she surely shouldn't have still been capable of flight. Could she have been held up by their guardian angel's wings? A romantic thought, I know, but it's a nice story and its revelation amused dad.

Due to their efforts in making the Veteran's and Memorial day exhibits available to the public, and through dad's availability and willingness to share his experiences in interviews they have both been recognized by the American Ex-Prisoners of War California North State Chapter several times. An American Patriotism Award in 2003. A Certificate of Special

Congressional Recognition from Congressman Wally Herger in Chico, California, in 1998, and a Senatorial Proclamation award in Fallon, Nevada, from Senator Dean Heller. He has been gifted with a United States Flag that had flown over the White House during President Reagan's administration. In 2012, Cecil was also gifted with a United States Flag which flew over the Navy's "Top Gun" school at Naval Air Station Fallon. Cecil's military awards include the Air Medal with one Oak Leaf Cluster, the European African Middle Eastern Campaign Medal with five battle stars, a Distinguished Unit Citation Ribbon for the 8 October 1943 Bremen raid, two Purple Heart Medals, a Prisoner of War Medal, and an aerial gunnery marksmanship badge.

This book has been a labor of love, for there is no better example of what a loving couple should be than these two people. Couples such as this are far too rare in our world today and I'm proud that I was able to witness their example through my formative years. Some would say that I matured late in life, and I'm forced to agree with that, but their message was not lost on me. I grew up idolizing fictional characters such as John Wayne. A fine persona to emulate, no doubt, but little did I know that down the hall was a real American hero, an "Iron Man" both physically and spiritually. A mother that is equal to the task also. I'm glad that they have been here long enough for me to see that. For me to see what a couple truly is and to prompt me to learn more about my family history. People have asked me from time to time over the years if I ever think about being adopted. In my younger years I'd have to say no. I was aware of it, my parents never kept it a secret, but it just wasn't something we dwelled on. Now, I think back on those years and realize how truly lucky I was. Most people are born into their family, right or wrong. I feel like I was hand-picked, by a couple that didn't have to pick another child at all. Dad was already 40 years old, but they had a lot of love left to give, and obviously a lot of longevity left. For that I am thankful. If there is an obvious religious overtone to this book, it's on purpose, for that is truly how they have lived their life every day that I have known them and have had memory to recall.

Dad told me a story about a Navy man that he met at a reunion. He didn't know why the Navy man was at a 381st Bomb Group reunion, but he struck up a conversation with him. The man told a story about being in a submarine in the Pacific during WWII. They had just torpedoed a Japanese ship and were sitting silently on the bottom of a bay while depth charges were exploding all around them. The ship was taking an awful beating, springing leaks everywhere. The man said he was a devout Atheist but he fell to his knees during the attack and prayed to God to spare him. He knew the end was surely at hand. Suddenly, the Japanese destroyers gave up the attack and moved on, sparing the U.S. submarine and all her crew. Dad told the man that was a fantastic story and asked him what he did now. The man said after the war he became an ordained minister and has been one ever since. He was at the 381st Bomb Group reunion to give the Invocation and Benediction. Dad's two word reply:

"Amen brother."

CPSIA information can be obtained at www.ICGtesting.com
Printed in the USA
LVOW08*1358310314

379649LV00002BA/2/P